Social Work Models, Methods and Theories

A Framework for Practice

Edited by

Paul Stepney and Deirdre Ford

Russell House Publishi

First published in 2000 by:
Russell House Publishing Ltd.
4 St. George's House
Uplyme Road
Lyme Regis
Dorset DT7 3LS

Tel: 01297-443948
Fax: 01297-442722
e-mail: help@russellhouse.co.uk

British Library Cataloguing-in-publication Data:
A catalogue record for this book is available from the British Library.

ISBN: 1-898924-83-X

Typeset by The Hallamshire Press Limited, Sheffield.
Printed by Redwood Books, Trowbridge.

Russell House Publishing

Is a group of social work, probation, education and youth and community
work practitioners and academics working in collaboration with a
professional publishing team. Our aim is to work closely with the field to
produce innovative and valuable materials to help managers, trainers,
practitioners and students. We are keen to receive feedback on
publications and new ideas for future projects.

Social Work Models, Methods and Theories

Contents

List of Abbreviations

EU   European Union

DSS   Department of Social Security

GNP   Gross National Product

GDP   Gross Domestic Product

NHS   National Health Service

OECD   Organisation for Economic Co-operation and Development

DoH   Department of Health

Preface

Professor Nigel Parton, University of Huddersfield

These are challenging times for social work, particularly in the United Kingdom. If the late 1960s and early 1970s could be seen as a period of optimism amongst social workers both about their capabilities and occupational futures, the years since have witnessed considerable changes. From the mid 1970s onwards social work has been subject to a series of child abuse inquiries and media opprobrium, which has had the effect of both undermining morale and undermining public confidence in its abilities. This was reinforced by fundamental changes in the political economy of most welfare states in the Western world, particularly in the UK. Increasingly, some of the basic assumptions of the post war welfare consensus, and thus many of the assumptions that underpinned the development of social work during that period, have not just been questioned but have been subject to fundamental reconfiguration.

The 1980s and 1990s have witnessed an increasing reliance on procedures and managerial oversight and audit, particularly within the local authority social services departments. While traditionally referred to as a semi-profession, more recent years have seemed to undermine any serious claims to professional identity. The growth of care management and the increasing emphasis on budgetary controls and budgetary decision making seem to have marginalised many of the values which previously characterised the occupation. Perhaps most significantly, however, the profession has been found wanting in key areas of decision making where its knowledge base and use of theory and research have been subject to critical appraisal. While this could be identified in the area of child abuse scandals, it was not limited to this alone. During the period, however, social work seemed to be singled out for much detailed critical attention.

However, as the 1990s progressed, this situation began to change. In particular the medical profession, teachers and a range of others in the field have found themselves subject to major public scrutiny and inquiry in the way that could be seen to characterise social work in the 1970s and early 1980s. In this respect, therefore, the crisis which seemed to characterise social work is no longer seen as specific to it. There is an increasing questioning of professionals and their knowledge base and science more generally. We are thus faced with something of a tension. On the one hand we are being encouraged to develop and invest in the 'knowledge society', while at the same time raising serious doubts about the current state of knowledge itself. Increasingly it seems that our experience is characterised by risk and uncertainty and that no longer is it possible to articulate clear-cut decision making and straightforward messages. The ability to deal with ambiguity and uncertainty is thus, perhaps more than ever, the area of transferable knowledge which is increasingly required at the start of the new millennium across many occupational groups and a range of tasks and skills.

Ironically, it is often in this area that much of social work's traditional strength could be seen to reside. Unfortunately, with our increasing emphasis on 'evidence-based practice' and 'effectiveness' we are in great danger of forgetting these histories and more traditional areas of expertise. Some of the central characteristics which can be seen to epitomise the development of social work from its birth are perhaps now required more than ever before (Parton, 2000).

Unfortunately, the last fifteen years have seen something of a decline in the availability of texts which make their prime concern the discussion of theories and knowledge which can be made usable for practitioners in their day-to-day practices. It is vital that practitioners are aware of the range of different approaches that are available and how these can be thought about and used. In many respects it is this relationship between the theory and practice which lies at the heart of social work itself and in some respects can be seen to make it distinctive. As Neil Thompson has argued:

> ...*the relationship between theory and practice can be seen as a direct parallel with that between thinking and doing. It hinges on the question, 'how do knowledge and thought influence or inform our actions?'*
>
> (Thompson, 2000: p4).

These are key issues for social work, particularly at this time.

It is in this context that this new book, edited by Paul Stepney and Deirdre Ford, is to be particularly welcomed. While it goes to considerable lengths to lay out a range of different methods and theories, which are of direct relevance to practice, this is done in a way which recognises that the nature of practice is itself crucially influenced by its changing political, economic and social contexts. Now more than ever it is vital that social workers recognise the need for not only handling the contemporary uncertainties and ambiguities which permeate their work, but in doing so give a voice to the people with whom they work. It is not simply a question of rediscovering the importance of professional judgement but in a way which attempts to empower the users and the groups and communities with whom they work. This book will provide a valuable addition to the literature and social workers will find much within it for helping them not only reflect on their practice but carry it out. The contributions are scholarly but accessible and, while never attempting to provide easy answers to difficult human situations, will provide an authoritative introduction to the field as well as an important resource for experienced practitioners. The book's publication is very much to be welcomed.

References

Parton, N. (2000). Some Thoughts on the Relationship Between Theory and Practice in and for Social Work. *British Journal of Social Work*, 30(4): pp449–463.

Thompson, N. (2000). *Theory and Practice in Human Sciences*. Buckingham: Open University Press.

Introduction

Paul Stepney and Deirdre Ford

Social Work…now finds itself in a world uncertain of whether or not there are any deep and unwavering principles which define the essence of its character and hold it together as a coherent enterprise.

(Parton and Marshall, 1998: p243)

An uneasy air of compliance has descended upon the world of social work. The sheer scale and intensity of the changes in human service organisations now exceed all previous expectations creating a growing sense of unease and ambiguity about the future. Social work has been systematically reshaped and repositioned within the restructured welfare state, only to become politically compromised and compliant: 'the dog that didn't bark', ironically in a policy climate tailor-made for its advance (Jordan, 2000). The result, not surprisingly, is increasing demoralisation, disorientation and uncertainty: the conditions of postmodernity which create a more de-contextualised and dismembered practice (Parton, 1996; Dominelli, 1996).

Perhaps one of the most notable changes that has taken place is the response to change itself. In the past the orientation of significant numbers of practitioners was informed by notions of challenge, resistance and refusal (Clarke, 1996). During the 1990s, that resistance has been eroded and in the political arena 'social work has largely been overwhelmed and routed' (Jones and Novak, 1993: p197). However, at the local level resistance strategies remain significant, both for personal survival and for developing more empowering relationships with service users.

In Britain the re-ordering of social priorities and restructuring of the welfare state has been dramatic, even though public expenditure on health, education and the personal social services has been maintained and between 2000 and 2002 looks set to rise (Glennerster and Hills, 1998; Brown, 1999). The residualisation of the public sector has been achieved through a combined policy of marketisation and fragmentation of provision, creating the mixed economy of welfare, and decentralisation of responsibility alongside centralisation of control (Walker, 1997). Allied to this, local authorities have been exposed to strong downward pressures on spending and staff subjected to increasing managerial control of their work (Clarke *et al.*, 1994). Introducing the discipline of the market and a 'contract culture' into welfare, supported by a presentational emphasis on consumer choice, has helped to create the conditions for the eventual privatisation of much social provision. We suggest that this is a global trend with similar developments in the USA, Australia and Europe (Jordan, 1998; George and Napier, 1997).

The election of a New Labour government in 1997, far from reducing the commodifying effects of the market on welfare, appears to be reinforcing them with the introduction of a significant programme of welfare reform, in particular, *A New Contract for Welfare* (DSS, 1998a), *Modernising the Social Services* (DoH, 1998), *Modernising Local Government Improving Local Services Through Best Value* (DETR, 1998) as well as a raft of proposals relating to the NHS and services in mental health, disability and so on. The documents are concerned with raising standards in the public sector through greater regulation to meet new performance targets. There is also emphasis on prevention through partnerships and competition to achieve 'best value' in the market. Here Tony Blair has drawn heavily on the programmes of the Clinton administration designed to 'end welfare as we know it'. New Labour seems firmly set on a policy path towards the confirmation of a more conditional and affordable welfare state which became such a hallmark of the Thatcher and Major years.

If the context for practice is increasingly shaped by global economic factors, the changing role of the nation state (Dominelli, 1996) and managerial imperatives (Clarke *et al.*, 1994), two sets of questions emerge. The first concerns the need to understand the precise way that global forces have impacted on social work and subjected it to competing pressures and claims. The second more practical concern is to explore what might be done to minimise the most negative and potentially oppressive aspects of globalisation, to reduce social costs, whilst enhancing the more positive and creative possibilities for empowering practice. By promoting a broader, more critical and constructive conception of practice (Parton and O'Byrne, 2000) encompassing community development, social regeneration and change, in line with international traditions (Midgley, 1997), social work might move forward beyond the rigid organisational culture it now finds itself in. This is the very general and perhaps most ambitious task we have set ourselves.

In Part One the focus is on four major themes which it is argued structure the debate and shape the agenda for practice:

1. An overview of the wider policy context.

2. Implications for social work in the new millennium.

3. The commitment to anti-racist practice.

4. The theory to practice debate revisited.

We readily acknowledge that, in exploring such themes, ideas about contemporary society, the nature of its problems and the orientation of social work become highly contested. Social work and social policy are the subject of much dispute which in turn is reflected in the work of social workers and the practice dilemmas they encounter. We take this lack of consensus as one of our starting points in seeking to develop a more reflective discourse about the place of theory in practice. We will be exploring this further in chapters Five–Fourteen through an examination of different practice theories, models and methods supported by case examples. These are intended to illustrate the nature of the dilemmas which emerge in the real world and why a sound theoretical foundation is essential for good practice. We invite you to join us in our journey into the disputed territory of social work methods, models and theory.

Models, methods and theories: a note about terminology

A brief note may be helpful as these terms are used fairly loosely in everyday speech and not always applied with consistency in the social work literature. For present purposes and at the risk of oversimplification we define a theory as a framework of understanding or cluster of ideas which attempt to explain reality. In the social sciences theoretical knowledge is highly contested because different theories offer competing explanations reflecting particular values and ideological positions. The crucial point here concerns the nature of the explanation why something is as it is and, according to Thompson, this is what distinguishes a theory from a model. 'A model seeks to describe...how certain factors interrelate, but it will not show why they do so' (Thompson, 2000: p22).

Methods represent the more formal written accounts about how to do the job of social work (Sibeon, 1990). This occurs when theory, or a combination of theories, is made concrete and applied in practice.

Where a group of theories is being discussed the term paradigm may be used. This originates from the work of Kuhn (1970) to denote an approach informed by a set of related theories and beliefs about the nature of the world and the individual's place within it (Mark, 1996).

For example, in community social work (which is a method) patch models have evolved describing how services are organised by local teams in particular communities. However, the patch model of working will not explain why services should be provided in this way. For an explanation about 'why', we need to refer to theory: in this case a paradigm consisting of systems theory, organisational/groupwork/networking theory and ideas associated with community empowerment.

Notes on Contributors

Wing Hong Chui is a Lecturer in the School of Social Work and Social Policy at the University of Queensland in Australia. He has researched and published in the area of social work and criminology in Hong Kong and England.

Lena Dominelli is Professor of Social Work and Director of the Centre for International Social and Community Development at the University of Southampton. She is President of the International Association of Schools of Social Work and has recently been elected as an Academician of the Association of Learned Societies in the Social Sciences. Her wide-ranging publications cover several aspects of social work and include seventeen books.

David Evans currently practices as a Social Worker for Devon Social Services. He has worked extensively with older people in the field of community care.

Frances Fleet is a Lecturer in Social Work at the University of Exeter and tutor for the Diploma in Probation Studies at the University of Plymouth. Until recently she was a Probation Officer in Devon.

Deirdre Ford is a Lecturer in Social Work at the University of Exeter and a Social Worker employed by Devon Social Services. She has researched and published works on community care and social work education.

Peter Ford worked in the Probation Service as a Court Welfare Officer after qualifying in social work. He is currently Director of Studies in the Department of Social Work Studies at the University of Southampton, and his recent publications include work on competence-based approaches to assessment and on the place of mediation in social work practice.

Delia Jack is a Social Worker for Children with Disabilities in a local authoriy Social Services Department in the South West of England. Her

particular interest is in working with local communities to promote the development of inclusive services, accessible to children of all abilities.

Gordon Jack is a Lecturer and Head of Social Work and Probation Studies at the University of Exeter. For many years he was a local authority social work practitioner and manager of children and family services. More recently he has taught and published widely on child welfare and social policy issues.

Bill Jordan is Professor of Social Policy at the Universities of Exeter and Huddersfield, Reader in Social Policy at the University of North London, and Visiting Professor at Charles University, Prague. He worked in the probation service and local authority social services from 1965–1985.

Bill Kenny has held a number of academic posts in British universities and polytechnics over the past thirty years. He is currently a part-time tutor for the Department of Social Work and Probation Studies, University of Exeter.

Lynette Kenny is an Approved Social Worker in a multi-disciplinary team providing care for older people coping with mental disorders. She has extensive experience of working collaboratively with health care professionals.

Karen Postle is a Senior Lecturer at University College, Chichester. As a social worker she worked generically before specialising in work with adults and older people. Her work as a care manager and interest in care management led to research for her PhD which she received in 1999.

Brian Sheldon is Professor of Applied Social Research, and Director of the Centre for Evidence-based Social Services at the University of Exeter. He has written widely on, and has conducted studies of the effectiveness of social work, and has a particular interest in the application of cognitive-behavioural methods to social and personal problems.

Paul Stepney is an Indepedent Researcher and Associate Consultant with *Avenue Consulting Ltd*. Prior to this he has been a Lecturer in Social Work and Social Policy at the Universities of Hull, Manchester and more recently, Exeter.

Neil Thompson is Director of *Avenue Consulting Ltd*. (PO Box 2060, Wrexham LL13 0ZG) and a Visiting Professor at the University of Liverpool. He is the author of several books, his latest being *Understanding Social Work: Preparing for Practice* (Palgrave, 2000).

Acknowledgements

To Gill Watson and Di Cooper for their characteristic reliability and assistance in completing the final typescript.

To Geoffrey Mann and Martin Jones for their support, good humour and patience in producing this volume.

Chapter One

An Overview of the Wider Policy Context

Paul Stepney

The paradox of Social Policy is a crisis of solidarity within the welfare state.

(Walter Lorenz, 1997)

The restructuring of welfare agendas, within parameters of cost containment, efficiency and affordability, has had a direct and immediate impact on social work. According to Dominelli, 'social work in a postmodernist world is characterised by fragmented service provision through specialisation and contracting out...today's shifts arise from international competitiveness which demands that government disengages from welfare provision', (Dominelli, 1996: p157). Social work then is strategically located at the intersection of global economic forces, European policy responses and local demands. It is also, in part, a product of its practitioners working with some of the most dispossessed and marginalised groups (Wilson, 1993). This creates tensions at a time when the language of the market has become the new currency of exchange in welfare. Social work must act out these contradictions and resolve the problem of embracing a system where the rewards for success in the market are mirrored by new patterns of exclusion and inequality.

Similarly, the growth of new user movements for change in the fields of mental health, disability and old age have generated expectations about rights and empowerment which social workers have readily endorsed. However, there is a sense of irony in noting that this has occurred at a time when practitioners feel increasingly disempowered by the changing organisational culture (Jones, M., 1996). Moreover, users are now articulating their demand for rights, access to information and improved services in the political arena at Westminster often without social work support (Beresford and Croft, 1993; Oliver, 1996).

At a time when social work appears to have few friends in high office and a number of critics, not to mention the effect of operating under the glare of a hostile media, the apparent rejection by user groups hurts, although this may in part be a reaction against outmoded paternalism as current practice. Added to this has been the growing public criticism for its failure to manage high risk clients especially in the areas of mental health and child protection (Parton, 1992; Franklin, 1989; Kent, 1996).

Whilst social work has been in the front line of politically imposed constraints to contain the rise in public spending, it has taken the brunt of criticism for devoting scarce resources to crisis work and protecting vulnerable clients at the expense of preventative work in the community (Jack and Stepney, 1995). Recent policy initiatives, especially the White Paper (DoH, 1998), recognise the problem but offer few constructive suggestions for creating genuinely preventative services. Significantly, social work barely receives a mention.

The current crisis is fundamentally about the future of social work as a professional activity, under the combined attack of an administrative system of care management and competence based training. What is at stake is 'the capacity for professional discretion and judgement being replaced by routinised procedures...dominated by business plans and budgets' (Jones, M., 1996: p1). All provide an impulse for a process of de-professionalisation. Under care management the social worker has been redesignated as a care manager, requiring a qualitatively different and less academic form of training, or indeed no training.

Competence based training courses reflect a political culture which stems from the world of business and financial management. As Howe notes 'Many of social work's theories and practices have become analytically more shallow and increasingly performance orientated' (Howe, 1996: p77) which, without a sustained effort to retain a critical perspective, will leave the newly trained professional ill-equipped to respond creatively to the complex needs of vulnerable people in troubled times.

A further objection to competence based training is that it leads to practice which may in turn become dismembered and de-politicised. The paradigm of competences ultimately means professional workers utilising their skills within a business environment, without having the autonomy or discretion to question the values that underpin it. Many of the new values from the market fit uneasily with either traditional social work values (Jones and Jordan, 1996) or notions of partnership, empowerment and anti-oppressive practice (Thompson, 1997; Adams, 1996).

Managerialism

One of the most potent connecting threads linking markets, partnerships and customers is managerialism (Clarke *et al.*, 1994). The new managerialism provides one solution which bridges the credibility gap between the rhetoric of needs-led services and the reality of increasingly mechanistic assessments, tighter eligibility criteria and resource driven service priorities.

The new managers play a central role in providing strategic leadership at a time of rapid change. This is designed to ensure broad commitment to centrally determined objectives whilst devolving responsibility to front line staff for making the organisation more user friendly. It intersects global economic imperatives of the market with the local and internal working lives of staff (Jones and May, 1992).

A further index of the problem is the extent to which questions of equity and justice still feature in organisational mission statements but are being swamped by bureaucratic procedures and are in danger of all but disappearing from professional social work agendas. Managerial priorities associated with the three E's (effectiveness, economy and efficiency) now permeate almost every aspect of the care management task and enable the manager to 'scientifically' appraise performance (Pollitt and Harrison, 1992).

In many important respects managerialism has played a strategic role in overseeing the fragmentation of provision and the development of a more de-politicised practice. In so doing social work staff have found it difficult to resist being co-opted into largely accepting these priorities at the expense of

professional autonomy and discretion. And this has created many schisms and tensions in local social services teams at a time of increased workloads and reduced budgets. The result, not surprisingly, has been high stress, low morale, surface compliance but a deeper mistrust about the future (Hadley and Clough, 1996; Balloch *et al.*, 1995). Thus the potential for more serious tensions erupting into conflict remains ever present. In the meantime practitioners continue to explore ways of meeting the challenge, by recording unmet need, assisting clients to appeal, and using what little discretion exists to maximise service provision within the tighter eligibility criteria which prevail in social services (Hadley and Clough, 1996).

Evidence of the unpromising climate shaping the outlook of front line practitioners can be found in research by Hadley and Clough together with government commissioned research. The community care reforms implemented in April, 1993 represent the most far reaching changes introduced into Britain's social services since they were set up in the early 1970s. In their research the authors report that 'for all the people we interviewed the experience of change has been one of loss: the loss of being valued, the loss of having a clear purpose and hope in the future, the loss of enjoyment and, for some, the loss of a career. Almost all identified new pressures to conform' (Hadley and Clough, 1996: pp176–177). Despite the rhetoric of enhanced provision and choice, the reality according to the workers in Hadley and Clough's sample is a 'situation in which they think the system of services has deteriorated rather than improved, with both users and workers losing out…Their reality is defined in terms of disappointment, confusion and frustration' (ibid: p183).

Further, these subjective responses correspond with research findings from studies designed to evaluate the community care reforms (Lewis and Glennerster, 1996; Henwood, 1995; Balloch *et al.*, 1995). The general picture which emerged was one of improvement in some areas but major problems in others. For example, improved inter-agency co-operation was developing which led to some creative responses for those clients with complex needs, evidence that individual practitioners can still make a significant difference.

However, according to Connolly and Johnson, 'concerns relating to finance and funding are quite apparent, so too are the constraints on providing preventative services. The boundary between free NHS care and means tested social services and the major question of who is responsible for long term care are significant concerns'. Moreover, this and other findings suggest that 'empowerment and user choice still remain more rhetoric than reality' (Connolly and Johnson, 1996: p8).

The European dimension

During the 1990s it became increasingly clear that governments throughout Europe faced a vast array of common problems. What is perhaps distinctive about the current situation 'is that the number, nature and severity of these problems demand solutions that are often beyond the scope of traditional forms of welfare provision' (George and Taylor-Gooby, 1996: p1). The nature and scale of the situation is worth briefly mapping out.

In very general terms the globalisation of the economy combined with the international-isation of the nation state provide the wider backdrop to the reshaping of practice. This is not to infer that globalisation is a distinctive process producing a 'new world order', but rather, the effect of different social, economic and political processes. Although such processes are commonly associated with the increasing mobility of capital, the information superhighway and so on, the effects of globalisation may be marked by partial, contradictory and highly conflictual tendencies (Clarke, 2000). Globalisation has occurred at a time when there has been a slowing down in the rise of GDP in most European nations (George, 1996) and a concomitant effort to constrain the rate of increase in public spending. As economies entered recession at the end of the 1980s and early 1990s unemployment rose and remained persistently high. This has led to renewed efforts to develop EU wide policies to tackle common economic and social problems, specifically to promote solidarity alongside subsidiarity (Spicker, 1991).

If we examine the demand side of European economies we find a trend towards growing casualisation and insecurity in the labour market especially in northern Europe (Hutton, 1996; George, 1996). This has created an expanding sector of low paid, part-time, casualised 'junk jobs' with a disproportionately high female workforce (Esping-Andersen, 1990).

To make sense of this, we need to recognise the consequences of a situation in which international companies can locate their operations anywhere in the world, combining technologies and human labour power in the most profitable ways. In Europe, returns on capital (dividends, profits) are at a historically high level, whilst those to labour have been declining (as a proportion of GDP) since the early 1970s. There is a surplus of unskilled labour all over the continent, but especially in the post-communist countries. Employers seek to use labour power 'flexibly', especially in the services sector, including human services. National governments compete for international investments as much in terms of low social costs as the high level of their social capital (education and skills of workers, trust, work ethic.) The UK has led the field in 'social deregulation' and the reform of welfare systems in line with these requirements. (Jordan, 1998).

Demographic changes are also significant as we witness a rise in Europe's ageing population—particularly the very old, those over 80. In the EU the proportion of the over 80 population, which was 10 per cent of older people in 1960, is projected to more than double by the year 2020 to approximately 22 per cent (Eurostat, 1993). Whilst the vast majority of older people look after themselves, with support (Wenger, 1993), as age increases so may disability and ill health (Johnson and Slater, 1993). This will inevitably place additional demands on resources for health and social care at a time when other social trends suggest that the number of informal carers, especially women in northern Europe willing and able to care, is set to fall. This is due to such factors as increasing mobility, family poverty, divorce rates, carers growing older (Abrams *et al.*, 1989). Thus, there is likely to be an impending crisis in care across the countries of northern Europe which will require action in the very near future.

It follows that the demand for welfare is set to rise given these predicted trends along with the increasing fragmentation of local communities, in both urban centres of population and rural areas. Here the articulation of need is already being expressed by a plurality of interest groups and new social movements demanding more empowering and democratic forms of provision (Beresford and Croft, 1993; Harloe *et al.*, 1990) and by users asserting their culturally diverse identities (Lorenz, 1997). Such demands cannot easily be satisfied by market consumerism or accommodated within existing structures at a time of severe resource constraints. The outcome paradoxically may be to perpetuate conditions of 'difference, doubt, dissatisfaction and diversity' (EU, 1994) at the local level which urgently require attention. Here, post-modernism offers rich descriptions but provides few solutions (Parton, 1996), although this is just the kind of challenging territory which social workers have traditionally been skilled at exploiting for the common good (Jordan, 1990).

Welfare states throughout Europe have been subjected to unprecedented criticisms and scrutiny from across the political spectrum (George, 1996) either for being overgenerous and a drain on resources (Murray, 1994) or for not doing enough to tackle poverty and reduce inequalities (Atkinson, 1991). This has left social work in an ambiguous position. The ever changing politico-economic climate presents new opportunities and dangers in exploiting the spaces and contradictions within post-modern market liberalism. Working with disenchanted and disaffected members of the community, on mutually negotiated terms rather than those of the market, can be a high risk strategy. However, the rewards are likely to be significant in enhancing citizenship rights, promoting solidarity and fighting oppression.

What social workers have hitherto found more difficult is to transcend the priorities of the nation state as part of a wider European project of transformation (Cannan *et al.*, 1992). Ultimately, according to Lorenz, social workers have a choice between 'fitting into a given agenda of exclusion and segregation and grounding their work on principles of social rights and solidarity' (Lorenz, 1994: pp10–11).

Policy responses

In all the OECD Countries, reform of welfare systems has been forced on governments by the erosion of collective institutions for protecting employment, and redistributing income providing social services.
(Scharpf, 1999, cited in Jordan, 2000: p4)

If the citizens of Europe face similar problems, then in contrast the policy responses from governments have hitherto been marked by enormous diversity and difference (Moran, 1988). This reflects different systems of social protection or welfare state regimes. Here the work of Esping-Andersen has been influential in identifying three configurations or broad clusters, which have been analysed in terms of commodification and stratification: the extent to which welfare can provide protection against the commodifying effects of the market and modify class related outcomes (Esping-Andersen, 1990).

Although these have been subject to some reformulation (Ferrera, 1994; Castles, 1993) the three original typologies are worth briefly outlining as they form a useful basis for evaluating subsequent policy change.

First, the liberal welfare states, epitomised by the USA (but with the UK in hot pursuit) have traditionally given rather ungenerous levels of social insurance benefits (retirement pensions, disability, sickness and unemployment benefits), and had extensive 'safety nets' of social assistance and means tested support for the working poor. Second, the corporatist welfare states such as Germany, have given much more generous social insurance benefits, but strongly related to employment and earnings: hence both perpetuating inequalities in the incomes of those outside the labour market, and favouring men over women (who participate less in employment than in the liberal regimes of USA and UK). Third, social democratic welfare states are those exemplified by Sweden, where every citizen has a strong stake in state benefits and services, and where redistribution and universalism continue to enjoy widespread political support (Esping-Andersen, 1990).

These regimes have responded rather differently to the challenge of globalisation and demographic change (Esping-Andersen, 1990). The liberal strategy has included these elements of social deregulation and privatisation mentioned above. The effect has been to polarise both incomes and employment opportunities, with falling real wages and a large sector of working households below the poverty line in the USA and UK. Both countries claimed to have achieved 'job miracles' in comparison with the rest of Europe. Indeed there was a large increase in employment in the US, and a small one in Britain. However, in both, the growth came mainly in low paid service work, including private social care, which contributed to the need for wage subsidisation. Recently the government claimed that labour market participation had increased by a total of 648,000, between May 1997 and September, 1999, as a result of the New Deals (Brown, 1999). A substantial number of these jobs will be part-time and low paid.

The growth in employment in social services is therefore a symptom of one of the problems of this model. (Ironically, many of the staff administering benefits, for example, are themselves claimants of working family tax credit and housing benefit.) Furthermore, the problem of casualisation and fragmentation of employment at the bottom of the labour market, low wages and lack of incentives, have contributed to the phenomenon of households with no member in regular employment (almost one fifth of all working households in the UK according to the Green Paper on Welfare Reform, DSS, 1998: p12). Hence the Clinton–Blair programme for welfare to work becomes enforcing by driving claimants into employment or training, where opportunities and incentives are lacking (Jordan, 1998).

By contrast, in the continental regimes epitomised by Germany, unemployment rates are now higher, and there is little sign of a growth in employment. Social exclusion rather than poverty is seen as the main problem. Social services in kind have not expanded as rapidly, and there are far fewer jobs, especially in community social care. In the Scandinavian countries, the 'Nordic Model of Welfare' retains a commitment to equality and solidarity (Jackobsson, 1998). This means that social welfare services are very extensive, and employees enjoy higher wages and better conditions. However, they are characteristically women, and this segmentation of female employment (often part-time) is increasingly seen as an unacceptable feature of the model. In the social democratic regime represented by Sweden, public services for social care predominate; in the corporatist one, voluntary agencies are the main providers.

There is some evidence of convergence in northern Europe towards a more liberal and residual welfare regime (George, 1996). In this Britain has set the pace. During the recession of the early 1990s traditional high spending Scandinavian countries cut back whilst Mediterranean countries, like Greece and Spain, with socialist governments and EU funding, increased social provision. In Britain, and to a lesser extent in Germany and France, cuts in benefit rates have occurred along with the gradual reform of pensions. It is significant that these have been high on the agenda of New Labour's welfare reforms. Less dramatic measures have been taken in the Nordic countries, which has slightly lowered the redistributional effect of welfare but without loss of public support or talk of 'retrenchment' (Kautto *et al.*, 1999). Hence 'globalisation does not necessarily lead to convergence...but welfare states are now on a shared trajectory of more limited social rights' (Timonen, 1999: p255).

It is only in central and eastern Europe where the state is being subject to more drastic modernisation policies, in collaboration with the creation of new markets, that a significant expansion appears to be taking place. Both social assistance and social work have grown rapidly, in an ironic imitation of the USA and UK. It is the residual 'safety nets', not the institutional features of a universal system of social protection, that have marked the transition to capitalism (Standing, 1996; Jordan, 1998). Perhaps this is a logical step along the road to closer European union.

In Britain the response, in terms of social policy, can be understood as a tactical retreat from universal provision accompanied by a redirection of expectations away from the state towards the market, the family and the community. New Labour's programme of welfare reforms, the 'Third Way', makes a virtue of such change. The reality is that this has placed a greater burden on informal carers, most of whom are women, at a time when they are subject to competing pressures in the labour market and the family (Langan and Day, 1992). In one sense this might be said to accord with the principle of subsidiarity, where seeking support from the state is seen as a last resort (Spicker, 1991). However, this may be a convenient and cheap policy option at a time when the family is under pressure and the community is subject to the forces of fragmentation and division. The result in the UK is growing poverty and exclusion.

New Labour's programme to reform the welfare state: the 'Third Way'

New Labour has skilfully mobilised a range of political interests in a project to modernise and reform the welfare state. At the core of the project is the aim to transform the welfare system around work and demand 'more from those who receive assistance', 'no rights without responsibilities', and which in exchange improves their incentives and opportunities' (Jordan, 2000: piii). However, what is not so clearly articulated is the quality of the work available and the type of inclusion on offer.

The set of principles underpinning the reform programme has been referred to by Tony Blair as the 'Third Way' (Blair, 1998): how to balance the freedom of the global market economy with a commitment to social justice. New Labour's 'Third Way' approach to welfare reform has three identifiable elements: first, a moral-political crusade against irresponsibility and deviance; second, the creation of a strongly conditional welfare regime based upon labour market activation, and third, a series of US-style enforcement measures (zero tolerance, three strikes and you're out, tough love). These elements neatly combine in the government's drive to promote responsible communities and tackle social exclusion. (Exclusion from work, family and community are seen as the priorities rather than poverty and inequality which represent Old Labour concerns.)

A plethora of policy initiatives have followed reflecting and indeed reinforcing 'Third Way' principles, including:

- Reform of the tax-benefit system including the introduction of Working Family Tax Credit to improve work incentives.

- Introduction of a modest minimum wage.

- New Deals to increase labour market participation for such groups as young unemployed, lone parents, disabled persons.

- Modernisation policies to transform local authorities and the NHS with specific proposals in the field of mental health, disability, children's services and criminal justice.

Two policy initiatives will be examined in greater depth: the Green Paper on Welfare Reform (DSS, 1998) and *Modernising the Social Services* (DoH, 1998a) as both have important implications for social work.

The Green Paper *A New Contract for Welfare* (DSS, 1998) insists that claimants have responsibilities that correspond with their rights and that all, including lone parents and disabled people, who can work should do so, reinforcing the message 'work for those who can, security for those who can't'. The various New Deals for claimant groups outline measures to enable, promote or enforce these obligations. Some of these, such as increased child care provision, training and the minimum wage, are aimed at improving incentives. Others, such as the plans to enforce benefit conditions and clamp down on 'fraud', are tougher sanctions against those seen as shirking their duties to contribute.

From the standpoint of social work, it is easy to recognise features of the earlier Conservative legislation in this programme. The DSS Green Paper speaks of 'flexible packages of help' which are 'tailor made' for individual claimants, but with an underlying threat of coercion if these are not accepted (DSS, 1998: p23). It is interesting, however, that social work is not mentioned in this context, as if the new system of 'advisers' will need to be built on a new spirit of constructive compulsion, which social work with its longstanding ties to the old welfare state cannot provide (Jordan, 1998).

Also familiar is the pledge to remould the 'old passive welfare state' into a more dynamic new model, from safety net to trampoline, in which both staff and service users will be recast as proactive and cost conscious, making choices and taking responsibility (DSS, 1998: p3). Here again we see the notion that any expansion of welfare spending is conditional on a new spirit of participation, flexibility and obligation. What is discouraging, from the point of view of neighbourhood social workers, voluntary agency project workers, volunteers and local activists alike, is the absence of any recognition of their struggles and successes in enabling the most deprived and excluded communities to survive the Thatcher years. Only formal employment in officially recognised jobs seems to count in New Labour's view of the contributions required for social justice and social inclusion. This reinforces the tendency for public sector social work to be used as an instrument of assessment, risk management and enforcement, rather than to support grass roots efforts at economic regeneration and social support (Stepney *et al.*, 1999).

The White Paper, *Modernising the Social Services* (DoH, 1998a), is concerned with the regulation of local authorities to raise standards and meet new performance targets. The social services will be subject to mechanisms which have been tried and tested in the NHS and education, including use of performance indicators, league tables and external audit with the establishment of a general social care council to enforce standards.

The White Paper outlines principles which, in themselves, are fairly uncontentious, for example, social care should 'promote independence' and 'respect dignity', 'meet individuals specific needs' and be 'organised, assessed, provided and financed in a fair, open and consistent way in every part of the country' (DoH, 1998a: para 1.8). However, it is extremely prescriptive about how these applied principles or proposals are to be implemented and the targets achieved. In fact the 'Third Way' becomes decidedly Benthamite in its regulatory approach and threats of penalties for non-compliance (Jordan, 2000).

The social services are criticised for a failure to promote independence and develop preventive strategies. But questions about the reasons for this, concerning the adequacy of central government funding, are quickly passed over. Similarly unacknowledged is the official approval given to local authorities for introducing eligibility criteria which limits services to those in the highest categories of need. The White Paper is confusing and unconvincing about the whole question of prevention. For example, it argues that more low level support is needed as a preventative strategy, but then contradicts this by adding 'for people most at risk of losing their independence' (DoH, 1998a: para 2.12). So, it seems that rationing will continue, but under the guise of prevention. In child care, the White Paper disappointingly has little to say on how resources might be redirected away from statutory interventions towards family support.

Overall, although there is potential in New Labour's programme for developing empowering practice to strengthen the position of oppressed groups, this is undermined by various factors, such as a conservative view of the community (based on narrow traditional values), rigid perceptions of what constitutes social exclusion, together with a somewhat paternalistic approach towards the re-integration and re-activation of such citizens.

New Labour seems determined to continue many of the Thatcherite populist themes, under a banner of social inclusion, including appeals to the middle ground of British politics. This might be seen to translate as 'fighting for the most effective means to inflame the irritable sensibilities of the nearly poor and almost rich' (Dean and Melrose, 1997). And by appeasing the popular prejudices of middle England, Tony Blair's 'Third Way' becomes preoccupied with clearing the streets of the underclass, with surveillance and control, rather than a genuinely new social contract rooted in justice and empowerment. Significantly, such responses have not gone unnoticed in Europe.

Traditional responses to the welfare crisis in Europe have been to either increase resources or dampen down demand. European governments appear to be following Britain's lead and adopting the latter course of action. With traditionally high rates of taxation and social protection contributions many governments faced difficult choices. Thus in the face of increasing global competition to create low cost economies, and with government borrowing already high, lowering expectations became the least painful option (Taylor-Gooby, 1996; OECD, 1994).

What has hitherto been lacking, is any sustained commitment to social investment on a scale commensurate with rising demand and social needs. This is especially the case given the high levels of unemployment in nearly all European countries. Britain now has amongst the lowest proportion of GDP available for social investment throughout the EU, financed through tax and national insurance contributions, (OECD, 1994). And this reluctance to use the state as a vehicle for investment, so central to New Right thinking during the Thatcher and Major years, has propelled New Labour policy towards public/private partnership which is likely to influence the rest of Europe. It follows that 'throughout Europe, the trend in policy has been towards greater commodification…whilst the position in relation to class is more complex, except in the UK where the redistributional aspect has been weakened' (Taylor-Gooby, 1996: p215).

Another important factor which social workers encounter in their daily working lives is the increasing feminisation and racialisation of poverty as part of the new pattern of exclusion (Hutton, 1996). In the past there was a lack of clear policy response to tackle this problem which meant that women had to rely on social security benefits or the labour market (or both) for income maintenance. Recently, as noted above, New Labour have begun to not only 'think the unthinkable' but translate this into policy, namely the abolition of lone parent premiums in income support alongside the various New Deals designed to push people into the formal labour market. Arguments about benefit dependency and social

responsibility, first deployed against black single mothers in the USA, now inform much of New Labour's 'tough love' welfare policy.

However, we know that women form the basis for developing networks of care and support in the community (Williams, F., 1997) and such resources need to be acknowledged and developed rather than exploited. A Eurostat report from the EU statistical office of information highlights that Britain now has more children living in poverty than any other EU country (*The Guardian*, April 28th, 1997). Consequently, social work has an important role to play in supporting all marginalised groups to tackle poverty and fight oppression at the local level whilst responding to pressures to become more cost effective and research minded. The problems and potential associated with achieving emancipatory change whilst demonstrating greater effectiveness are explored in the next section.

Chapter Two

Implications for Social Work in the New Millennium

Paul Stepney

We have noted in the previous section how the context for practice has become increasingly shaped by forces which stem from the global economy. Here international comparisons of performance and competitiveness, as measured by the OECD, have come to be dependent on high rates of growth and productivity which require low social maintenance costs. The problem in Britain is that whilst labour productivity (and investment) still lags behind the USA and most of Europe (Elliot, 1998) efforts to remedy this have produced wider inequalities, greater insecurity and exclusion (Jordan, 1998; Hutton, 1996). This provides the backdrop to recent welfare reforms and highlights the nature of the structural constraints on social work.

One of the problems with this kind of analysis is that such considerations may seem somewhat distant from the world of practice. Of course, this is not the case. For example, in the summer of 1998, 1,100 job losses were announced in the North East by a multi-national firm little more than a year after launching its UK operation with some £50 million in regional aid. The social costs in the area are likely to be catastrophic (Milner and Hetherington, 1998). In the same week the minister for welfare reform Frank Field resigned following a cabinet reshuffle. He complained that his reform programme was blocked and that, whilst he had been encouraged to 'think the unthinkable', the government was unwilling to translate his recommendations into concrete policy proposals (Brindle, 1998). Almost simultaneously, the media reported that three generations of children from one family in the South West had been subjected to systematic abuse during the past 35 years (Davies, 1998).

These three stories selected from news reports over a couple of days will all have significant implications for social workers and yet in the reporting of these events, with the exception of the child abuse case, social work hardly received a mention. More recently media coverage of the government aid package to help workers due to be made redundant at Rover and Ford made no reference to social work. In other European countries the contribution of social work to economic regeneration is recognised (Kautto et al., 1999). The local/global connections which now underpin so many of the problems social workers in the UK encounter also need to be understood and acknowledged. Whilst this doesn't make the task of finding a way forward any easier or offer any quick fix solutions, it does offer a more viable framework for working with service users on politically sound and mutually negotiated terms. Such an approach may also offer some insights into the road social work is being propelled along, the tensions which emerge in practice and whether any alternatives might exist.

In the restructured and marketised welfare state, social work is now required to have a narrower and more instrumental focus (Howe, 1996), operate within increasingly proscribed parameters (Walker, 1997; DoH, 1998a) and demonstrate evidence of effectiveness (MacDonald et al., 1992). New legislation in terms of Community Care, Criminal Justice and the Children Act has accelerated this process. Alongside this social services have introduced new systems of care management for delivering services involving the separation of purchasing from providing responsibilities. As Payne notes, the relationship between care management and social work is disputed. 'Care management, according to one view, is a form of social work, another view represents it as service management, whilst a third view locates it as a management technique for reforming social work so that it deals more effectively with situations where co-ordinated service provision is required rather than therapeutic help' (Payne, 1997: p280). And it is this third view which, it was argued, has been instrumental in creating a climate where social workers experience the reforms in terms of loss—loss of skills, opportunities to implement the range of methods for which they have been trained, erosion of professional identity and so on (Hadley and Clough, 1996).

Whatever view is adopted the reforms have had a major impact with the employment of care managers in social services purchasing teams whose role and duties subsume many of the tasks previously performed by social workers (Coulshed and Orme, 1998). This had opened the way for the recruitment of unqualified staff to carry out much of the so-called routine care management work. The establishment of 'Help Desks' in some areas based upon the financial services call centre model will only accelerate this trend.

It is quite a short step from this to a situation where substantially less professionally qualified staff will be required, principally to undertake the more high risk work: for example child protection investigations, mental health assessments, complex risk assessments. However, the problems inherent in such an approach are slowly beginning to emerge: first it may contribute to a general process of de-skilling and de-professionalisation (Clarke, 1996); second, it leads to a more mechanistic and bureaucratic practice (Howe, 1996); third, there is no reliable way of separating complex work from the more straightforward, leaving unqualified staff quite exposed and reliant on highly skilled supervision which may or may not be readily available (Parton and Small, 1989); fourth, high risk work may not receive the resources it merits, increasing the probability of mistakes. (There has been increased public awareness in the number of violent incidents involving mental health users being discharged into the community without adequate supervision and support, as evidenced by the case of Christopher Clunis resulting in the tragic death of Jonathon Zito (Zito Trust, 1995).) Fifth, there is a strong case for thinking that the policy direction being followed is in the name of cost containment rather than quality and is at odds with the values of delivering needs-led, empowering services.

In other words, social work has been subjected to competing pressures and claims. On the one hand it has become more limited, defensive (especially in child protection work), and constrained by strict budgetary control and eligibility criteria. On the other hand it has reaffirmed its commitment to developing anti-oppressive practice, challenging discrimination, and promoting programmes of social justice designed to enhance the citizenship rights of service users. In community care, as Wistow notes, the aims of empowering practice are 'founded upon holistic assessments of the needs of individual; individualised care packages; and the empowerment of users to make informed choices about their future life styles' (Wistow, 1995: pp234–235).

The problem is that such claims contain a fundamental tension between practice which is empowering and facilitative and the underlying policy of social discipline and cost containment (Payne, 1997). The success of the system is clearly dependent upon each element of the care management task being performed adequately, sufficient funding and the ability of care managers to link into and strengthen informal networks (Challis, 1992). However, evidence from research suggests that only some of these objectives are being met, that community care funding is inadequate and that relationships with informal carers remain tenuous (Henwood, 1996; Wistow, 1995). Further, enormous regional variations exist between local authorities in the way the community care reforms have been implemented (Lewis and Glennester, 1996).

One potentially powerful way of querying the welfare circle (George and Miller, 1994) has been the search for greater effectiveness in social work. This element is central to the movement for evidence-based practice and the establishment of research centres at a number of universities including Stirling, Huddersfield and Exeter to name but three, specifically to promote a culture of evaluation and research minded practice in the personal social services.

Evidence-based practice

Such a development has obvious attractions for practitioners, managers and service users in helping to improve accountability and deliver more effective services informed by research evidence about what works (Cheetham, 1998). The wider challenge is that, whilst this may be perceived (by government) as having considerable potential in the quest for efficiency savings and securing better value for money services, its contribution to tackling oppression and a wider programme for social justice is less clear cut.

In the past, as MacDonald *et al.* (1992) note, there has been a certain amount of ambivalence if not complacency about conducting research into effectiveness, a situation not confined to social work. However, more recently, although arguments about methodology continue, in particular the respective contribution of qualitative and quantitative approaches, practical difficulties in carrying out practice-based research, the value of small scale studies together with a certain amount of professional scepticism, social work has begun to embrace the need to be 'both research literate and politically wary' (Cheetham, 1998: p15). This may assist it to resist the ideologically driven pendulum swings of policy fashion (Sheldon and MacDonald, 1999).

Clearly, research has the capacity to influence the quality of the policy/practice debate and contribute to more informed programmes of action. In the past this was referred to as experimental social policy (Smith, 1975) or action-research (CDP, 1977). However, for this to happen in the new millennium will require rational, open and democratic controls to be put in place to ensure research is part of a process of critical enquiry rather than cost control. Used wisely, research has the potential to be used as a 'basis for critical review and reflection, perhaps including comparison of different ways of providing similar services, an analysis of factors which influence quality and a pointer to unintended or unexpected outcomes' (Cheetham, 1998: p26).

However, the relationship between research and practice is problematic in several respects. This can be illustrated from the many well funded and justifiably influential projects in the field of child care and child protection. (Packman *et al.*, 1986; Millham *et al.*, 1986; Freeman and Cleaver, 1995; Packman and Hall, 1998). These have formed the basis of DoH guidelines and local authority policies in this field, which have become increasingly prescriptive over time. In this they have tended to serve the purposes of top down managerial methods, and restricted the scope for professional initiatives and judgement. However, on one thing all these studies have agreed: the importance of the quality of the relationship between social worker, parents and children. This repeated finding contains a paradox. First, it is not always clear how researchers have reached their conclusions from their methodology, it sometimes seems more of a post-hoc policy. Second, the prescription it entails is often vague and generalised, in terms of honesty and good faith, rather than specific methods. In other words, an emphasis on good practice is often undermined by considerable fogginess about how this is recognisable and how it can be learned.

During recent years practitioners have begun to redress the balance concerning their exclusion from the research process and practice-based research has slowly advanced (Fuller and Petch, 1995). Various developments are significant here, including improvements in methodologies which are more responsive to the needs of practitioners; a certain amount of methodological synthesis and pluralism; and increasing collaboration between practitioners and researchers (Kazi, 1998). It is necessary, as Karvinen reminds us, to develop a range of research strategies which 'should be sensitive enough to uncover not only general tendencies, but also contextual particularities' (Karvinen, 1999: p282). Nonetheless social work still faces some formidable hurdles if practitioner/researchers are to combine evaluation concerned with effectiveness alongside a commitment to emancipatory change (Shaw, 1998). There are at least three general factors which can be identified as structuring the research agenda: the internal market, managerialism and methodological disputes or paradigm wars (Everitt and Hardiker, 1996; Pawson and Tilley, 1997).

Internal market

Whilst practitioners may have been criticised in the past for not being sufficiently research literate, the impact of the internal market on the research enterprise has been largely overlooked. If practitioners have internalised the policy message to contain costs and improve efficiency then in this context research can easily be seen as something of a luxury. In fact as Everitt reminds us, the Culyer review of research in the NHS was initiated by just these concerns (Everitt, 1998). The Culyer Report made a raft of positive proposals for encouraging practitioner research and acknowledged there was an urgent need to bridge the gap between policy and practice.

It is perhaps ironic to note at this juncture that the reforms to the health service outlined in *Working for Patients* (Cm. 555, 1989), which under Mrs Thatcher's leadership created the internal market, were themselves implemented without any corresponding research to evaluate outcomes. And it was much later that subsequent research was carried out to evaluate their effectiveness with support from the King's Fund Institute (Robinson and Le Grand, 1994).

Managerialism

Whilst most practitioners would concur with the need to develop research minded and policy orientated practice 'there seems little doubt that recent initiatives have been experienced as part of a process of increasing managerial control' (Everitt, 1998: p106). The emphasis on technical recording, systematic information gathering, performance indicators, of which there are now more than 400 in the NHS (Pollitt and Harrison, 1992), all tend to reinforce mechanistic practice rather than creativity and innovation.

It follows that there is an urgent need to recognise the different interests that exist in the research enterprise and combine rigorous scrutiny of practice with public debate (Everitt, 1998), otherwise there is a danger that the critical cutting edge of research will become subordinate to managerial concerns and control. Another way of reinforcing this aim is to establish collaborative partnerships with users and community members so that research questions address the problems of disadvantage and oppression. In this context the disability rights movement provides a good example of what can be achieved (Campbell and Oliver, 1996).

Methodological disputes and 'paradigm wars'

Another problem with research in a market economy is that marketised assumptions may encourage a higher value to be placed on hard, empirical, outcome based methodologies which are seen to be objective and neutral, rather than softer qualitative approaches, action-research or

policy orientated studies. The strengths and scientific validity of experimental designs is not disputed here although their usefulness in social science research is more contentious (Usher, 1997). However, the value placed on alternative methodologies often involves making a political as well as a professional judgement. Significantly, qualitative methods may allow for more empowering and reflective evaluations of practice (Shaw, 1998). Consequently, we need to make the epistemological and ontological criteria for exercising such judgements about methodology more explicit (McKenzie *et al.*, 1997; Thompson, 2000). This raises some fundamental questions about what counts as knowledge, in what way is it known and what is the nature of 'reality' (Guba, 1990; Usher, 1997).

In a telling contribution to the debate, Shaw challenges much conventional wisdom by calling on social workers to develop 'a critical, reflective and enabling practice' anchored in an exploration of how experienced practitioners evaluate their work. He suggests that this offers a valid foundation for building on existing expertise rather than importing 'off the shelf' research designs (Shaw, 1998). Clearly much here depends on the quality of the experienced practitioner and their capacity to reflect critically and abstract from individual practice examples to general theory and back to another real situation (Pawson and Tilley, 1997). Notwithstanding the problems inherent in identifying good practice and distinguishing it from 'convincing stories' about practice, Shaw draws up a manifesto for evaluation in practice. Here social workers should be encouraged to:

- Exploit the potential of reflective methods to reflect hard on both process and outcomes.

- Make theoretical assumptions explicit, including taken for granted knowledge about culture, identity, class, gender, disability etc.

- Get close to service users' experiences, and respect these as authentic accounts of resilience in the face of oppression.

- Develop genuinely participatory and dialogical forms of evaluation as critical enquiry (Freire, 1972).

- Ground research evaluation in different practice theories and methods.

(from Shaw, 1998: pp214–215)

Whilst Shaw makes a strong case for practitioners developing qualitative methods such as participant observation, life histories and focus group work, a case can be made here for methodological pluralism: utilising quasi-experimental designs if appropriate, but drawing largely on critical theory and qualitative approaches through a 'realistic' approach to methodological issues (Kazi, 1998; Pawson and Tilley, 1997). This has the potential for combining experimental rigour, to discover what works for whom in what context, with user participation towards more emancipatory practice. The challenge as always with a pluralistic approach is to create a structure which 'conveys a sense of explanatory synthesis' and ontological coherence (Pawson and Tilley, 1997).

Responding to uncertainty

Another problem in constructing a valid framework or manifesto for evaluating practice is the degree of uncertainty and unpredictability which permeates much of the terrain of social work. As Thompson has usefully reminded us, before embarking on a new piece of work expect the unexpected and predict the unpredictable (Thompson, 2000). Flexibility has always been the key to the social worker's survival if not success, but the challenge is to use this purposefully in a world where there are few benchmarks of truth and certainty.

In social work this may not create as many problems as it might in other professions (such as medicine, law, teaching even) for the notion of universal truth has long been abandoned in favour of treating knowledge as socially constructed, partial, fragmented and encoded with contested meanings, thereby contributing to a sense of disorientation and difference (Parton, 1996; Guba and Lincoln, 1989). What is at stake here is social work's capacity to operate effectively in situations of uncertainty —especially for its clients, who remain amongst the most marginalised and excluded groups in society.

There have been two broad responses to the problem of uncertainty. One embraces a discourse of competences (CCETSW, 1996) the other reflective practice (Adams et al., 1998). The issue here is whether the latter can be adequately developed within a paradigm dominated by the former.

The development of competence based training, at both qualifying and postqualifying level, and its influence on practice emerged during the early 1990s following a succession of child abuse scandals. The enquiry reports highlighted deficiencies in training and agency procedures. Both have been addressed through the language of competences permeating professional agendas. However, this response was a reaction to wider global pressures and the new market in welfare to try and maintain reliable standards in an uncertain world. It also answered the call for improvements in services and enhancing consumer choice. What is more problematic is deciding in what sense competence based approaches may be empowering and the extent to which they reinforce managerial control (Adams, 1998). Further, it has been argued that they undermine the movement towards anti-oppressive practice (Dominelli, 1996).

Adams identifies six major criticisms of competence based approaches including arguments that they are more suited to work in stable, bureaucratic organisations rather than the organic milieu of social work; they fragment practice into artificially discrete elements; they are outcome-based and encourage convergent and mechanistic thinking; they concentrate exclusively on measurable aspects of job performance; and overemphasise techniques and skills at the expense of values and critical reflection (Adams, 1998: p258). The result is what Pearson once described as welfare technicians reducing complex socio-political issues to the problems of administration (Pearson, 1975). These limitations are neatly captured by Orme when she argues that 'the competence based approach requires certainties; that if one is dealing with A, you can intervene with B and that will secure an acceptable outcome…but the outcome is often that the required form has been completed' (Coulshed and Orme, 1998: p8).

If social workers are going to be trained to 'approach each situation respectful of difference, complexity and ambiguity' (Parton and Marshall, 1998: p246), as well as provide a competent level of service, then it is the capacity for critical enquiry and reflection that must be enhanced. Critical enquiry as we have noted above can be developed by practitioners becoming more research minded and policy orientated, and importantly, integrating these elements into their practice. Developing discerning powers of critical reflection are essential if social work is to combine effectiveness in its traditional helping and care managing role with a commitment to social justice and empowerment (Lishman, 1998; Everitt and Hardiker, 1996).

In common with all worthwhile journeys in social work there are no easy roads, or blueprints for success. Moreover, if the somewhat pretentious sounding 'less travelled road' is taken, as by the traveller in Robert Frost's poem, then the destination is likely to be disputed even if the journey has 'made all the difference'. Anti-racism has been a central tenet of social work in the UK and has been instrumental in the evolution of professional values. Its continuing relevance in wider society is under scrutiny, however, and will be examined in the next section.

Chapter Three

The Commitment to Anti-racist Practice

Deirdre Ford

Human rights and social justice serve as the motivation and justification for social work action. It strives to alleviate poverty and to liberate vulnerable, excluded, and oppressed people in order to promote empowerment and social inclusion.

(International Federation of Social Workers, 2000)

The IFSW declaration encapsulates some of the themes that have emerged in the preceding chapters. Of particular concern in this section is the profession's commitment to social justice together with the strategies needed to utilise the spaces and contradictions of neo-liberalism identified above. For Dominelli the 'value commitment to the realisation of social justice' finds expression in anti-oppressive practice (Dominelli, 1998: p4). As a radical, and emancipatory form of social work, anti-oppressive practice challenges dominant power relations. It confronts social divisions and the processes of categorisation that sustain structural inequality, while seeking to understand the connections that result in 'the layering of oppressions within individual experience' (Williams, 1999: p220). At times the use of the term 'anti-oppressive practice' is vague and it is deemed to be synonymous with anti-discriminatory measures. Conversely:

It could be argued that the concept of discrimination derives from political analyses of fair/unfair distribution of goods and services within a given system, while the notion of oppression derives from political analyses of structural patterns of mistreatment.

(Harlow and Hearn, 1996: p102)

Thompson, however, makes the link between discrimination as 'the process (or set of processes) that leads to oppression. To challenge oppression it is therefore necessary to challenge discrimination' (Thompson, 1997: pxii). It is important to recognise that challenge in either context will involve activity of a political nature.

Within the overarching concept of anti-oppressive practice, a distinctive form is that of anti-racism (Phillipson, 1992). Against all the forces and attacks described earlier to which the profession is subject, social work's focus on anti-racist practice has endured nevertheless both in the UK and worldwide. In reviewing the critiques of anti-racist theory Williams cites Smyth and Campbell (1996) who outline the potential of anti-racist analysis and action to inform resistance against other forms of oppression (Williams, 1999). As such, the approach seeks to identify and understand the processes through which racism operates, whether overtly or in more insidious ways; it examines how these processes are sanctioned by, and within institutions; it locates social work as a form of state activity, and applies the overall analysis to local practice. (Dominelli, 1997).

Power

Central to the anti-oppressive framework and to anti-racist theory is the concept of power, as noted. Studies of empowerment informed by the writings of Freire (1972), Lukes (1974) or Rees (1991) have encouraged a reappraisal of the radical view of power as wholly negative, as well as a recognition of the complexity of power relations as shifting and contextualised. Anti-racist practice is necessarily concerned with inequalities that stem from the exertion of power, whether structurally or at the level of the individual. Gould offers an analysis, which illustrates the importance of theorising anti-racism in this way in order to develop practice (Gould, 1992; quoted in Baldwin, 1996). Gould identifies four dimensions or modalities of power:

The 'behaviouralist modality' engages us in the identification of prevailing interests in decision-making processes. The 'non-decision-making modality' notes the way in which powerful groups can deny access to resources through negating the interests of disadvantaged groups. The modality which rests on the theory of hegemony describes the way in which conflict can be pre-empted through compromise on minor issues, and the creation of belief systems which are internalised by disadvantaged people. In the post-structuralist modality, power is described as being exercised through 'forms of knowledge which define and proscribe human identity.'

(Baldwin, 1996: p25)

The application of this analysis can lead to the empowerment of individuals and representative groups, involving them in decision making processes, for instance.

Increasingly, as Williams observes, issues of power in social work are problematised but the concept merits further attention and vigilance in the anti-racist project (Williams, 1999). New ideologies surface from specific social structures and power relations (Husband, 1991). In turn, 'through the use of prevailing dominant discourses, scientific and professional, racist ideology constantly seeks to obscure, and naturalise relations of dominance.' (Singh, 2000: p8).

At a time therefore when the Macpherson Report into the death of Stephen Lawrence has finally endorsed CCETSW's much contested assertion of 1991 that racism is endemic in the institutions of British society, it is perplexing to witness the almost careless ease with which notions of diversity and difference are now favoured in place of anti-racism. (Macpherson, 1999; CCETSW, 1991). Whilst surviving the charges of 'political correctness' from the New Right (a term which has been further appropriated to contest any form of unpalatable truth in the mainstream) as well as other contemptuous epithets such as 'the Race Industry' and accusations of 'playing the Race Card', anti-racist social work currently faces challenges from within the profession itself. Gilroy's earlier criticisms of municipal anti-racism were rightly influential and, as Humphries observes, continue to beset social work education (Gilroy, 1990; Humphries, 1997). Not least of these are the 'crucial ambiguities' that contribute to the confusion surrounding the meaning of racism, as well as the failure to make links between racism and other social divisions (Humphries, 1997).

Practice in a predominately white rural area such as the South West of England has occasioned struggles to recognise the need to develop anti-racist social work where service users are not perceived to be characterised by ethnic diversity (Baldwin, 1996). Substantial

expertise has accrued in some spheres, as anti-racist theory and practice are the focus for development by specialist staff groups, notably practice teachers, and local government officers responsible for the placement of asylum seekers in the region (Development Forum for Anti-Racist Practice, 2000). Nevertheless, the response that 'there is no problem here' documented in the Jay Report of 1992 persists in welfare provision and sadly remains a feature of the South West peninsula in general (Jay, 1992; Dhalech, 1999). As many writers have commented, the absence of clear definitions rooted in the lived experiences of black people, not only serves the agenda of the Right. It has reduced anti-racist practice to the level of concern for language and representation instead, culminating in the 'sewers of R.A.T or Race Awareness Training' (Sivanandan, 1991). As a consequence of these factors liberal white practitioners, who are not informed by black perspectives, seek to avoid discourses of race and hence marginalise the discrimination against black people at both personal and institutional levels. Particular avoidance strategies are fully recognised by Dominelli (1997), and result in the practices described in the Smith Report on the Probation Service (Smith, 2000).

The social workers who have struggled with the issues in this way are better disposed to embrace formulations of identity and difference. Identity politics, premised on the idea of identity that is constructed dialogically and through intersubjectivity, concern the politics of recognition. Fraser asserts, however, that the primary focus is one of the misrepresentation of culture rather than redistributive justice, leading to an over-simplification and reification of group identity and interaction across social divisions (Fraser, 2000). Significantly, the politics of identity do not invite forms of collective action that are the hallmark of anti-racist movements. Fiona Williams meanwhile examines difference from three perspectives; the market's view of 'consumer choice', administrative devices used to categorise need, and the means to establishing a political identity. Again the analysis is not conducted within the context of power (Williams, 1996, quoted in Williams, 1999).

In mitigation, ideas of diversity, identity and difference accord not only with the realities of practice and the complexities enshrined in personal constructs of self (Somers, 1994; Lloyd, 1998). They are also congruent with traditional aspects of the profession's value base that commend respect for persons and individual self-worth (Biestek, 1961; BASW, 1996). 'Black' as an organising term is troublesome in this context, nevertheless its history and significance are well recorded. Sivanandan describes how black as a 'political colour' was deconstituted by multiculturalism (Sivanandan, 1991). Elsewhere 'the emergence of ethnically distinctive and exclusive professional and political groups' contests black identity as a broadly inclusive term that is acceptable to all Asian and Chinese populations (Husband, 1992: p94). Concern for ethnically sensitive practice creates ambivalence in the use of the category, justification for which features in almost all writings on the subject. Neither in such binary opposition to white oppression does it address the situation of asylum seekers from Eastern Europe facing discrimination in the UK.

Such political constructs employed to strengthen and mobilise oppressed groups are further undermined by the flagrant individualism of market principles sustained under New Labour which fail to acknowledge commonalities among people. Writing about coalition building as a vehicle for teaching anti-discriminatory practice, Razack cites Alperin regarding the need for 'oppressed groups with different standpoints to form alliances in order to understand how different types of oppression interact', in this instance through 'analysis of colonialism, imperialism and systemic inequalities' (Razack, 1999: p238 and p248). Black as a political category, therefore, denotes not only 'the common experiences of racism and marginalisation in Britain' but also resistance amongst groups characterised by ethnic diversity and difference (Hall, 1992). In contrast as Williams observes, social constructionist analyses often do not take account of power relations that are central to anti-oppressive practice, and the 'structuring of inequality' by such means is not recognised (Williams, 1999).

Thus while some practitioners have yet to make the local and global connections outlined in Chapter Two, and are in danger of not recognising racism as 'a structural phenomenon with a long history and ideology, developed and applied at a number of levels',

the profession is not ready to relinquish anti-racist social work in favour of more positive-sounding constructs (Patel, 1995: p18).

New racism

Gilroy is confident that 'the era of New Racism is emphatically over' (Gilroy, 2000: p34). Be that as it may, the time lag with which new theorising is operationalised ensures that the lessons learned from the processes of new racism remain highly pertinent to the current appraisal of anti-racist practice.

While not universally acknowledged as such, certainly race is identified as an artificial construct in social work literature, formerly aligned with biological determinism. (The irony has not passed unnoticed that while races do not exist as such, racism is all too real. Husband, 1992.) Discredited by associations with fascism, specifically Nazi theories of eugenics and race, thereafter the discourse of race appropriated culture as an immutable set of characteristics that neatly upholds the nation state, through notions of difference. This process was termed 'new racism' (Barker, 1981). Husband records the ease with which, in this arena, the New Right moved to perceptions of alienness and inferiority, 'In defining nation through culture the New Right inevitably define 'different' as 'alien'' (Husband, 1991: p64). Thus culture may serve as a smokescreen to obscure discrimination (Patel, 1995) while Thompson identifies the more 'covert shift' from ethnic difference to race (Thompson, 1997). Such evaluations do not detract from the importance of ethnically sensitive practice responding to the needs of service users (Dutt, 1990). Initially however, the approach may not extend beyond a preoccupation with differing religious practices and diet, shaped by stereotypical assumptions of black people as care-givers and other misconceptions. While information about beliefs and ethnicity can form the basis for the development of anti-racist practice (Gourvish, 1995) the situation of black people as service users must not be decontextualised. The interconnections of race, gender and class, together with an understanding of the impact of racism on individuals in terms of anger or internalised beliefs need to inform ethnic sensitivity in practice.

As the current backlash engendered by the New Right is designed to maintain inequalities of power by trivialising, and detracting from anti-racist activity, so new racism supports mutually exclusive concepts of nationality and citizenship epitomised by the Apartheid system of South Africa (Gilroy, 2000). In this scheme the defence of culture and tradition is perceived as natural, as 'common sense'; hence the call to stem the tide of multiculturalism in the South West made by a parliamentary candidate during the last election, echoing the title of the Jay Report. Gilroy's concern is to de-nature and deconstruct race, to find a different political language and a new way of conceptualising the relationships between groups of people which inevitably would dispense with the term 'anti-racism'. It is my view that social work cannot safely adopt this position as yet.

> We would like to conclude that there has been a dramatic shift in both attitudes and behaviour across the region and there is widespread recognition that issues pertinent to rural race equality have been widely accepted and acted upon. **Sadly, we cannot.**
> (Dhalech, 1999)

The election success of the Far Right, most notably in Austria as well as France, provides the European backdrop for this. The contemporary UK context is that of institutional racism which is the subject of reporting almost on a daily basis, replicating the findings of the Macpherson Report (Home Office, 2000; Smith, 2000). New Labour's asylum and immigration policies are perceived to be the latest manifestation of this process, responsible for fuelling racism and creating the 'climate of fear' described by Bill Norris, general secretary TGWU (Wintour, 2000). Neither are welfare services as a social institution exempt from such charges. Patel cites Jones (1993) to remind us that:

> If racist consequences accrue to institutional laws, customs or practices the institution is racist whether or not the individuals maintaining those practices have racist intentions.
> (Patel, 1995: p29)

The paradox that finds black people under-represented as service users in receipt of preventive social care but over-represented in systems of social control is well documented (Skellington, 1996; Thompson, 1997). Owusu-Bempah provides a powerful illustration of how social work unwittingly colludes with the processes of racism in pathologising individuals to the neglect of inequalities that are induced by the system. Efforts to bolster the self-concept of black children in the care system epitomise the failure to address the more significant impact of racism on life chances of black people (Owusu-Bempah, 1997). Similarly, the findings of the Smith Report regarding racism in the Probation Service have resonances for social work, whether in relation to the poorer quality of pre-sentence reports for ethnic minority offenders or the discrimination experienced by black professionals in the service (Smith, 2000).

The way forward

Dominelli attests to the expansion of anti-oppressive practice in tandem with new social movements organised around the rights of women, and of black people. She describes how initially it represented a critique of practice as a function of middle-class values (Dominelli, 1998; Lloyd, 1998). Despite its 'radical mandate' it is hardly surprising, however, that anti-oppressive social work has not begun to address the iniquities within welfare provision. Located within organisational and bureaucratic structures that espouse white liberal values, social work's potential for political action is constrained and subject to competing claims (Williams, 1999).

Professionalism is also identified by some writers as a barrier to developing broader structural perspectives 'or non-individualistic ways of working' (Lloyd, 1998: p715). Social workers employ casework methods which do not invite challenges to the social structures that discriminate against service users. Furthermore, 'being political is synonymous with being unprofessional' in public sector services where professional detachment and its function in maintaining power relations are accepted uncritically (Husband, 1991: p66). The challenge to the profession in this instance is to develop a concept of professionalism that sanctions and affirms the political dimension to practice in pursuit of social justice.

The imposition of care management on social work practice has compounded these factors, as acknowledged in the previous chapter. Consumerist values, while conducive to assessments and services that are ethnically sensitive, discourage a more radical approach to social care characterised by notions of social justice and inclusion.

The equivocal nature of a liberal welfare state that seeks to promote the freeplay of the market economy, while retaining a centralised system of power and control, is one which finds expression in the delivery of community care. Commenting on social work in Vietnam former BASW director Clive Walsh writes:

> It is about enabling and transacting with individuals at a community level: something we have lost. Our community care is about economics. Theirs is about care. Ours says we can no longer afford dependency: Theirs simply says people must be helped.
>
> (Walsh, 1996)

In contrast, however, Lloyd sets out to examine the opportunities afforded by new configurations of power and the changing contexts for practice (Lloyd, 1998). Her endorsement of community development as a model for anti-oppressive practice is a reminder that black communities and groups have continued to gain political influence (Husband, 1991; Dhalech, 1999; Macpherson, 1999). Lloyd argues that the contract culture can be harnessed to create 'new alliances between professionals and the communities in which they work' (ibid: p723).

Above all, this analysis aims to confront the New Right from a position of strength, whereby anti-oppressive practice is defined and theorised in the context of the changes that result from globalisation. With reference to social divisions Williams takes up the point:

> What is needed, therefore, is a more precise analysis of theories of interconnection or intersection; a more rigorous look at how anti-racist approaches and the more illusive 'black perspectives' connect within the framework of anti-oppressive practice.
>
> (Williams, 1999: p226)

While the issue of 'black perspectives' is not unproblematic (Sivanandan, 1991; Humphries, 1997), the 'emergence of a black perspectives agenda' has been crucial to the development of anti-racism (Singh, 2000: p14). Black perspectives represent the means to progress debates surrounding identity, commonalities of experience and the structural factors that perpetuate oppression. In affirming the histories of black people and challenging dominant white modes of thought, they underpin emancipatory practice.

The presence of asylum seekers in a region like the South West exposes the prevalence of racism in all sectors of society. Yet the 'invisibility' of racism, allied with under-reporting of racial incidents and inadequate systems of ethnic monitoring, perpetuate the 'No Problem Here…' myth, as does the race-blind approach adopted by many agencies (Henderson and Kaur, 1999). In this climate, surrendering 'anti-racism' as a practice principle will permit the survival of 'race' as a construct that sanctions oppression. Its demise will fuel the lingering denials that racism does exist in white, rural areas and is endemic in social institutions.

Crucial to the development of anti-racist perspectives is a capacity for reflection in the process of integrating theory to practice. Reflective practice will be explored in the next chapter together with a reappraisal of the relationship between theory and practice.

Chapter Four

The Theory to Practice Debate Revisited

Paul Stepney

A text which invites the reader to embark on a journey of exploration into the world of social work methods and models must necessarily address the central problem of relating theory to practice. However, a word of caution might be in order, especially as anyone seeking neat or simple answers is soon likely to become frustrated. The nature of the relationship is far more complex than it may first appear and it is doubtful whether it is as yet fully understood (Sawdon, 1986).

The starting point adopted here is to risk stating the obvious by acknowledging that theory informs and enlarges practice (Coulshed and Orme, 1998; Curnock and Hardiker 1979) by providing the essential 'raw material' as a basis for understanding and action (Thompson, 2000). As Coulshed reminds us 'whether we recognise it or not, theoryless practice does not exist; we cannot avoid looking for explanations to guide our actions, whilst research has shown that those agencies which profess not to use theory offer a non problem solving, woolly and directionless service' (Coulshed, 1991: p8).

However, whilst the connections are undoubtedly there and the potential for creative thinking very considerable, this is something which the vast majority of practitioners find difficult to articulate. The end result is all too often muddled thinking, confusion or perhaps we just give up and quietly eject theoretical concepts from our mental formulations about practice. Theory in turn becomes rationalised and reinterpreted as 'unnecessary baggage' which complicates the picture, something the hard pressed and streetwise practitioner can well do without.

This debate highlights the tension between two models of practice. The first draws on a notion of practice which presents the social worker as a kind of maintenance mechanic with stress on such qualities as technical competence, hard skills and knowledge of the law. The alternative view suggests that social work has more in common with the art of gardening (organic of course) which emphasises the need to achieve sustainable growth and change through a process of critical exploration. Davies has put the case well for the social maintenance approach arguing that it is a crucial, but rather undervalued role 'for the practice of social work a knowledge of the social sciences is less crucial than training in basic skills' (Davies, 1994: p205). Variations on the social gardening model have been proposed by various writers in both social work and adult education (Freire, 1972; Knowles, 1973). For example, Vickery used this approach to outline her vision of community social work and the development of a patch system in the early 1980s (see Chapter Eleven) 'to practice her art (the worker) needs to stay put in one geographical area for long enough to understand it, work with it and increase its capacity as a fertile environment for growth and well being' (Vickery, 1982).

For patch working to be viable, as Sawdon and others have noted, social workers need to work as a team and acquire the necessary skills to adopt a problem solving, research minded approach and engage in enquiry based action learning (Sawdon, 1986; Knowles, 1972).

The preference here is very much for this latter approach, although clearly as workers we need to acquire the core skills to enable us to become competent and credible practitioners. Service users will rightly expect nothing less: so perhaps we must find some fresh links and connections between basic competence and critical enquiry.

The meaning of 'theory': theoretical knowledge versus practice wisdom

In exploring what is 'theory', the term is placed in inverted commas to denote that it is a contested concept. In social work many of our ideas are borrowed from the human sciences, philosophy, law and so on, which means that inevitably our theoretical knowledge base is very broad. It also needs to be recognised that such ideas may be at a highly abstract level of analysis, quite speculative and fiercely contested (Parton, 1996).

Sociology, psychology and social policy, the new social sciences, whatever merits and insights they bring, do not offer any neat and consistent theory about human behaviour. The latter derives from an epistemological position that certain truth does not exist. And whilst academics can usefully debate such theoretical dilemmas the practitioner can only afford such luxuries if they bring some tangible benefits and lead to positive outcomes. Consequently, over time, abstract theory from the social sciences has tended to be subject to a process of professional adaptation and refinement. In the case of social work, as it slowly developed in the USA and Europe, gradually and hesitantly, a professionally derived body of knowledge was established. This is clearly subject to ongoing change and reformulation reflecting the results of empirical research and scholarship. It is also an attempt to span the divide between the personal and the political explaining how our thoughts about the social world connect with individual feelings and experience. Theory implies 'rational thinking, distance and objectivity which contrasts with feelings and the living reality of social work encounters' (Coulshed and Orme, 1998: p7).

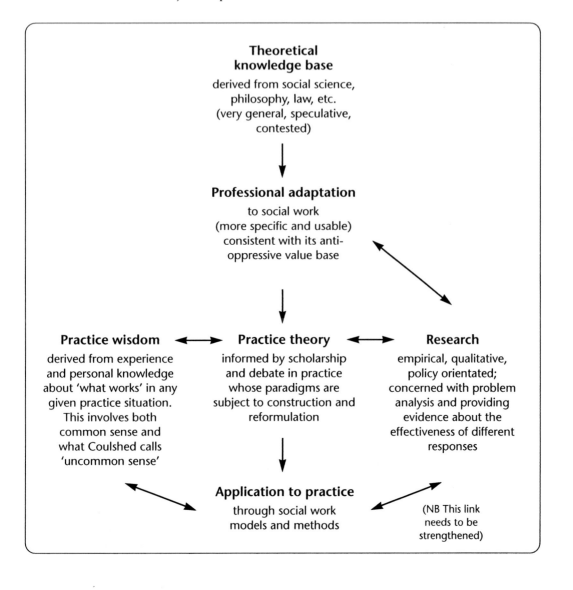

Theoretical knowledge base

derived from social science, philosophy, law, etc.
(very general, speculative, contested)

Professional adaptation

to social work
(more specific and usable)
consistent with its anti-oppressive value base

Practice wisdom

derived from experience and personal knowledge about 'what works' in any given practice situation. This involves both common sense and what Coulshed calls 'uncommon sense'

Practice theory

informed by scholarship and debate in practice whose paradigms are subject to construction and reformulation

Research

empirical, qualitative, policy orientated; concerned with problem analysis and providing evidence about the effectiveness of different responses

Application to practice

through social work models and methods

(NB This link needs to be strengthened)

Hence, it is now convenient to refer to this as practice theory. This is not to infer that such knowledge is fixed or unproblematic and devoid of internal contestation and dispute, but represents a genuine attempt to combine reading and research to create a more usable and accessible knowledge base. This has variously been described as 'an assemblage of sign posts' or 'a knowledge bank of useful ideas available to the practitioner to dip into and use' (Curnock and Hardiker, 1979: p160).

However, practice theory also derives its applicability and resonance from other less elevated and recognisable sources. In particular, knowledge and experience of what might work in any given situation. If we do this then experience suggests that will happen. Some writers refer to this kind of knowledge as practice wisdom which is built up over time and passed on through word of mouth about doing the job. Others refer to this as working class knowledge to denote how the views of service users get absorbed into the professional culture. A more popular description might be just to call it common sense.

Practice theory as common sense dressed up

The notion of common sense contains a certain paradox: it is something which in a general sense is very real and compelling, with the potential for wide application, yet remains essentially quite personal and idiosyncratic. The end result is that common sense is riddled with ambiguity and is one of those concepts which tends to be all things to all people. Thus in recognising its strength and capacity for infusing practice theory with everyday knowledge about experience 'at the sharp end', we also need to recognise its weaknesses and limitations. For example, common sense may descend into parochialism and popular prejudice which has led Coulshed to suggest that we may need to harness common sense with 'uncommon sense' (Coulshed, 1991).

Common sense may reflect highly discriminatory and racist attitudes which clearly need to be exposed and challenged. For example, social workers sometimes encounter racism amongst people who comment on the decline of their neighbourhood by saying 'this used to be a nice area before they came…' and prefixing it with 'its only common sense' or 'that's what we all think if we're being honest'. Clearly this kind of gut reaction is informed by particular values which need to be challenged with a very different kind of common sense. Here we are concerned with the less visible but common experience of oppression which has roots in perpetuating existing social divisions on the basis of race, class, gender, or ability in local communities. Of course, these two kinds of common sense may not be easily reconcilable which indicates why it is important that taken for granted knowledge and popular assumptions be subjected to the same critical analysis and scepticism as would be applied to other forms of knowledge. The methods we employ in practice will need to do all this and more.

Practice theory and critical reflection

Practice theory, as has been noted, will be subjected to a range of influences, not least a practitioner's self-reflection about what the job entails. In this sense theory will need to be reflexive and adaptable to changing practice constructions. Conversely, reflection is the way practitioners weigh up the possibilities in any given situation and evaluate the extent to which existing theory is adequate (Payne, 1997). This is closest to what Schön referred to as having a 'reflective conversation with the situation' (Schön, 1983: p163). We all implicitly do this much of the time but often without having the space to record the content or process involved.

However, for reflection to become meaningful and significant for practice it will need to be translated into positive action. Here Thompson draws our attention to Kolb's (1984) model of experiential learning which encourages both reflection and active experimentation (Thompson, 2000). The model has four stages:

1. **Concrete experience:** which includes all life experiences, not just formal training.

2. **Reflective observation:** standing back and considering the significance of the experience.

3. **Abstract conceptualisation:** considering broader and deeper issues which stem from reflection. According to Thompson

this involves 'hypothesis formation' as we try and place the experience in a wider context.

4. **Active experimentation:** where new learning begins as we put our abstract concepts into practice.

The cycle can then begin again as active experimentation becomes the next concrete experience to reflect upon (Thompson, 2000: pp5–6).

Payne identifies three meanings associated with being a reflective practitioner 'thinking things through, questioning our guidelines and developing our theories to respond to new situations' (Payne, 1998: p124). Clearly, reflection must be placed in its appropriate social context amidst competing formulations about the role of social work, which are taken up below. Since the very nature of social work is contested, practice theories provide a useful framework for reflecting on the nature of the task, alternative courses of action, underlying assumptions, predictions about possible outcomes and what Sheppard (1995) has referred to as the problem of 'disconfirming evidence'. Here as elsewhere critical reflection may help us to avoid jumping to superficial conclusions, based upon tradition and routine (Coutts-Jarman, 1993), which support the three

c's—conformity, consensus and conventional wisdom. Given the foregoing, 'critical reflection' also signifies a 'melting pot' in which values play a prominent part. The responsive, creative and critical practitioner will need to be morally as well as conceptually fluent.

Locating social work methods and developing a structure for practice

It is argued that social work methods are informed by a very broad spectrum of ideas, theoretical knowledge and what might be referred to as practice wisdom. And to deconstruct particular approaches requires considerable energy and skill. Hence, it is hardly surprising to find that the end result is a continuously evolving map of different methods and models. These can usefully be conceptualised in terms of a two dimensional diagram first proposed by Burrell and Morgan (1979). Social thinkers since Marx have argued that society can be understood in terms of a tension between the forces of change and stability, and the extent to which subjective experience contradicts objective reality. These were combined by Burrell and Morgan with the following result:

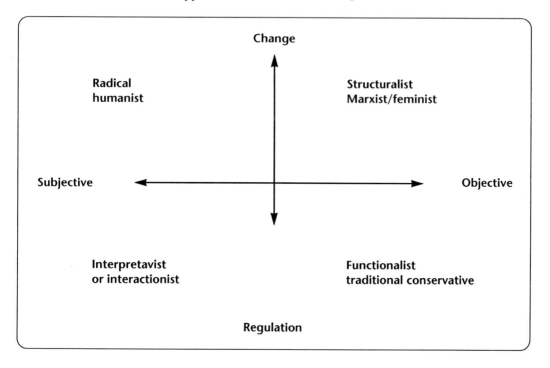

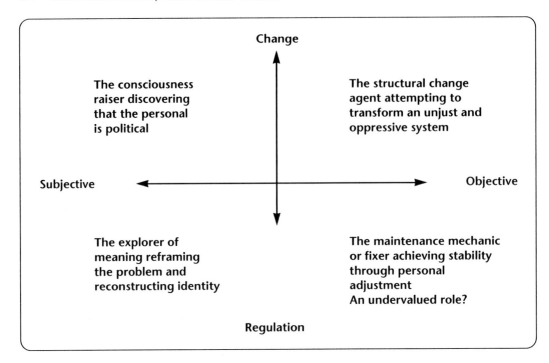

This generates four paradigms which have subsequently been reworked and applied to social work by various writers (Rojek, 1986; Sawdon, 1986; Howe, 1987).

The second diagram displays the general orientation which might be taken by the social worker operating within a particular paradigm.

There are at least three problems which can be identified when using such a model. First, it is doubtful whether each of the methods currently in use can be equated with a particular paradigm. Whilst some may fit quite well, for instance radical social work within a paradigm of subjective change, others remain problematic. One of the reasons for this is that a number of methods are concerned with both regulation and change, which in practice are not mutually irreconcilable.

Second, some methods such as community social work and ecological approaches derive from a number of different but interdependent traditions which cannot adequately be located without adding further dimensions to the model. These might include:

```
powerlessness  ◄──►  empowerment

collectivism   ◄──►  individualism
```

Third, such models might be seen as reductionist and social work is hopefully more than the sum of its component parts. As Rojek notes the social work task is so complex and fluid that it cannot be reduced in this way without losing the very essence of what the job is about (Rojek, 1986).

Notwithstanding these criticisms such a model may still be useful provided we recognise that it represents broad clusters and a general theoretical orientation rather than a template for innovative practice. The view proposed here is that mapping our practice in this way can still be helpful as an initial starting point which confirms broader patterns and opens up possibilities for combining methods in a clear yet constructive way (Coulshed and Orme, 1998; England, 1986). As Coulshed reminds us 'if we have a variety of tools in our workbag, we are more able to offer a service which is determined by client need rather than our own' (Coulshed, 1991: p9).

However attractive it is to contemplate the integration of theory and practice, Sheldon reminds us of the many obstacles in the way of achieving it (Sheldon, 1978). At least three problems can be identified: Firstly, 'theory' and 'practice' originate from two different sub-cultures, one academic and the other work based, and tensions are likely to re-emerge when points of dispute arise. Secondly, the social work curriculum encourages an eclectic, supermarket approach where all theories are treated as potentially of equal status and value. Thirdly, the professional culture of social work has not hitherto embraced a strong research tradition and staff have had few opportunities to conduct routine empirical evaluations of their work.

These criticisms have in part been answered by developments identified in the previous section, including Sheldon's own work at the Centre for Evidence-based Social Services, University of Exeter. The cultural divide between research and practice is now breaking down, as are the barriers confronting social workers who seek to conduct evaluations of their work and practice-based research (Cheetham and Kazi, 1998) although resources for this remain limited. New courses in research methods are also developing both within initial training as well as on post qualifying programmes. What continues to be more problematic, however, is achieving a critical understanding of the place of theory in practice given the constraints imposed by competence based training and marketised services.

In searching for some helpful criteria to find a way forward we can empathise with the dilemmas described by White (1998) as she attempted to combine an academic career whilst continuing in practice. Both the editors have experienced similar pressures within dual posts of being pulled in different directions by the conceptual and organisational demands of academia and practice. This certainly produces fertile conditions for unpacking many of social work's taken for granted assumptions and representations within a discourse of practice theories and professional ideology (White, 1998).

The terrain which social workers occupy is contested, uncertain and marked by political conflict (Payne, 1997). The contradictions and dilemmas encountered reflect this tension, which is why a sound theoretical framework is essential for good practice. As Howe usefully reminds us, 'to show no interest in theory is to travel blind' (Howe, 1987: p9). In Part One we have outlined a broad framework which stresses the need to make our values and commitment to anti-oppressive practice explicit, to recognise the wider policy context and the increasing requirement to become more research active. Social work in its international context (Midgley, 1997) draws on such a framework and develops in areas where sometimes other professionals might fear to tread—for example, supporting minorities and defending the rights of the oppressed. The increasing demand for new knowledge and a critical approach to its application is consistent with this tradition.

It follows that we need to utilise skills of critical engagement in relation to each of the social work methods and practice theories in the chapters which follow in Part Two. A good working knowledge of different models and methods, and the theories which inform them, open up opportunities for progressive practice—working with service users to develop a shared understanding of a social world characterised by oppression and exclusion, so that we might be better placed to transform it.

References (Chapters 1–4)

Abrams, P., Abrams, S., Humphrey, R., and Snaith, R. (1989). *Neighbourhood Care and Social Policy*. London: DoH/HMSO.

Adams, R. (1996). *Social Work and Empowerment* (2nd edn.). Basingstoke: Macmillan.

Adams, R. (1998). Social Work Processes. In Adams, Dominelli, and Payne (Eds.). *Social Work: Themes, Issues and Critical Debates*. Basingstoke: Macmillan.

Adams, R., Dominelli, L., and Payne, M. (Eds.) (1998). *Social Work: Themes, Issues and Critical Debates*. Basingstoke: Macmillan.

Atkinson, A. (1991). *Poverty, Statistics and Progress in Europe: A Discussion Paper*. LSE, Welfare State Programme.

Audit Commission (1994). Taking Stock: Progress with Community Care. *Community Care Bulletin*, No. 2. London: HMSO.

Baldwin, M. (1996). White Anti-racism: Is it Really 'No Go' in Rural Areas? *Social Work Education*, Vol. 15: No. 1.

Balloch, S., Andrew, J., Ginn, J., McLean, J., Pahl, J., and Williams, J. (1995). *Working in the Social Services*. London: NISW.

Barker, M. (1981). *The New Racism*. London: Junction Books.

Beresford, P., and Croft, S. (1993). *Citizen Involvement: A Practical Guide for Change*. Basingstoke: Macmillan.

Biestek, F. (1961). *The Casework Relationship*. London: George Allen and Unwin.

Blair, T. (1998). *The Third Way: Politics for the New Century*, Fabian Pamphlet 588. London: The Fabian Society.

Bornat, J. *et al.* (1997). *Community Care: A Reader* (2nd edn.). Basingstoke: Macmillan.

Braye, S., and Preston-Shoot, M. (1995). *Empowering Practice in Social Care*. Buckingham: Open University Press.

Brindle, D. (1998). *The Guardian*, July 28th, 1998.

British Association of Social Workers (1996). *The Code of Ethics for Social Work*. Birmingham: BASW.

Brown, G. (1999). The Chancellor's speech to the Labour Party Conference reported in *The Guardian*, September 28th, 1999.

Burrell, G., and Morgan, G. (1979). *Sociological Paradigms and Organisational Analysis*. London: Heinemann.

Campbell, J., and Oliver, M. (1996). *Disability Politics*. London: Routledge.

Cannan, C., Berry, L., and Lyons, K. (1992). *Social Work and Europe*. Basingstoke: Macmillan.

Castles, F. (Ed.) (1993). *Families of Nations*. Aldershot: Dartmouth.

CCETSW (1996). *Assuring Quality: in the Diploma in Social Work - 1. Rules and Requirements for the DipSW* (second revision). London: CCETSW.

CDP (1977). *Guilding the Ghetto: The State and the Poverty Experiments*. London: CDP Inter Project Team.

Challis, D. (1992). Community Care of Elderly People: Bringing Together Scarcity and Choice, Needs and Cost. *Financial Accountability and Management*, 8(2): Summer, 1992.

Cheetham, J. (1998). The Evaluation of Social Work: Priorities, Problems and Possibilities. In Cheetham, J., and Kazi, M. Op. cit.

Cheetham, J., and Kazi, M. (Eds.) (1998). *The Working of Social Work*. London: Jessica Kingsley.

Clarke, J. (1996). After Social Work. In Parton, N. (Ed.) (1996). *Social Theory, Social Change and Social Work*. London: Routledge.

Clarke, J. (2000). A World of Difference? Globalisation and the Study of Social Policy. In Lewis, G., Gewirtz, S., and Clarke, J. (Eds.). *Rethinking Social Policy*. Sage.

Clarke, J., Cochrane, A., and McLaughlin, E. (Eds.) (1994). *Managing Social Policy*. London: Sage.

Connolly, N., and Johnson, J. (1996). *Community Care as Policy: Emerging Issues*. Supplement to K259 Workbook 2. The Open University.

Coulshed, V. (1991). *Social Work Practice: An Introduction* (2nd edn.). Basingstoke: Macmillan.

Coulshed, V., and Orme, J. (1998). *Social Work Practice: An Introduction* (3rd edn.). Basingstoke: Macmillan.

Coutts-Jarman, J. (1993). Using Reflection and Experience in Nurse Education. *British Journal of Nursing*, (2).

Curnock, K., and Hardiker, P. (1979). *Towards Practice Theory*. RKP.

Davies, M. (1994). *The Essential Social Worker: A Guide to Positive Practice* (3rd edn.). Aldershot: Arena.

Davies, N. (1998). Lives that were Beyond Belief'. *The Guardian*, August 1st, 1998.

Dean, H., and Melrose, M. (1997). *Poverty, Riches and Citizenship*. London: Macmillan.

Department of Health (1989a). *Caring for People: Community Care in the Next Decade*, Cm. 849. London: HMSO.

Department of Health (1995). *NHS Responsibilities for Meeting Continuing Health Care Needs* (HSG(95)8). HMSO.

Department of Health (1998a). *Modernising the Social Services*. London: HMSO.

Department of Health (1998b). *Our Healthier Nation*, Cm. 3852. London: HMSO.

Department of Health (1999). *The New NHS: Modern, Dependable*. London: HMSO.

Department of Health, Social Services Inspectorate (1991). *Care Management and Assessment: Practitioners Guide*. London: HMSO.

Department of Social Security (1998). *A New Contract for Welfare*, Cm. 3805. HMSO.

DETR (1998). *Modernising Local Government Improving Local Services Through Best Value*. London: HMSO.

Development Forum for Anti-racist Practice (2000). *Anti-racist Standards within Anti-oppressive Practice*. Unpublished standards for practice teachers in Far South West.

Dhalech, M. (1999). *Challenging Racism in the Rural Idyll*. Final Report of the Rural Race Equality Project. National Association of Citizens' Advice Bureaux.

Dominelli, L. (1988). *Anti-Racist Social Work*. Basingstoke: Macmillan.

Dominelli, L. (1994). *Anti-Racist Social Work Education*, paper presented at 27th Congress, International Association of Schools of Social Work, Amsterdam, July, 1994.

Dominelli, L. (1996). De-professionalising Social Work: Anti-oppressive Practice, Competencies and Postmodernism. *British Journal of Social Work*, 26: pp153–175.

Dominelli, L. (1997). *Anti-Racist Social work* (2nd edn.). Basingstoke: Macmillan.

Dominelli, L. (1998). Anti-oppressive Practice in Context. In Adams, R. Dominelli, L., and Payne, M. (Eds.). *Social Work: Themes, Issues and Critical Debates*. Basingstoke: Macmillan.

Dutt, R. (1990). *Black Communities and Community Care*. London: Race Equality Unit, National Institute for Social Work.

Elliot, L. (1998). *The Guardian*, May 21st, 1998.

England, H. (1986). *Social Work as Art: Making Sense of Good Practice*. London: Allen and Unwin.

Esping-Andersen, G. (1990). *The Three Worlds of Welfare Capitalism*. Cambridge: Polity Press.

Esping-Andersen, G. (1996). *Welfare States in Transition*. London: Sage.

Etzioni, A. (1995). *The Spirit of Community*. New York: Free Press.

EU (1994). *European Social Policy—A Way Forward for the Union*. Luxembourg: EU Commission.

Eurostat (1993). *Rapid Reports: Population and Social Conditions*. Luxembourg: EU Commission.

Everitt, A. (1998). Research and Development in Social Work. In Adams, Dominelli, and Payne. Op. cit.

Everitt, A., and Hardiker, P. (1996). *Evaluating for Good Practice*. Basingstoke: Macmillan.

Ferrera, M. (1994). *Welfare in Southern Europe*, International Seminar on Social Policy, University of Madrid, October, 1994.

Franklin, B. (1989). Wimps and Bullies: Press Reporting of Child Abuse. In Carter, P. *et al.* (Eds.). *Social Work and Social Welfare Yearbook*. Buckingham: Open University Press.

Fraser, N. (2000). Rethinking Recognition. *New Left Review*, (3): pp107–120.

Freeman, P., and Clearer, H. (1995). *Parental Perspectives in Supervised Cases of Child Abuse*. London: HMSO.

Freire, P. (1972). *Pedagogy of the Oppressed*. Harmondsworth: Penguin.

Fuller, R., and Petch, A. (1995). *Practitioner Research: The Reflective Social Worker*. Buckingham: Open University Press.

George, J., and Napier, L. (1997). Speaking what we Feel: Diversity and Social Work Education, paper presented at International Conference, *Culture and Identity: Social Work in a Changing Europe*, Dublin.

George, V. (1996). The Future of the Welfare State. In George, V., and Taylor-Gooby, P. (Eds.). Op. cit.

George, V., and Miller, S. (Eds.) (1994). *Social Policy Towards 2000*. London: Routledge.

George, V., and Taylor-Gooby, P. (Eds.) (1996). *European Welfare Policy*. Basingstoke: Macmillan.

Gilroy, P. (1990). The End of Anti-racism. In Ball, W., and Solomos, J. (Eds.). *Race and Local Politics*. London: Macmillan.

Gilroy, P. (2000). *Between Camps*. Harmondsworth: Allen Lane.

Glennerster, H., and Hills, J. (Eds.) (1998). *The State of Welfare* (2nd edn.). Oxford University Press.

Gourvish, S. (1995). Learning about 'Race' and Anti-racism: The Experience of Students on a Diploma in Social Work Programme. *Social Work Education*, Vol. 14: No. 1.

Guba, E.G. (Ed.) (1990). *The Paradigm Dialog*. Newbury Park: Sage.

Guba, E.G., and Loncoln, Y. (1989). *Fourth Generation Evaluation*. London: Sage.

Hadley, R., and Clough, R. (1996). *Care in Chaos: Frustration and Challenge in Community Care*. London: Cassell.

Hall, S. (1992). New Ethnicities. In Donald, J., and Rattansi, A. (Eds.). *'Race', Culture and Difference*. London: Sage.

Harloe, M. *et al.* (Eds.) (1990). *Place, Policy and Politics: Do Localities Matter?* London: Unwin Heinemann.

Harlow, E., and Hearn, J. (1996). From Rhetoric to Reality: Historical, Theoretical and Practical Complexities in Educating for Anti-discriminatory and Anti-oppressive Social Work. In Ford, P., and Hayes, P. (Eds.). *Educating for Social Work: Arguments for Optimism*. Aldershot: Avebury.

Henderson, P., and Kaur, R. (Eds.) (1999). *Introduction: Rural Racism in the UK. Examples of Community-Based Responses*. London: Community Development Foundation.

Henwood, M. (1995). *Making a Difference? Implementation of the Community Care Reforms Two Years On*. Nuffield Institute for Health and King's Fund Centre.

Henwood, M. (1996). *Continuing Health Care: Analysis of a Sample of Final Documents*. NHS Executive.

HMSO (1989). *Working for Patients*, Cm. 555. London: HMSO.

Home Office (2000). *Race Equality in Public Services*. London: HMSO.

Howe, D. (1987). *An Introduction to Social Work Theory*. Aldershot: Wildwood House.

Howe, D. (1996). *Surface and Depth in Social Work Practice*. In Parton, N. (Ed.). Op. cit.

Humphries, B. (1997). The Dismantling of Anti-discrimination in British Social Work: A View from Social Work Education. *International Social Work*, Vol. 40: pp289–301.

Husband, C. (1991). 'Race', Conflictual Politics, and Anti-racist Social Work: Lessons from the Past for Action in the '90s in Northern Curriculum Development Project (No. 1) *Setting the Context for Change*. Leeds: CCETSW.

Husband, C. (1992). Racism, Prejudice and Social Policy. In Coombe, V., and Little, A. (Eds.). *Race and Social Work. A Guide to Training*. London: Routledge.

Hutton, W. (1996). *The State We're In*. Vintage.

International Federation of Social Workers (2000). Redefining the Nature of Social Work. *Professional Social Work*. BASW.

Jack, G., and Stepney, P. (1995). The Children Act 1989: Protection or Persecution? Family Support and Child Protection in the 1990s. *Critical Social Policy*, 43: pp26–39.

Jackobsson, G. (1998). The Politics of Care for Elderly People in Scandinavia. *European Journal of Social Work*, 1(1): pp87–93.

Jay, E. (1992). *Keep them in Birmingham: Challenging Racism in South West England*. London: Commission for Racial Equality.

Johnson, J., and Slater, R. (Eds.) (1993). *Ageing and Later Life*. London: Sage.

Jones, A., and May, J. (1992). *Working in Human Service Organisations: A Critical Introduction*. Melbourne, Cheshire: Longman.

Jones, C. (1996). Anti-intellectualism and the Peculiarities of British Social Work Education. In Parton, N. (Ed.). Op. cit.

Jones, C., and Novak, T. (1993). Social Work Today. *British Journal of Social Work*, 23: pp195–212.

Jones, M. (1996). *Bridging the Worlds of Professionals, Managers and Users in the Personal Social Services: Culture, Politics and Partnership*, Proceedings of Crisis in the Human Services Conference, Cambridge, September, 1996.

Jones, M., and Jordan, B. (1996). Knowledge and Practice in Social Work. In Preston-Shoot, M., and Jackson, S. (Eds.). *Educating Social Workers in a Changing Policy Context.* London: Whiting and Birch.

Jordan, B. (1990). *Social Work in an Unjust Society.* Hemel Hempstead: Harvester Wheatsheaf.

Jordan, B. (1998). *New Politics of Welfare.* London: Sage.

Jordan, B. (2000). *Tough Love: Implementing New Labour's Programme: Social Work and 'the Third Way'.* London: Sage.

Karvinen, S. (1999). The Methodological Tensions in Finnish Social Work Research. In Karvinen, S., Pösö, T., and Satka, M. *Reconstructing Social Work Research,* SoPhi. University of Jyväskyla Press.

Kautto, M., Heikkilä, M., Hvinden, B., Marklund, S., and Ploug, N. (Eds.) (1999). *Nordic Social Policy: Changing Welfare States.* London: Routledge.

Kazi, M. (1998). Putting Single-case Evaluation into Practice. In Cheetham, and Kazi. Op cit.

Kent, I. (1996). Reporting Back. *Community Care,* February 22nd–28th: pp18–19.

Knowles, M. (1972). Innovations in Teaching Styles and Approaches Based on Adult Learning. *Journal of Education for Social Work,* Vol. 8: No. 2.

Knowles, M. (1973). *The Adult Learner: A Neglected Species.* Gulf.

Kolb, D. (1984). *Experimental Learning.* Englewood Cliffs, NJ: Prentice Hall.

Kuhn, T. (1970). *The Structure of Scientific Revolutions.* University of Chicago Press.

Langan, M., and Day, L. (Eds.) (1992). *Women, Oppression and Social Work: Issues in Anti-discriminatory Practice.* London: Routledge.

Lewis, J., and Glennerster, H. (1996). *Implementing the New Community Care.* Buckingham: Open University Press.

Lishman, J. (1998). *Personal and Professional Development.* In Adams, Dominelli, and Payne. Op. cit.

Lishman, J. (Ed.) (1991). *Handbook of Theory for Practice Teachers in Social Work.* London: Jessica Kingsley.

Lloyd, L. (1999). The Post- and the Anti-: Analysing Change and Changing Analyses in Social Work. *British Journal of Social Work,* 28: pp709–727.

Lorenz, W. (1994). *Social Work in a Changing Europe.* London: Routledge.

Lorenz, W. (1997). Social Work in a Changing Europe, Keynote address and paper presented at an International Conference, *Culture and Identity: Social Work in a Changing Europe,* Dublin.

Lukes, S. (1974). *Power: A Radical View.* London: Macmillan.

MacDonald, G., Sheldon, B., and Gillespie, J. (1992). Contemporary Studies of the Effectiveness of Social Work. *British Journal of Social Work,* 22(1): pp615–643.

Macpherson, W. (1999). *The Stephen Lawrence Inquiry,* Cm. 4262-1. HMSO.

Mark, R. (1996). *Research Made Simple: A Handbook for Social Workers.* Thousand Oaks, CA: Sage.

McKenzie, G., Powell, J., and Usher, R. (1997). *Understanding Social Research Perspectives on Methodology and Practice.* London: Falmer Press.

Midgley, J. (1997). Social Work in International Context. In Reisch, M., and Gambrill, E. *Social Work in the 21st Century.* USA: Pine Forge Press.

Millham, S., Bullock, R., Hosie, K., and Haak, M. (1986). *Lost in Care.* London: Gower.

Milner, M., and Hetherington, P. (1998). Jobs Blow to Hi-tech Hopes. *The Guardian,* August 1st.

Moran, M. (1988). Crises of the Welfare State: Review Article. *British Journal of Political Science,* Vol. 18: pp397–414.

Munday, B. (1989). *The Crisis in Welfare—an International Perspective on Social Services and Social Work.* Hemel Hempstead: Harvester Wheatsheaf.

Murray, C. (1994). The New Victorians…and the New Rabble. *Sunday Times,* May 29th.

OECD (1994). New Orientations for Social Policy. *Social Policy Studies,* No. 12. Paris: OECD.

Oliver, M. (1996). *Understanding Disability: From Theory to Practice.* Basingstoke: Macmillan.

Owusu-Bempah, J. (1997). 'Race'. In Davies, M. (Ed.). *The Blackwell Companion to Social Work.* Oxford: Basil Blackwell.

Packman, J., Randall, J., and Jaques, N. (1986). *Who Needs Care? Social Work Decisions about Children.* Oxford: Blackwell.

Packman, J., and Hall, C. (1998). *From Care to Accommodation.* London: HMSO.

Parton, N. (1992). The Contemporary Politics of Child Protection. *Journal of Social Welfare and Family Law,* 2: pp100–113.

Parton, N. (Ed.) (1996). *Social Theory, Social Change and Social Work.* London: Routledge.

Parton, N., and Marshall, W. (1998). Postmodernism and Discourse Approaches to Social Work. In Adams, Dominelli, and Payne. Op. cit.

Parton, N., and O'Byrne, P. (2000). *Constructive Social Work.* Basingstoke: Macmillan.

Parton, N., and Small, N. (1989). Violence, Social Work and the Emergence of Dangerousness. In Langan, M., and Lee, P. (Eds.). *Radical Social Work Today.* London: Unwin Hyman.

Patel, N. (1995). In Search of the Holy Grail in Hugman, R., and Smith, D. (Eds.). *Ethical Issues in Social Work.* London: Routledge.

Pawson, R., and Tilley, N. (1997). *Realistic Evaluation.* London: Sage.

Payne, M. (1995). *Social Work and Community Care.* Basingstoke: Macmillan.

Payne, M. (1997). *Modern Social Work Theory* (2nd edn.). Basingstoke: Macmillan.

Payne, M. (1998). Social Work Theories and Reflective Practice. In Adams, Dominelli, and Payne. Op. cit.

Pearson, G. (1975). *The Deviant Imagination.* Basingstoke: Macmillan.

Phillipson, J. (1992). *Practising Equality. Women, Men and Social Work.* London: CCETSW.

Pollitt, C., and Harrison, S. (1992). *Handbook of Public Services Management.* Oxford: Blackwell.

Razack, N. (1999). Anti-discriminatory Practice: Pedagogical Struggles and Challenges. *British Journal of Social Work,* 29: pp231–250.

Rees, S. (1991). *Achieving Power: Practice and Policy in Social Welfare.* Sydney: Allen and Unwin.

Robinson, R., and Le Grand, J. (1994). *Evaluating the NHS Reforms.* King's Fund Institute.

Rojek, C. (1986). *A Way of Being.* London: Routledge.

Sawdon, D. (1986). *Making Connections in Practice Teaching.* Heinemann, NISW.

Schön, D. (1983). *The Reflective Practitioner: How Professionals Think in Action.* New York: Basic Books.

Shaw, I. (1998). Practising Evaluation. In Cheetham, and Kazi. Op. cit.

Sheldon, B. (1978). Theory and Practice in Social Work: A Re-examination of a Tenuous Relationship. *British Journal of Social Work,* 8(1): pp1–22.

Sheldon, B., and Macdonald, G. (1999). *Mind the Gap.* Centre for Evidence-based Social Services. University of Exeter.

Sheppard, M. (1995). *Care Management and the New Social Work: A Critical Analysis.* London: Whiting and Birch.

Sibeon, R. (1990). Comments on the Structure and Forms of Social Work Knowledge. *Social Work and Social Sciences Review,* 1(1).

Singh, G. (2000). *Developing Black Perspectives in Practice Teaching.* Conference and Research Findings. London: CCETSW.

Sivanandan, A. (1991). Black Struggles Against Racism in Northern Curriculum Development Project (No. 1), *Setting the Context for Change.* Leeds: CCETSW.

Skellington, R. (1996). *'Race' in Britain Today* (2nd edn.). London: Sage.

Smith, G. (1975). Action Research: Experimental Social Administration. In Lees, R., and Smith, G. *Action Research in Community Development.* London: Routledge.

Smith, G. (2000). *Thematic Inspection Report. Towards Race Equality 2000.* HM Inspectorate of Probation. London: HMSO.

Somers, M. (1994). The Narrative Constitution of Identity: A Relational and Network Approach. *Theory and Society,* 23: pp605–649.

Spicker, P. (1991). The Principle of Subsidiarity and the Social Policy of the European Community. *European Journal of Social Policy,* Vol. 1: No. 1.

Standing, G. (1996). Social Protection in Central and Eastern Europe: A Tale of Slipping Anchors and Torn Safety Nets. In Espring-Andersen, G. (Ed.). *Welfare States in Transition.* London: Sage.

Stepney, P., Lynch, R., and Jordan, B. (1999). Poverty, Exclusion and New Labour. In *Critical Social Policy,* 19(1) 58: pp109–127.

Taylor-Gooby, P. (1996). The Response of Government: Fragile Convergence? In George, V., and Taylor-Gooby, P. (Eds.). Op. cit.

The Guardian (1997). Britain has Highest Number of Children in Poverty in Europe, April 28th, p1.

Thompson, N. (1997). *Anti-discriminatory Practice* (2nd edn.). Basingstoke: Macmillan.

Thompson, N. (2000). *Theory and Practice in Human Services* (2nd edn.). Buckingham: Open University Press.

Timmonen, V. (1999). A Threat to Social Security? The Impact of EU Membership on the Finnish Welfare State. *Journal of European Social Policy,* 9(3): pp253–261.

Usher, R. (1997). Introduction. In McKenzie, G., Powell, J., and Usher, R. *Understanding Social Research Perspectives on Methodology and Practice.* London: Falmer Press.

Vickery, A. (1982). Settling into Patch Ways. *Community Care,* January 14th.

Walker, A. (1997). Community Care Policy: From Consensus to Conflict. In Bornat *et al.* (Eds.) *Community Care: A Reader* (2nd edn.). Basingstoke: Macmillan.

Walsh, C. (1996). *The Ties that Bond us Across the World: Professional Social Work.* BASW, September.

Wenger, C. (1993). The Formation of Social Networks: Self-help, Mutual Aid and Old People in Contemporary Britain. *Journal of Ageing Studies,* 7(1), pp25–40.

White, S. (1998). Analysing the Content of Social Work: Applying the Lessons from Qualitative Research. In Cheetham, and Kazi. Op. cit.

Williams, C. (1997). Towards and Emancipatory Pedagogy? Social Work Education for a Multi-cultural and Multi-racial Europe, paper presented at an International Conference, *Culture and Identity: Social Work in a Changing Europe,* Dublin.

Williams, C. (1999). Connecting Anti-racist and Anti-oppressive Theory and Practice: Retrenchment or Reappraisal? *British Journal of Social Work,* 29, pp211–230.

Williams, F. (1997). Women and Community. In Bornat, J. *et al.* (Eds.). Op. cit.

Wilson, R. (1993). *Poverty, Powerlessness and Dispossession: A Personal Guide.* BBC2 programme, March 21st.

Wintour, P. (2000). Whitehall Mandarins 'Balking' Black Staff. *The Guardian,* April 15th.

Wistow, G. (1995). Aspirations and Realities: Community Care at the Crossroads. *Health and Social Care in the Community,* 3(4): pp227–240.

Zito Trust (1995). *Learning the Lessons.* London.

Chapter Five

Psychodynamic Theory in Social Work: A View from Practice

Lynette Kenny and Bill Kenny

Do you know the theological term kenosis? The idea from Greek means vain, hollow, fruitless, void, empty...Kenosis seems now the only political way to be, emptied out of certainty. Otherwise you become a fundamentalist with an almighty ideology, protected from above by a cause. Therapy is just one more of the current ideologies keeping its believers from the panic of kenosis, the panic that comes when the whole structure of guarantees has collapsed. Therapy becomes one more salvational ideology.

(Hillman, and Ventura (1993). *We've Had a Hundred Years of Psychotherapy and the World's Getting Worse*)

In the beginning...psychodynamic casework was almost the only articulated theory available to professional social work practitioners, and was perhaps equally influential within the UK and the US. (Hollis, 1964; Perlman, 1954). By the late 1960s and early 1970s however, the method had come to be critically examined in America by Reid and Shyne (1969) and criticised in Britain by Mayer and Timms (1970) who believed it to be 'intrusive'. In 1972, Reid and Epstein declared that Freudian based methods '...appear to consist of explorations, mostly inquiries into the client's problems, behaviour, feelings, current situation and early history' and considered this to be an unsatisfactory state of affairs. They were particularly concerned with the difficulties that psychodynamic casework posed in terms of generating results that were equally 'measurable' by practitioner and 'client' alike and they argued ultimately for something more demonstrably effective. Task-centred casework was born and led in due course to a variety of other short-term approaches, all of which claimed measurable outcomes and successes (see Chapter Seven).

It seems to us that social work is currently divided (we hesitate to say ambivalent) about the usefulness of psychodynamic method. On the one hand, well-established authors of social work textbooks point out that the psychoanalytic theories of Sigmund Freud and related ideas have had a considerable influence in the formulation of social work practice and

are therefore still worthy of study. (see Payne, 1997, Coulshed and Orme, 1998) Against this, however, psychoanalysis and the social work method that arises from it do not seem to be particularly popular among recent generations of students. Complaints about it that we have heard in recent years, are that psychoanalysis is too 'Eurocentric' to be useful in a multi-cultural society, that its principle of 'psychic determinism' implies that 'clients' are incapable of expressing their own needs clearly, and (perhaps commonest of all) that it is 'patriarchal' and discriminatory to women. According to these latter views, psychodynamic theory in social work has become outmoded, and does not fit at all well with contemporary demands for 'evidence based practice.' Are any of these diverse views correct?

In the remarkable series of letters published by James Hillman, a respected American psychotherapist and the journalist Michael Ventura in 1993 (Hillman and Ventura, op. cit.), the authors discuss the psychological problems of the post-modern Western world. The main difficulty of living nowadays, they say, is that most people lack a true sense of community because virtually all former traditions and assumptions about life and its meaning have been severely eroded. There are no 'guarantees' any more and the sense of psychological and spiritual emptiness (kenosis) that results from their absence causes people to cling desperately to anything that seems to offer some kind of uneasy certainty. In America, Hillman and Ventura say, one such manifestation of the search for this kind of 'salvational ideology' is an over-inflated notion of the value of 'therapy'. We are tempted to suggest here that parallel phenomena are currently visible in the UK, although they may manifest themselves differently. The current preoccupations of some politicians and social work managements with the need for 'solutions' to all of our social problems, with value for money, with 'evidence based practice' and perhaps even with over-simplified notions about 'empowerment' do sometimes seem to be expressed with an almost evangelical zeal.

We are deeply suspicious of evangelism generally, but especially so when it comes to social work, where we often deal with problems that are neither readily soluble nor even capable of much immediate relief. And insofar as we are defending or advocating reconsideration of psychodynamic method here, it is only as one more useful tool, which may be helpful in some (but by no means all) social work situations. Furthermore, it is not the case either that we are advocating unquestioning acceptance of all the concepts found within psychoanalytic theory. In the 'hundred years of psychotherapy' that have passed by so far, many ideas have been tested, have been found wanting and then (quite properly) have been abandoned. It remains the case however that bath-water is one kind of thing while babies are something else.

Relationship in social work practice

Whatever else professional social work might be about, it is clearly concerned for people of almost infinite diversity and their equally diverse difficulties. The current emphasis on the importance of social work values and ethics remind us of this (see Banks, 1995; Thompson, 1997). We are also concerned with oppression in all its forms: a growing body of literature guides us through the tricky issues involved in 'anti-oppressive practice' (Dalrymple and Burke, 1995) and 'empowerment' (Dominelli, this text; Braye and Preston-Shoot, 1995). Each of these ideas requires us to reconsider some fundamental elements of our current practice; one of which is social work theory. It is clear that in order to deal competently with the undoubted diversity of 'clients' and their needs we must hold in our minds a considerable variety of frameworks and perspectives to be appropriately helpful to everyone seeking our services. Arguably however, there is one true constant among all this diversity: the social worker–client relationship.

Relationships between social workers and their clients happen, however hard we may sometimes have to struggle to define their precise purposes. Directed by a fairly stable system of social work values (see below), the importance of relationship is perhaps one of the few things about which all social workers can agree and, within the profession's fairly short history, relationship has been the subject of an immense amount of commentary within the 'technical' literature. (See Biestek, 1957; Ferrard and Hunnybun, 1962 as early examples.) Payne (1997: p89) summarises how professional social work relationships differ from non-professional ones, because:

- Client need forms the basic focus of the interactions, instead of the needs of both parties.
- Workers involve themselves in the relationship in a disciplined and controlled way, rather than from personal inclination or personal emotional response.
- Social work values are always involved, so that expanded tolerance of clients' behaviours and extended viewpoints are offered which exceed the tolerances offered in ordinary non-professional relationships.
- The influence of past experiences (both clients and workers) is acknowledged to account for *irrational* (our italics) aspects to the progress of the relationship.

The acknowledgement of an irrational element within professional social work relationships and the significance of past experiences are perhaps particularly important ideas here. Some relationships certainly do not develop exactly as we expect; they produce unanticipated consequences, positive or negative, for the parties involved, for clients and social workers alike, and we suspect that most experienced social workers will have met clients who seem to misinterpret their actions and intentions almost at every turn. Other clients, by contrast, seem to derive almost excessive comfort and support from things that social workers say apparently casually, or at the least without intending any special significance to them. Relationships can be hard to fathom, even with hindsight.

Professional social work relationships and their meaning have to be made sense of by all the parties involved in them and are potentially open to different and divergent interpretations by each. Some social workers, and certainly some clients, find that ideas from psychoanalysis and its related theories are useful in interpreting the transactions of relationship, particularly in relation to making sense of unanticipated or even seemingly irrational occurrences. When clients and social workers make sense together however, then shared understandings may develop and new perspectives on the tasks in hand may open up. This is perhaps the principal reason for thinking about aspects of relationship psychoanalytically.

Psychoanalysis as science: theory, empathy and experience

To judge by the degree of influence that his ideas have had on Western thought and culture, (there is hardly a medium that has not been influenced by psychoanalysis) Sigmund Freud's achievements may fairly be ranked alongside those of Darwin or Einstein (see Yellold, 1980). Freud trained as a medical doctor and consequently believed that his theories were based on scientific principles, in particular biology and pre-relativistic physics.

Nowadays, thinking about what constitutes scientific method has moved on to some degree and it is clear that from a modern standpoint psychoanalysis fails to meet the minimum standards by which scientific validity is currently judged. Psychoanalysis has little predictive integrity for example and does not easily generate hypotheses that are easily falsifiable. An additional problem about Freud's theorising was that it was inextricably linked to the behavioural and moral conventions of the society in which he lived. As the works of one of Freud's contemporaries, the Austrian playwright Arthur Schnitzler illustrate graphically, some of these conventions, particularly those concerned with the status of women and of doctors are seriously out of step with modern ideas. This is nowhere clearer than with regard to many of Freud's ideas about personality development, psychosexual development and his more controversial notions about the development of femininity (see Joan Rivière, *Womanliness as a Masquerade* in Ruitenbeek, 1966). It is unquestionably these aspects of Freudianism, which have led (probably quite correctly) to fierce and often scornful criticism from psychologists of other schools, and from some

feminist writers. And it has often been exactly these topics which have been taught to generations of slightly confused social work students, many of whom have surely been very uncertain as to their relevance to social work practice.

The problem with the overemphasis on Freudian personality and psychosexual development in much social work teaching has been that the (perfectly valid) objections that can made to these ideas tend to promote 'baby and bath water' rejection of some other Freudian ideas which are useful when making sense of social work relationships. In particular, Freud's ideas about personality *structure*, about anxiety and about the nature of the 'irrational' elements in helping relationships may be particularly helpful. We can illustrate this best by considering the problem of 'empathy' within relationships, and by referring to the work of another of Freud's contemporaries, the German (and definitely non-Freudian) psychiatrist and philosopher Karl Jaspers (Jaspers, 1913 and 1963).

Jaspers, a disciple of the phenomenological philosopher Edmund Husserl, maintained that there are important differences between trying to 'understand' people and 'explaining' their problems theoretically. In his terms 'understanding' (*verstehen* in German) is an empathic process requiring considerable descriptive and imaginative ability, which needs practice and development to become useful. Jaspers believed that empathic understanding should always *precede* attempts at theoretical explanation (*erklären*) and he also maintained that the subjective connections that people make between various aspects of their experiences (their ' meaningful connections' as he called them) were a critical aspect of developing understanding. Jaspers' ideas about empathy and theorising seem to us to be particularly relevant to social work.

In Jasperian terms, empathic understanding requires both a facility for describing personal experiences (often by using *analogy*) and a capacity for imagination. When we describe experiences to someone else (especially experiences of our own thoughts, feelings and awareness of ourselves) we often try to find analogies that make sense to the other person we are talking with. A trite example might be to describe a toothache as being like 'hot needles' in the jaw. A dentist, who presumably knows a lot about the physiology of pain, might be unimpressed by the analogy but the point of it is that it tries to convey the subjective experience of toothache. If the dentist tries even superficially to imagine what 'hot needles' might feel like, he might (just) be moved to treat the problem more sympathetically and with urgency.

The assumption that the experience of pain is similar for all human beings, including dentists, may seem reasonable, but it may be much less easy to assume that other people share other kinds of personal experiences at all. Additionally, people who are not particularly introspective may be unused either to thinking consciously about their experiences or may be unused to trying to describe them. Some clients (and some social workers) may struggle very hard indeed to find ways of expressing their experiences clearly enough, to allow a listener to imagine what they feel like. And in the same way, the listener may have equal difficulty in finding the right words with which to demonstrate her/his empathy. To show that we grasp another person's experience, to convey that we can imagine what it is like to be in their position sometimes means working hard to help them clarify or refine their descriptions until a shared sense emerges. We may not always succeed.

Jaspers' argument that empathic understanding should precede theoretical 'explanation' of troublesome experiences is made for a sound reason: if it doesn't, then theoretical explanation can too easily degenerate into a process of judgmental tidying up or 'explaining things away.' It is only when empirical explanation is watertight that empathic enquiry becomes unnecessary, and this can rarely be the case in the field of complex human experiences. Additionally, empathic relationship generates a sense of feeling valued and 'understood' in many people, which may be valuable in itself. Our non-empathic dentist who draws on his 'objective' and theoretical understanding of pain, might reasonably conclude that most people don't die of toothache, and dismiss his patient's plight with advice to take aspirin until a slot is vacant in the dentist's busy schedule. The patient won't feel very 'cared for' however.

It is our contention that because social workers deal with the subjective a good deal of the time, it may be that the emotional

significance of the 'meaningful connections' that clients make between different aspects of their experiences is at least as important as more 'objective' explanations of these same experiences. Two people suffer much the same kind of heart attack: one takes up jogging while the other takes to bed. Why? The answer may lie in the significance or meaning that the heart disease has for each person: a challenge to be transcended or a reason for defeat.

From this kind of standpoint, it may be relatively unimportant that psychoanalytic views of relationships and their application to social work theories are 'unscientific' in the strictest of senses. What may be more important is whether psychodynamic perspectives promote a sense of feeling 'understood' in the client. Since, as Jaspers points out, empathy depends on finding analogies that allow us to be reasonably clear that we 'grasp' our clients' diverse and problematic experiences, the concepts that underpin psychodynamic theory (anxiety, ego-defences, transference and so on) may best be considered as an interlinked set of analogical descriptions that can make sense to some (but by no means all) clients, when they struggle with difficult thoughts, feelings and memories. Human experiences may not fit neatly into 'science'; if they did, then valuing 'diversity' might become redundant.

Anxiety and personal functioning

Freud's ideas about the significance of anxiety in disturbing a person's abilities to function competently are central to psychodynamic social work. According to Freud, human behaviour is driven initially by the biological energies that he called 'instincts' without which survival and reproduction would not be possible. In Freudian theory however, human beings differ from other animals because we have the capacities for consciousness of the self, for abstract thinking and for self expression using complex language. The expression of 'instinct' can therefore be mediated and moderated by thought and language and, because we need to live socially, the 'instincts' constantly require such moderation.

The classical division of the personality structure by Freudians into three separate components called Id, Ego and Super Ego is well known. Id (the reservoir or well-spring of instinctive energy) is 'unconscious' and can have no contact with the external world, unless its instinctive energies are directed and channelled by the Ego (the conscious aspect of personality by means of which we perceive the world, ourselves as individuals and other people who surround us.) Super Ego, the third aspect of the personality structure is also 'unconscious' but is a learned element, acquired initially from parents but also from significant others: it contains rules or standards which govern acceptable/unacceptable expressions of instinct and therefore is roughly equatable with a moral code for 'correct' behaviour towards others ('conscience'), and also with a blueprint for all aspects of personal behaviour (the 'ego ideal').

Ego, the conscious sense of self, is constantly bombarded by potentially overwhelming anxiety either because the external world presents it with real and objective dangers to its survival (everyday hazards to life, competitive attacks from others etc.) or because the conscious feelings produced by uncontrolled instinctive desires (sexuality, aggression etc.) become too intense for comfortable expression in the external (social) world. Additionally, Ego is also attacked by a third source of anxiety whenever it fails to match up to the exacting standards required by the internalised conduct-standards contained in the Super Ego.

Whenever these combined anxieties (or the intensity of any one of them) become unmanageable, the Ego's sense of its own integrity may become weakened to the point of panic. Then the Ego attempts, and needs desperately, to lower anxiety to levels that can be experienced comfortably and it does this by adopting the evasive manoeuvres that Freud called mental defence mechanisms. The defence mechanisms do reduce anxiety to manageable proportions but they also distort the Ego's perceptions of what is 'really' happening to it so that its judgement about itself and the external world is impaired. The Ego survives in a distorted reality.

Defensive perceptions and defensive behaviours

Freud posited three types of anxiety; Reality Anxiety (threats to the Ego from external hazards), Moral Anxiety or Guilt (injunctions to the Ego from the Super Ego) and Neurotic Anxiety (Instinctual threat to the Ego from the Id: often manifested as the experience of being overwhelmed by the sudden intensity of sexual or aggressive feelings). Many people (perhaps all of us, according to Freud) will experience all three, and most of us will be able to recognise each type when their manifestations are pointed out.

A person in a near-miss car accident may say that the (Reality Anxiety) experience 'scared them shitless', unless the Super Ego steps in with an injunction against 'bad language' (Moral Anxiety or Guilt): then the person may feel better by saying that the experience 'scared them witless.' The same person may also describe their neurotic anxiety when talking the incident over with a friend: 'I don't know what came over me,' they might say, 'All I wanted to do afterwards was to kick the bastard's head in. The impulse was really strong, I was horrified to feel so aggressive towards someone I'd never met.' It might well be horrifying; according to Freud, the experience of neurotic anxiety is always disturbing.

Because a good deal of Freudian theory has become part of popular culture, the idea of the mental defence mechanism is familiar to many of us. People say for example that someone they know is 'in denial'; rationalising, projecting, sublimating or whatever and these terms may be used critically or even disparagingly in everyday speech. This kind of connection between 'defensive behaviours' and some kind of character defect, seems to us to overlook three important points; Freud taught that mental defences are unconscious, are adaptive survival mechanisms, and are common to everyone at sometime or another. All egos need defending at sometime, either temporarily or for longer.

Since defences protect the Ego's integrity by dealing with unmanageable anxiety, they can only be given up when the Ego feels safe. Mental defence mechanisms are not the same kind of phenomenon as deliberate (or wilful) evasiveness, and defences can only be 'lowered' when the Ego can cope with the anxiety that provokes them. In practical terms this means, perhaps, that a person's sense of safety has three components: they must be safe enough first of all to experience their anxieties consciously, then to discover that their sense of self remains intact while they are doing this, and then safe enough perhaps to examine the sources or origins of the anxieties that were so disturbing originally. All of this may take some considerable time to accomplish, even in circumstances where the 'client' does not perceive the person nominally helping them as a source of additional threat.

Transference and counter-transference

Just as relationships happen, then the irrational emotional responses to another person known as transferences happen too: and may well colour our perceptions of what is 'really' happening within the relationships. The phenomenon of transference can be fairly easily demonstrated by setting up a slightly artificial situation as an experiment. Talking to someone about any subject you like for a few minutes, but arranging for them not to respond to anything you say while they sit outside of your direct line of vision is likely to lead to curious results. The probability is that within a fairly short space of time you will begin to talk to the other person as if they were someone else, most probably as if they were someone significant in either your past or your present life. You can catch yourself doing this quite quickly and often with remarkably little introspection: the process is not usually difficult for most people, but the results may be surprising if the experience is unfamiliar.

Classical psychoanalysis depends on the development of the transference and its examination by the analyst/therapist. In prolonged sessions of analysis, the 'patient' may express a wide variety of emotions, relating to the analyst by turns as 'the doctor', either or both parents, and perhaps a variety of other significant people. The skill of the analyst lies in teasing out the relationships between the emotions expressed, the content of the conversation and the problems that brought the person into analysis in the first place. The interpretation of the transferences offered by 'the patient' will depend on the significance of

all of these within the particular theoretical frameworks for personality development and for emotional problems that the analyst respects. In classical Freudian terms these might be about the stages of so-called psycho-sexual development, and emotional 'fixations' at one or other of these stages. There are many different schools of analytic or psychodynamic thought however which modify these initial formulations.

Transferred emotions may be both 'positive' and 'negative.' People in analysis may be angry and hostile towards the therapist or alternatively may idealise them and become irrationally attached to them. It is clearly important that the analyst can distinguish between emotions related to the significant others in the person's life and those that relate directly to themselves. Analytic therapists may need supervision by an experienced colleague of the same theoretical persuasion to make these distinctions accurately.

Therapists themselves are never immune to transference problems of their own. Counter-transference occurs when it is the therapist who acts irrationally towards the client. Any client may unconsciously remind the therapist of a previous client (or their problems) for example, and may lead to complicated and misleading interpretation of a current situation. Once again regular and skilled supervision for the therapist is necessary to minimise such risks.

Psychodynamic social work

Although psychodynamic social work uses ideas taken from psychoanalysis, it differs from analysis in a number of important ways. Social work practice:

- Concentrates on the present rather than the past.

- Attempts to help people achieve equilibrium between their inner emotional states and the pressures that they face in the outside world.

- Uses the client's relationship with the social worker actively.

Additionally, whereas psychoanalysts are often extremely passive and offer no practical help with matters of concern to the client outside the consulting room, social workers are concerned with troublesome aspects of the client's environment and work with the client to achieve desired changes (Payne, 1997: ibid).

In Britain psychodynamic social work has never quite developed the sophistication or elaborate typologies which have characterised its practice in the USA. Even at its zenith, the variants of psychodynamic theory, *diagnostic theory* (Hollis, 1964; 1972) versus *functional theory* (Smalley, 1970), tended not to be taught as separate and contrasting approaches in any kind of systematic way. Considerable attention was often given however to Hollis' *Psychosocial Casework* (Hollis, 1964; 1972; and latterly Woods and Hollis, 1990) and the 'problem solving' approach of Helen Harris Perlman (Perlman, 1957; 1971).

Of these two approaches, Hollis' method is by far the most elaborate and most closely founded on 'classical' psychoanalysis. It comprises a complex classification of casework procedures, which are classified as 'Procedures for Client-Worker Communications' and 'Procedures in Environmental Work'. Many of these, 'exploration, description and ventilation' for example, which was aimed at obtaining an understanding of the clients' view of their situation and themselves, together with bringing out their feelings, were regarded for many years as the corner-stones of social work method. They can reasonably be seen as precursors of more modern counselling techniques.

In Helen Perlman's formulation of method (Perlman, ibid) a *person* is said to require help with a *problem*, at a *place* where social work is done. The client then becomes subject to a social work *process* by means of which professional help is offered. Clients are assumed to be unable to solve problems themselves, since many of them say that this is the case, and help is directed at enhancing their capacities to cope. Although firmly based on psychodynamic principles, Perlman's method, as Payne points out (ibid), was an important forerunner of task-centred casework.

For the purposes of this current discussion, the psychodynamic method influenced by ego-psychology and called 'Ego orientated Casework' (Goldstein, 1984; Parad, 1958; 1963) seems particularly appropriate. This approach concentrates on helping the client develop sufficient ego strength or integrity to deal with external relationships and difficulties occurring in the world. Within the approach the relationship formed with the social worker and the personal insights gained by the clients are believed to be essential factors in the help that is offered.

According to Goldstein (ibid) the phases in the helping process are as follows: first, *assessment*, looking at the person's present and past ways of coping or managing their lives. This includes emotional (inner capacities, habitual emotional responses to stress) as well as practical aspects of coping with practical requirements of life. *Defining the problems* to be tackled is the second phase: sharing the problem, assessing ways that clients have already tried (presumably unsuccessfully) to resolve it (them) and looking for other possible ways of dealing with it. Thirdly, *action* means either:

- Improving the clients' internal capacities to cope (by understanding why they are weakened and then finding strategies to strengthen them).

- Changing outside circumstances affecting the client.

- Improving how the internal and external worlds experienced by the client fit together.

Since the study of ego functioning is held to be paramount in the problem solving method, the helping process comprises interventions which are either *ego supporting* or *ego modifying*. Ego supporting interventions (Goldstein, ibid; and also Hollis, ibid) focus on present behaviours, conscious thought and environmental change. They involve the client in learning new skills or developing old skills, through the medium of the relationship with the worker, who may use directive or educational techniques, which are more likely to be short rather than long term (c.f. task-centred method once again). Ego modifying interventions, by contrast, focus on past and present unconscious feelings and drives or impulses, concentrating on giving insight into the client's feelings and so helping to resolve emotional conflicts. Understanding transferences in the client–worker relationship is important in this process, which uses non-directive and reflective techniques and is often longer term.

Using psychodynamic method

In the past a psychoanalytic orientation appeared to invite social workers to 'do therapy' which not only failed to meet the key criterion of relevance, it also left workers feeling inadequate to the task.

(Nathan, J., (1996). Psychoanalytic Theory. In Davies, M. (Ed.). *The Blackwell Companion to Social Work*, p231)

Is social work 'therapeutic'? And if so, how does it differ from the 'therapeutic' activities of other 'helping' professionals? As Nathan points out, it is very easy to see psychoanalytic theory as an area that is too complex for social workers to engage in nowadays without undergoing further lengthy (and costly) training. Additionally, Nathan says that other types of professional may currently see such activity as infringing on their territory, giving new impetus to debates about roles and boundaries, which are often time-consuming and sometimes acrimonious.

It is clearly true that social work has undergone enormous changes over recent years and it is obviously equally true that more changes are likely in the future. Colleagues of ours have said that the introduction of care management has caused them to feel 'de-skilled' and the emphasis on bureaucratic activity that seems to prevail everywhere certainly appears to raise 'stress' levels in social workers. So what price 'therapy' within this kind of context? Are social workers equipped to do it? Should we even attempt it within the policy frameworks of the present day?

Nathan's comment concerning the management of conflicts arising between social workers adopting psychodynamic method and other professionals is more relevant nowadays than it might have been formerly. Structural changes to health care and to social care provision over the past ten years have meant that where social work methods appear to enter the arena of 'therapy', particularly in the field of adult mental health service provision, some health care professionals may see this as an invasion of their traditional territory. In similar fashion, the rise of counselling as an independent and reasonably strictly accredited profession in the past twenty years or so means that a new group of workers are also laying claim to an area of expertise which in times past was very clearly encompassed within social work, at least in some settings.

We can think of no obvious reason to suppose that any group of professionals is entitled to claim any psychological method of helping people as their exclusive property. The mystique that often surrounds terms like 'therapy' and 'counselling', which the Barclay Committee certainly regarded as a social work activity (Barclay, 1982), can sometimes obscure the fact that the knowledge upon which these helping methods are built, is shared by many different types of professional 'helpers'. Including social workers.

If social work depends on understanding and using relationships to produce its results then we see no obvious technical difference between social work and other kinds of helping activity that use relationships consciously. Such differences as exist between 'social work method' and 'counselling' or even 'therapy' as practised by other professionals have more (in our opinion) to do with values than method. (See Fleet, this volume, for further discussion of this topic.)

Jack Nathan's other point (that psychoanalysis requires lengthy and expensive specialised training) is of course true; but psychodynamic social work method has never set out to produce fully-fledged psychoanalysts. Traditionally it has used everyday supervision and what we nowadays call ' reflective practice' to help social workers apply some psychoanalytic ideas to their practice and to themselves, especially in terms of gaining 'insight' into their own emotions and behaviours within their relationships with clients. Psychodynamic social work is *social work*; a method for 'improving relationships among people within their life situation.' (Payne, 1997: p80).

This particular point may need emphasis within the context of care management regimes. An older woman whose husband has developed dementia, for example, and who can no longer communicate with him or offer him the physical care he needs, will be faced with what feels like the death of her spouse, but will not be allowed the outward forms of parting which go with death. Her grief might be overwhelming and might take on any of the forms described by experts in this field (Murray Parkes, 1982; Worden, 1988 for example). The worker who goes to help effect the process of her husband's move to a nursing home needs to be able to respond appropriately to these feelings not least because the woman's distress may cloud her judgement about the proposed admission. There are other considerations however: in such a circumstance, unless we understand this person's emotions, unless we *help her* to acknowledge her anxieties (of which psychodynamic theory would say there might be several different types at work at the same time) we will probably neither meet her needs nor empower her however much we think otherwise. And if we do these things well, if we help her to maintain her ego-integrity as we might say, then who is to argue that this work is not 'therapeutic' or that what we are doing is not 'counselling'. Very few we suggest.

The question of results

Reid and Epstein's original objections to psychodynamic theory (being over concerned with experience and too little with concrete outcomes) still resonate today, when services have to be cost effective. And again, Mayer and Timms' (Mayer and Timms, op. cit.) criticism of the method (over-intrusiveness into clients' lives) and certain feminist critiques of psychoanalysis (Mitchell and Ruitenbeek, op. cit.), undoubtedly have their own meanings and validity. But these kinds of criticisms can also be connected with more profound questions about what social work is or perhaps about what it should be. Are 'social work' and 'social care', one and the same thing; are certain perspectives on human problems unacceptable in practice if they cannot apply equally to everyone or if the theory that underpins them is flawed at least in part; is 'client satisfaction' ever wholly attainable? What about results?

It is clear that 'evidence based practice' can ask (and can answer) many sensible questions about some important aspects of practice. Does residential care for older people for example, prolong life or improve its quality and does residence ease the burden on carers, more or less well than domiciliary care overall? Are (reasonably matched) recipients of contrasted care regimes equally satisfied with the care they receive? It is not too difficult to think of research designs that could go some way to tackling these issues or to envisage that results from such studies might guide future policy.

But the problem of respecting the diversity of clients, grasping their troublesome experiences empathically and of defining the boundaries of professional social work expertise remain, so that practice questions about psychodynamic method may be rather harder to settle. What can (or should) we do for clients whose problems have no ready solutions? Does empathy really matter in social work? Is 'gaining insight' into a personal problem helpful and is it always a quick 'eureka' experience? Is this 'insight' a necessary quality for professional social workers?

There are other questions still. Does initial dissatisfaction with a social work service indicate enduring dissatisfaction with it and does the whole notion of 'satisfaction' have something to do with feeling 'understood' rather than 'explained'? Perhaps or perhaps not. We may note however, that sometimes the immediate satisfactions experienced by both clients and workers do not sustain them either, and that there are indeed problems for which we social workers have no ready solutions. The truth will make us free, someone said, but first it will make us miserable. There may be very many different truths within social work.

References

Banks, S. (1995). *Ethics and Values in Social Work*. London: Macmillan.

Barclay Report (1982). *Social Workers: Their Role and Tasks*. London: Bedford Square Press.

Biestek, F.P. (1957). *The Casework Relationship*. London: Unwin Hyman.

Braye, S., and Preston-Shoot, M. (1995). *Empowering Practice in Social Care*. Buckingham: Open University.

Coulshed, V., and Orme, J. (1998). *Social Work Practice: An Introduction* (3rd edn.). London: Macmillan.

Dalrymple, J., and Burke, B. (1995). *Anti-oppressive Practice: Social Care and the Law*. Buckingham: Open University.

Dominelli, L. (2000). *Empowerment*, this volume.

Fleet, F. (2000). *Counselling and Contemporary Social Work*, this volume.

Ferrard, M., and Hunnybun, N. (1962). *The Caseworkers Use of Relationship*. London: Tavistock.

Goldstein, E.G. (1984). *Ego Psychology and Social Work Practice*. New York: Free Press.

Hillman, J., and Ventura, M. (1993). *We've Had a Hundred Years of Psychotherapy and the World's Getting Worse*. London: Harper Collins.

Hollis, F. (1964) and (1972). *Casework: A Psychosocial Therapy* (2nd edn.). New York: Random House.

Jaspers, K. (1913). *Allgemeine Psychopathologie*. Translated by Hoenig, J., and Hamilton, M. (1963) as *General Psychopathology*. Manchester: Manchester University.

Mayer, J.E., and Timms, N. (1970). *The Client Speaks: Working Class Impressions of Casework*. London: Routledge and Kegan Paul.

Mitchell, J. (1974). *Psychoanalysis and Feminism*. London: Allen Lane; New York: Pantheon.

Murray Parkes, C. (1972). *Bereavement: Studies of Grief in Adult Life*. London: Tavistock.

Nathan, J. (1996). Psychoanalytic Theory. In Davies, M. (Ed.). *The Blackwell Companion to Social Work*. London: Blackwell.

Parad, H.J. (1958). *Ego Psychology and Dynamic Casework*. New York: Family Service Association of America.

Parad, H.J. (1963). *Ego-oriented Casework; Problems and Perspectives*. New York: Family Service Association of America.

Payne, M. (1997). *Modern Social Work Theory* (2nd edn.). London: Macmillan.

Perlman, H.H. (1954) and (1971). *Social Casework: A Problem-solving Process*. Chicago: University of Chicago.

Reid, W.J., and Epstein, L. (1972). *Task Centered Casework*. New York: Columbia University.

Reid, W.J., and Shyne, A.W. (1969). *Brief and Extended Casework*. New York: Columbia University.

Rivière, J. (1966). Womanliness as a Masquerade. In Ruitenbeek, H.M. (Ed.). *Psychoanalysis and Female Sexuality*. New Haven: College and UP.

Smalley, R. (1970). The Functional Approach to Casework Practice. In Roberts, R., and Nee, R.H. (Eds.). *Theories of Social Casework*. Chicago: University of Chicago.

Thompson, N. (1997). *Anti-Discriminatory Practice*. London: Macmillan.

Warden, W.J. (1988). *Grief Counselling and Grief Therapy*. London: Routledge.

Woods, M., and Hollis, F. (1990). *Casework: A Psychological Process* (2nd edn.). New York: Random House.

Yelloly, M.A. (1980). *Social Work Theory and Psychoanalysis*. Wokingham: Van Nostrand Reinhold.

Chapter Six

Crisis Intervention as Common Practice

Wing Hong Chui and Deirdre Ford

Introduction

Social workers, social services management, and social work trainers do not have to be reminded that the crisis task in social services constitutes the most formidable and expensive challenge.

(O'Hagan, 1986: p12)

In day-to-day practice, it is not surprising that the vast majority of social workers come into contact with people in states of crisis. Almost every individual, in one way or another, experiences crises and participates in the crises of others at different stages in life (Calhoun, Selby and King, 1976; Robinson, 1979; Stephen and Woolfe, 1982; Young, 1983; Hoff, 1995). While some may cope with crises on their own, others may seek help from family and friends or turn to professionals for practical and emotional support. Encountering various forms of crisis is generally recognised as one of the integral parts of direct practice within the range of social work settings. The manifestation and characteristics of a crisis, however, vary from one to another, so that there is no consensus regarding what constitutes a crisis. Additionally, crisis situations generally require immediate responses from practitioners and managers alike to give advice and to arrive at decisions within a short period of time. As such, crisis work may provoke anxieties and induce a sense of helplessness amongst trained workers, not to mention those who are inexperienced and not prepared for it. A sound knowledge of the concepts and principles of crisis theory therefore is important in order to take up the challenges, along with service users, of confronting crises, and avoiding the less satisfactory outcome of mere 'crisis survival' (Thompson, 1991).

While there is no one prescription for dealing with crises, crisis intervention is seen as one of several therapeutic models that offers a clear framework for understanding the salient features of crises and principles to guide intervention. According to Ewing:

Social scientists speak of crisis intervention as a conceptual model for understanding human adjustment, family dynamics, and even organisational development. Community mental health workers view it variously as a strategy for the prevention of mental disorder and psychiatric hospitalisation, a form of short-term psychotherapy, a model for community consultation, and as a rationale for new self-help and paraprofessional programmes.

(1978: p3)

One assumption of this model is that every person has a potential for growth and an ability to solve problems. What social workers can do is to facilitate those who are in distress so that they can discover and develop coping strategies to meet life demands. Caplan (1964), Carkhuff (1969), Rapoport (1970), Shneidman (1972) and Golan (1974) amongst others proposed that the right kind of minimal intervention during a brief crisis period can achieve a maximum effect. Another pragmatic argument in favour of crisis services in the last decade, particularly in the British context, is that budget cuts and pressures on resources place emphasis on the great value of employing 'brief' therapies or time-limited intervention rather than traditional longer term psychotherapy (Monach and Monach, 1993). By no means do we argue that crisis intervention itself provides us with all solutions to sophisticated crisis contexts but it is a mode of brief treatment for the immediate threats imposed on an individual, and if necessary, follow-up services can and should be provided after the critical moment.

The concepts and development of crisis theory, which derived from the practice of psychiatry in America, have been written about extensively since the 1960s (Lindemann, 1965; Parad, 1965; Rapoport, 1970; Golan, 1978; Ewing, 1978; Burgess and Baldwin, 1981; Roberts, 1990; Thompson, 1991; Coulshed and Orme, 1998; Payne, 1998). There is an abundance of literature to illustrate how crisis intervention has been applied in relation to service users such as older people with dementia (Marshall, 1991; Thompson, 1991;

Parker, 1992); people who are dying or bereaved (Berman, 1978; Sharer, 1979; Burgess and Baldwin, 1981; Smith, 1982; McConville, 1990); suicidal clients (Lewis, Walker and Mehr, 1990); people who misuse substances (Cocores and Gold, 1990; Gilliland and James, 1997); victims of violence and their abusers (Bard and Ellison, 1974; Warner, 1979; Kilpatrick and Veronen, 1983; Petretic-Jackson and Jackson, 1990; Roberts and Roberts, 1990; Roberts and Dziegielewski, 1995); and those with health related and mental health related problems (Robinson, 1979; Hess and Ruster, 1990; Mitchell, 1993). Admittedly most of these are American texts and it is questionable whether crisis intervention is still regarded as an important model of social work practice in Britain. It is timely therefore to revisit the concepts of crisis intervention and to illustrate how it can be applied in practice with the person-in-crisis.

This chapter is structured into six sections. Relying on social work and health literature, the first and second sections deal with the concepts of crisis and the basic assumptions underlying this time-limited crisis intervention approach. The third section briefly summarises different phases or stages of crisis intervention in helping service users work through traumatic events. Sections four to six examine how crisis intervention can be used constructively with people and communities who suffer acute crisis as a result of large-scale accidents or disasters.

Defining crisis

> *A crisis refers to…A crisis occurs when…A crisis affects…Crisis has been viewed as…*
>> (Umana, Gross and McConville, 1980, cited in O'Hagan, 1986: p14)

Any attempt to look for a universal definition of crisis is doomed to failure (Langsley *et al.*, 1968; Umana *et al.*, 1980; Thompson, 1991). O'Hagan for instance recognises that the term 'crisis' is indeed elusive and vague in its meaning and is subject to personal interpretation:

> *A set of circumstances or conditions which constitute a crisis for one individual, may not do so for another. An unmanageable problem may render Mr Smith in a state of panic, and may be a matter of indifference to Mrs Brown. The sight of a spider could provoke a massive phobic reaction which we may justifiably call a crisis for the person concerned, whilst the birth of a mentally handicapped child may be perfectly manageable determinants, and it is easy to understand why many of the pioneers gave up the task of definition.*
>> (1986: p14)

Another similar explanation offered by Johnson is that 'crisis' and 'stress' are commonly used interchangeably by practitioners and students alike, and indeed there should be a distinction between the two terms:

> *Stress by itself isn't crisis: not even severe stress. Nor is a stressful event like job loss or illness a crisis, although such an event may precipitate a crisis. In some cases, an event that triggers a crisis in one person may scarcely even affect another. So much depends on the person's feelings about the situation, as well as their ability to cope with it at that time. The same situation occurring at another time in the person's life may not upset them unduly.*
>> (1979: pp15–16)

Thus it is important to be aware that different people may think of a crisis in many different ways and the cornerstone in understanding the nature and impact of a crisis situation depends largely on the feelings, perceptions and responses of an individual. Social work practitioners thus need to be open-minded and sensitive in order to understand the immediate concerns and worries of those involved rather than rigidly classifying crises according to the practitioners' frame of reference (Specter and Claiborn, 1972; Sebolt, 1972; Cohen and Nelson, 1983; Parker, 1992).

While there are many definitions of crisis and crisis may be perceived in different ways according to different experiences, most of them entail a negative connotation and certainly interpret crisis as a form of danger and destructive forces to individual and social functioning. Some examples are as follows:

> *Crisis results from impediments to life goals that people believe they cannot overcome through customary choices and behaviours.*
>> (Caplan, 1964: p40)

> *Crisis is a subjective reaction to a stressful life experience, one so affecting the stability of the individual that the ability to cope or function may be seriously compromised.*
>> (Bard and Ellison, 1974: p68)

Crises are personal difficulties or situations that immobilise people and prevent them from consciously controlling their lives.

(Belkin, 1984: p424)

A crisis brings about a temporary state of disorganisation in which people experience disruption of their normal functioning, and due to the inability to cope they can become frustrated, distressed, and angry. A number of authors such as Aguilera and Messick (1982), Young (1983), Thompson (1991), Roberts and Dziegielewski (1995) and Payne (1998) however draw attention to the positive dimension in viewing crisis by borrowing ideas from the two Chinese characters—*Wei Chi* that represent the word 'crisis'. These two characters indicate the presence of both 'danger' and 'opportunity', and literally mean the possibility of growth and impetus for change. Aguilera and Messick further emphasise that crisis can be seen as a turning point for better or worse in the person's well being:

> *Crisis is a danger because it threatens to overwhelm the individual or their family, and it may result in suicide or psychotic break. It is also an opportunity because during times of crisis individuals are more receptive to therapeutic influence.*

> (1982: p1)

At the point of crisis, it may be easier to admit that problems are beyond control and to be more receptive to change if defences collapse. Thus this gives a person a chance to look for new skills to meet demands in living (Gilliland and James, 1997). Recognising crisis as a turning point, the primary aim of crisis work is 'not simply to minimise the harm of a crisis, to 'cut losses', but rather to maximise the positive potential of crisis' (Thompson, 1991: p28).

Another key term related to crisis theory and practice is 'homeostasis'. It refers to 'self-regulation and the need to preserve a balance: in this case in affective (emotional) and cognitive (thinking) function which is dependent upon an individual's coping mechanisms' (Parker, 1992: p44). In the normal course of events every individual attempts to maintain a steady state of feeling and being mostly by utilising customary methods of problem solving or defence mechanisms:

> *The principle of homeostasis is borrowed from physiology and is defined by the need to preserve stable chemical or electrolyte balances within the body necessary to sustain life. When the balances are upset, self-regulatory mechanisms are triggered that help to return these balances to healthy levels for the individual.*

> (Burgess and Baldwin, 1981: p24)

Nonetheless, no one is immune to crises and at times our homeostatic equilibrium or normal functioning is disrupted for various reasons. Janosik (1984) opines that every crisis, whether universal or idiosyncratic, is accompanied by disequilibrium or disorientation. Heightened emotions, affective discomfort, cognitive confusion, and a sense of helplessness and powerlessness are often experienced. In this respect, it is essential for crisis workers to be sensitive to the signs of upset, enabling service users to understand the causes for crises and to arrive at a healthy process of recovery or restoration.

What are the events that produce stress and vulnerability? At the outset it should be emphasised that every crisis is a unique experience and yet attempts have been made to generalise possible factors to explain crisis situations. According to Rapoport, 'a crisis is an upset in a steady state caused by hazardous events' (1970: p276), and broadly speaking, hazardous or precipitating events can be experienced by an individual as a loss, a threat or a challenge. Nonetheless, Rapoport provides a rather vague definition of these three domains:

> *A threat may be directed to instinctual needs or to an individual's sense of integrity or autonomy. A loss may be that of a person or an experience of acute deprivation. A challenge may be to survival, growth, mastery, or self-expression.*

> (1970: p277)

Loss, threat and challenge result in differing affective reactions: for example loss often produces anger and protest. Threat may result in anxiety, fearful anticipation and uncertainty. Challenge may produce feelings of hopeful anticipation but at the same time panic may be experienced. In contrast, a simpler way of classifying crisis has been offered by Gilliland and James (1997), Coulshed and Orme (1998) and Payne (1998). There are two basic types of crisis in general terms, namely developmental or maturational crises and accidental or situational crises. While developmental crises can usually be anticipated and are seen as a normal part of human development and maturation such as pregnancy, marriage, retirement and ageing (Erikson, 1977), accidental crises are either unexpected or tragic events such as sudden bereavement, loss of health, hospitalisation and accidents. Butler and Elliott (1985) outline foreseeable changes to both external and internal patterns of living and in turn these natural crisis points to life transitions will induce periods of upset which call for readjustments. Given the fact that most developmental crises can be expected there is huge scope for social workers in prevention work. On the other hand, crisis intervention such as that undertaken by rape crisis services, women's refuges and suicide prevention centres should be readily available in the community to handle those unforeseen situational crises (Coulshed and Orme, 1998).

Basic assumptions of crisis theory and practice

> *Understanding the variations and sequences of emotions, with the accompanying defences, is at the heart of crisis intervention.*
>
> (Cohen, 1990: p284)

This section aims to revisit the theoretical base and assumptions of crisis intervention. The major conceptual development of crisis theory and practice is attributed to the work of Erich Lindemann, Gerald Caplan, Lydia Rappaport and Howard Parad (Ewing, 1978; Roberts, 1990). Golan uses ten statements to summarise the basic tenets of crisis theory, as shown below (Golan, 1974; 1978).

Tenets of Crisis Theory

1. An individual (or family, group, or community) is subjected to periods of increased internal and external stresses throughout their normal life span which disturb his/her customary state of equilibrium with their surrounding environment...The hazardous event may be a single catastrophic occurrence or a series of lesser mishaps which have a cumulative effect.

2. The impact of the hazardous effect disturbs the individual's homeostatic balance and puts them into a vulnerable state.

3. A precipitating factor can bring about a turning point, during which self-righting devices no longer operate and the individual enters a state of active crisis, marked by disequilibrium and disorganisation.

4. As the crisis situation develops, the individual may perceive the initial and subsequent stressful events primarily as a threat...as a loss of a person or an ability...or as a challenge to survival, growth, or mastery.

5. Each of these perceptions calls forth a characteristic emotional reaction that reflects the subjective meaning of the event to the individual.

6. Although a crisis situation is neither an illness nor a pathological experience and reflects a realistic struggle to deal with the individual's current life situation, it may become linked with earlier unresolved or partially resolved conflict.

7. The actual state of active disequilibrium, however, is time-limited, usually lasting up to four to six weeks.

8. Each particular class of crisis situation seems to follow a specific sequence of stages which can be predicted and mapped out.

9. During the unravelling of the crisis situation, the individual tends to be particularly amenable to help.

10. During the reintegration phase, new ego sets may emerge and new adaptive styles may evolve, enabling the person to cope more effectively with other situations in the future. However, if appropriate help is not available during the critical interval, inadequate or maladaptive patterns may be adopted which can result in weakened ability to function adequately later on.

(Extracted and modified from Golan, 1974: pp500–501)

Put simply, a crisis reaction will involve shock, emotional responses and resolution in the reconstruction of a new equilibrium. Other than basic crisis theory, Janosik (1984, also cited in Gilliland and James, 1997) acknowledges that contemporary crisis intervention strategies are drawn from psychoanalytic theory, systems theory, adaptational theory and interpersonal theory. One major assumption of psychoanalytic theory is that early childhood fixation is the major reason for turning an event into a crisis, and this theory argues for the importance of gaining access to the unconscious and past emotional traumatic experiences to understand a person's crisis. Using systems theory may not only enable the helping professional to conceptualise the wider conflicting processes impinging on a specific circumstance but also to look at the crisis event in the total social and environmental settings (Haley, 1976; O'Hagan, 1986; Cormier and Hackney, 1987; Parker, 1992). With reference to adaptational theory, both maladaptive behaviours and adaptive behaviours are learned, and when applied to crisis work, the person-in-crisis should be encouraged to replace maladjusted functioning such as negative thoughts and destructive defence mechanisms with new, self-enhancing ones by reinforcing their successful experiences (Gilliland and James, 1997). Finally, interpersonal theory (Rogers, 1977) places a great emphasis on the value of promoting a sense of internal control and enhancing the personal self-esteem of those who have lost confidence and are self-defeating as a consequence of experiencing acute crisis. This can be achieved by employing counselling techniques such as unconditional positive regard, empathy and genuineness in the helping process (Thorne, 1992; Howe, 1993). Thus crisis intervention is often regarded as an eclectic approach that generously comprises ideas and concepts from a number of psychological and developmental theories.

Thompson (1991) is rightly critical of traditional crisis theory, not least for its dissociation from the structural factors of oppression and its reliance on clinical terms which serve to pathologise the individual experiencing trauma. A community oriented approach to the theory however enables a reappraisal of the crisis response to be made with due regard for the cultural values of a society, its belief systems and socio-economic factors that might shape reactions. Cohen for instance draws attention to the experience of immigrant families in the United States in the aftermath of disaster (Cohen, 1990). Broader perspectives can be gained from 'community crises' which are considered in the second part of the chapter.

Process of crisis intervention

In the light of the basic assumptions of crisis theory and practice, two models conceptualise the process of crisis work. They are Caplan's three phases of crisis (1961) and Roberts' seven stages of working through crises (1990). Both appear to see crisis as having a structure which can be broken down into specific phases or stages for intervention. In practice, these phases are not clear-cut or mutually exclusive. Moreover, they are unlikely to proceed in a linear sequence. Nevertheless, the models provide a direction for social work practice and have particular relevance for intervention but their use requires practitioners' sensitivity and flexibility in relation to the actual crisis situations and individuals' responses to crises.

Caplan's three distinct phases are the impact stage, the recoil stage, and adjustment and adaptation (1961, cited in Thompson, 1991). Generally speaking, an onset or initial phase of a crisis is initiated when a hazardous event results in a state of confusion and disorientation from increased internal or external stress. During the impact phase the first and most important concern of a crisis worker is to attend to the immediate effect and perception of the crisis on an individual. This involves the person-in-crisis in defining the nature of problems openly and examining the detrimental effects of a crisis on himself or herself. Getting to grips with issues arising from the situation is one means of encouraging participation right at the beginning of the intervention process. Young (1983) provides a list of three main intervention activities in the impact phase, which are the management of heightened emotions, the restructuring of the crisis situation and the activation of coping responses. Given that the stage is usually short, these three activities may need to be addressed at the same time. Quick reactions and intense counselling work may also be required.

The second phase of the crisis intervention is called the recoil stage. It occurs when the individual attempts to use customary coping mechanisms to regain a state of equilibrium but these attempts to cope fail. As mentioned before, the experience of failure leads to a period of upset and disorganisation. Thompson (1991) reports that 'physical symptoms can also feature at this stage of the crisis process, such as fatigue, headaches, stomach disorder' (p10).

The final phase of crisis intervention is adjustment and adaptation which is also a stage of 'breakthrough or breakdown' (Thompson, 1991) or a crisis integrative phase (Young, 1983). This phase is particularly important simply because it involves the individual and a practitioner working together to confront crises and evaluate these experiences or results of the actions which have been taken.

> Basically, the integrative phase is concerned with accepting or assimilating the implications of the crisis into the individual's life. Integrative activities include working through:
>
> ● Current issues which continue to appear and demand attention throughout the crisis resolution phase.
>
> ● Past issues associated with the current crisis which have arisen and underlying past issues that are being reawakened.
>
> ● Implementing the decisions and actions initiated in the restructuring process.
>
> (Young, 1983: p42)

Once new coping mechanisms have been developed, the crisis has been resolved and normal functioning is resumed. However, the pace of integrative work should take into account of a number of factors such as the individual's readiness and motivation, and the availability of both tangible and intangible resources. Termination needs to be dealt with explicitly, and an evaluation is very useful in consolidating the gains of crisis intervention, reinforcing the experience of handling crises and discussing how this experience can be transferable into the future.

Further to Caplan's model, Roberts's (1990) seven stages of crisis intervention are also of practical use when working with individuals who have experienced accidental crisis. The stages are:

1. Assessing lethality and safety needs which aims to tease out the perception and meaning of crisis on an individual.

2. Establishing rapport and communication by showing acceptance of and genuine respect for those who receive help.

3. Identifying the major problems or the precipitating events and old ineffective coping methods that cause intense emotion and distress.

4. Dealing with feelings and providing support by active listening and facilitation of expression in a safe environment which is conducive to self-disclosure.

5. Exploring possible alternatives by examining the past, less adaptive responses to the crisis events and defining what are more adaptive coping behaviours to resolve them.

6. Formulating an action plan by restoring cognitive functioning and giving positive reinforcement for the willingness to face problems and commitment.

7. Providing follow-up by making referrals or informing of the availability of crisis work in the future.

(Roberts, 1990; 1991)

Among the limitations of crisis intervention (Payne, 1997; Thompson, 1991) it should be noted that the response of different ethnic groups to the crisis event will be culturally determined. For example in Chinese philosophy excessive emotions are considered harmful to the balance of Yin and Yang causing poor health. In this context an individual would habitually suppress their emotions in the onset phase at the optimal point for intervention, and thereby mask the true nature of the crisis.

Nevertheless the framework can be employed effectively to relieve emotional distress and offset stress-related disorders in the long term.

Crisis intervention, emergency planning and disaster work

It is surprising that crisis intervention is often neglected in the UK literature about social work methods. Local authorities are increasingly required to plan for, and respond to larger scale emergencies, almost as a matter of routine. Most social workers located in the public sector are likely to be involved in this relatively new area of work at some time in their career, either as staff nominated to form emergency planning teams, or as a result of working with individuals affected by a disaster, such as the relative of a victim killed in a train crash or a member of a community traumatised by the loss of a fishing vessel's crew. Together with the more orthodox use of crisis intervention in field work services described earlier, emergency planning and, at times, disaster work form a significant part of social work practice in the new century. Core social work skills are deemed to be appropriate and of real worth in responding to disasters (Newburn, 1996). The lack of a corresponding and robust literature regarding social work's expertise in this field may stem from a failure to respond to Thompson's earlier challenge to reformulate crisis theory and crisis intervention for the new era (Thompson, 1991).

This part of the chapter reviews crisis intervention as a framework for practice in community crises and disasters with reference to the authors' own experience. It argues for the development of the model in the context of community while acknowledging the achievements of emergency planning in providing a blueprint for multidisciplinary, and preventive practice.

The global society, the power of the media, the current preoccupation with the management of risk, are all factors that force everyone of us to confront trauma on a large scale at regular intervals. The cult viewing of disaster movies during the last two decades might be judged as a corollary to the morbid fascination of crowds who gather at the scene of some local catastrophe and whose interest is fuelled by incessant media activity. In the crisis framework an explanation for such processes offered by developmental psychologists is that of 'desensitisation' as a means of developing coping abilities (Franklin, 1983).

Community crises and emergency planning

Notwithstanding such phenomena, Britain's 'decade of disasters' not only heightened public awareness of, and concern for the community's response to major tragedies. It also accelerated developments in the knowledge and practice of agencies providing support to those affected. The legacy of the 1980s was the aftermath of tragic events marked by the Bradford football stadium fire in May, 1985 and ending with the sinking of the 'Marchioness' river boat in August, 1989.

At this time one of the authors of this chapter encountered the potential for such forms of crisis work when local authority social workers were recruited as 'counsellors' to support families in the event of service personnel being killed in the Gulf War. While the sequence of 'national' disasters unfolded (so that sadly names like the 'Herald of Free Enterprise', Kings Cross, Piper Alpha, Lockerbie, Kegworth, Hillsborough and Dunblane are now forever associated with major tragedy), the experience of responding to what might be termed 'community crises' grew almost imperceptibly as an element of routine practice undertaken by a local social services department. Social workers were asked to provide counselling, for instance, to a school community following the death of a pupil from a sports injury. Support was also mobilised for families of students who died in the Lyme Bay disaster and again for a school, as well as the wider community, coming to terms with the murder of a teenager. As part of the organisation of social services, social workers have been involved in the evacuation of sections of the community as a result of fires in factories containing explosive, and toxic materials respectively, a gas explosion, and as a consequence of an unexploded wartime bomb. Like those in many agencies, social workers have been alerted to the possibility of relatives of commuters killed in rail accidents needing support, as occurred at the time of the Paddington rail crash in October, 1999.

Emergency team workers have been placed on alert following the suspicion of terrorist activity at a major public event and possible mass evacuation. Perhaps the most famous recent examples of emergency planning in the South West, however, have been in relation to the total eclipse of the sun in August, 1999 and the millennium celebrations.

These illustrations represent a fraction of the work that might be subsumed under the heading of crisis intervention in which social workers play a significant and varied role.

Organisations in which practitioners are located, whether statutory or voluntary, have clearly defined responsibilities under arrangements for emergency management. Emergency planning is now a familiar term for front-line social services managers and their staff, enabling 'the organisation to deal effectively with a major or minor emergency, whether foreseen or unforeseen' (Home Office, 2000: p3). The local authority remit developed out of Civil Defence regulations but is not supported by central government funding (in contrast to the assistance available in the United States through the terms of the Federal Disasters Relief Act 1974). Nevertheless, emergency plans are governed by principles of crisis intervention in as much as they are proactive, preventive and flexible in operation. They must be integrated into everyday practice to ensure an immediate response. Effective inter-agency co-operation is vital and may involve co-ordination with neighbouring authorities (Home Office, 2000).

Planning for the foreseen in areas, for instance, at risk of flooding has been informed in no small measure by the experience of local councils gained incrementally as a result of the incidents described above. Debriefing following such events, simulated exercises to rehearse procedures, and staff training have all contributed to the development of local expertise in the management of community crises. These measures also provide opportunity for reflection on the lessons learned from major disasters such as Hillsborough where survivors' accounts, as recipients of services, were very powerful (Newburn, 1993).

As a result, progress has been made in identifying the specific role of social services in emergency planning, contrary to earlier findings (Thompson, 1991). Tasks may include the identification of:

> *Counselling and other support needs as they emerge. This may involve psychological and emotional support for victims and relatives of victims arriving in the area…Immediate counselling and support will be provided where necessary and arrangements made for continuing appropriate support after the crisis.*
>
> (Source: *Emergency Plan,* Devon Social Services, 1997).

Staff with the necessary experience and professional training are assigned to reception centres and emergency rest centres providing levels of support according to the magnitude of the trauma. While social work is likely to predominate as a profession in response teams, nevertheless social workers have yet to gain full recognition of their particular expertise within practice and policy guidance.

Emergency plans reveal the importance of local knowledge and understanding regarding the needs of the community involved, so that district councils for instance in rural areas have a significant part to play and can be mobilised in quick succession according to the scale of the crisis. In the absence of additional resources from central government, localised responses to the events described have been largely successful, while the involvement of community members assists the recovery phase as control is retained (Franklin, 1983; Young, 1995).

Social work practice in the aftermath of disaster

Corporate failures and acts of terrorism as well as natural catastrophes, however, have become features of the age. The proliferation of 'socio-technical' disasters (or situational crises) in recent years, heightens awareness that emergency planning has to anticipate the worst.

> *The Air India 747 which crashed off Cork in 1985 caused 325 fatalities. If the incident had happened 15 minutes later the aircraft would have been over Devon.*
>
> (Source: Devon Social Services training material)

Disaster is defined as:

> *any event…causing or threatening death or injury, damage to property or to the environment or disruption to the community, which because of the scale of its effects cannot be dealt with by the emergency services and local authorities as part of their day-to-day activities.*
>
> (Home Office, 2000)

The term 'major incident' is also used by the emergency services. Thompson (1991) differentiates between conventional applications of crisis intervention and disaster work in terms of the scale of the impact which can incapacitate both worker and organisation. A longer term perspective is adopted by Eyre (1998) who is mindful of the sustained public interest in questions of accountability and corporate responsibility for disasters. She argues that rehabilitation and recovery phases need to be reconfigured to understand the enduring psycho-social factors for survivors and relatives. These stem from protracted systems of inquiry and legal processes in the UK as well as the persistence of the media. (Recent private prosecutions against police chiefs involved in the Hillsborough disaster accentuate this point as television coverage of the tragedy is replayed throughout the trials and the trauma is relived.)

Modified emotional responses to disaster are also observed as a development of crisis theory. The initial phase of the impact can be described as 'heroic', characterised by reflexive behaviour as well as altruism to ensure the immediate survival of self and others. The honeymoon phase involves acute awareness of survival with others at a time when support from disaster agencies is available. Disillusionment occurs as anger and loss are experienced, crises services are withdrawn and the sense of community engendered among survivors may diminish. Blaming and scapegoating will represent attempts to regain control at this time. Finally reconstruction reflects the integrative phase of crisis theory which enables survivors to rebuild their lives and reaffirm their beliefs in personal coping strategies (Hartsough, Zarle and Ottinger, 1976, cited in Franklin 1983).

While the police hold strategic command for major incidents and together with the emergency services control the initial response, social services are quickly mobilised to assist in the assessment of the situation and planning for the recovery phase. Although different in their application, the basic professional knowledge and skills of daily practice are deemed to be essential at this stage of the crisis (Cohen, 1990). Public interest in post-traumatic stress disorder has heightened awareness of the psychological effects of trauma in the long term (Turnbull, 1997). A rapid and proactive response within a crisis framework seeks to pre-empt future problems of this nature. Thus survivors with adequate coping mechanisms prior to the disaster may be assisted to regain effective strategies without long term sequelae (Franklin, 1983).

Guidelines for a crisis intervention service in the aftermath of disaster have been developed by an American project, the National Organisation for Victim Assistance (Young, 1995):

Safety and security

1. Survivors need help in regaining a sense of safety and security, while avoiding the humiliation and dependency that might be incurred by needing to rely entirely on the emergency services for food, shelter and clothing (Cohen, 1990).

Ventilation and validation

2. The opportunity for expression of feelings together with conformation that such reactions are normal and to be expected are both important components of the work. Following the example set by Bradford Social Services after the fire, many local authority offices now routinely display leaflets about coping with a major personal crisis which provide information regarding common emotional responses to such events.

Prediction and preparation

3. Assistance should be offered in helping survivors to plan for the future. A task-centred approach may be adopted with the survivor or victim to encourage self-care or address practical matters such as memorial services, legal proceedings, relocation and so on (see Chapter Seven).

Rehearsal and reassurance

4. Survivors may need to rehearse and discuss events on the horizon such as an inquest or inquiry: visiting the scene of the disaster may be an aspect of this.

Education and expertise

5. Finally, the importance of information is recognised following a large-scale crisis event, together with the development or strengthening of support networks (Young, 1995).

Research by Newburn revealed similar categories of assistance provided by social workers which are regarded as crucial by service users. These are: advice, support, validation, reconstruction, facilitation and mitigation (Newburn, 1996).

The interpersonal skills of the individual worker are also identified as determinants of effective intervention. The ability to listen and a sense of the worker's credibility emerge as significant qualities, the latter assisted by the provision of practical support and the completion of tasks which enable trust to develop. A flexible approach is regarded as essential not only towards the needs of the individual survivor or victim but also to the community. Services must be culturally appropriate 'to incorporate the affected people's world-views…geographical, religious and historical implications…these aspects of the trauma experience and people's recovery are often overlooked entirely, or inappropriately minimised' (leaflet produced by the International Trauma Recovery Institute, LLC, Arizona).

Conclusion

The substantial body of literature identified at the beginning of this chapter reveals the rapid development of crisis intervention skills and knowledge over the last two decades of the twentieth century. Planning for the disaster that it is hoped will never happen has precipitated the growth of effective inter-agency co-operation and training. From such levels of co-operation learning might be usefully extended to other arenas where multi-disciplinary practice is essential to service delivery.

Within this framework social work is well placed to contribute to progress. Just one example where social work has much to offer is that of relationships. By virtue of the magnitude of the event and needs of those involved, relationships between survivors or victims and workers differ in terms of intensity and duration from those proscribed by conventional professional boundaries (Cohen, 1990). Personal friendships will emerge in the extraordinary circumstances created by a major disaster (Newburn, 1996). A relation-based approach might be regarded as a particular attribute of professional practice in this context (Howe, 1998).

With regard to the development of the theoretical model, the tradition of community work described in Chapter Eleven, systemic perspectives, and the ascent of anti-oppressive practice can all inform the understanding of crisis in relation to community. Indeed it is a prerequisite of the global society and technical achievement that a broader analysis of crisis provides the focus for intervention. The Lockerbie disaster epitomises the way in which the communities of several countries are suddenly linked by just one event.

It is therefore apparent that social work has a responsibility to promote its considerable expertise and skills in the practice of crisis intervention and to engage with other professions in the relief of emotional distress following a traumatic event.

References

Aguilera, D.C., and Messick, J.M. (1982). *Crisis Intervention: Theory and Methodology* (4th edn.). St Louis, Missouri: C.V. Mosby.

Bard, M., and Ellison, K. (1974). Crisis Intervention and Investigation of Forcible Rape. *The Police Chief*, 41(May): pp68–73.

Belkin, G.S. (1984). *Introduction to Counseling* (2nd edn.). Dubuque, IA: William C. Brown.

Berman, L.E. (1978). Sibling Loss as an Organiser of Unconscious Guilt: A Case Study. *Psychoanalytic Quarterly*, 47: pp565–587.

Burgess, A.W., and Baldwin, B.A. (1981). *Crisis Intervention Theory and Practice: A Clinical Handbook*. Englewood Cliffs, NJ: Prentice-Hall.

Butler, B., and Elliott, D. (1985). *Teaching and Learning for Practice*. Aldershot, Hants: Gower.

Calhoun, L.G., Selby, W., and King, H.E. (1976). *Dealing with Crisis: A Guide to Critical Life Problems*. Englewood Cliffs, NJ: Prentice-Hall.

Caplan, G. (1961). *An Approach to Community Mental Health*. New York: Grune and Stratton.

Caplan, G. (1964). *Principles of Preventive Psychiatry*. New York: Basic Books.

Carkhuff, R.R. (1969). *Helping and Human Relations: A Primer for Lay and Professional Helpers* (Vol. 2). New York: Holt, Rinehart and Winston.

Cocores, J.A., and Gold, M.S. (1990). Recognition and Crisis Intervention Treatment with Cocaine Abusers: The Fair Oaks Hospital Model. In Roberts, A.R. (Ed.). *Crisis Intervention Handbook: Assessment, Treatment and Research*, pp177–195. Belmont, CA: Wadsworth.

Cohen, L.H., and Nelson, D.W. (1983). Crisis Intervention: An Overview of Theory and Technique. In Cohen, L.H., Claiborn, W.L., and Specter, G.A. (Eds.). *Crisis Intervention* (2nd edn.), pp13–26. New York: Human Sciences Press.

Cohen, R.E. (1990). Post-disaster Mobilisation and Crisis Counseling: Guidelines and Techniques for Developing Crisis-oriented Services for Disaster Victims. In Roberts, A.R. (Ed.). *Crisis Intervention Handbook: Assessment, Treatment and Research*, pp279–298. Belmont, CA: Wadsworth.

Cormier, L.S., and Hackney, H. (1987). *The Professional Counselor: A Process Guide to Helping.* Englewood Cliffs, NJ: Prentice-Hall.

Coulshed, V., and Orme, J. (1998). *Social Work Practice* (3rd edn.). London: Macmillan.

Davies, M. (Ed.) (1997). *The Blackwell Companion to Social Work.* Oxford: Blackwell.

Erikson, E. (1977). *Childhood and Society.* London: Fontana.

Ewing, C.P. (1978). *Crisis Intervention as Psychotherapy.* New York: Oxford University Press.

Eyre, A., (1998). More than PTSD: Proactive Responses Among Disaster Survivors. *Australian Journal of Disaster and Trauma Studies,* Vol. 1998–2.

Franklin, T. (1983). Crisis Intervention in Community Disasters. In Cohen, L.H., Claiborn, W.L., and Specter, G.A. (Eds.). *Crisis Intervention* (2nd edn.), pp147–164. New York: Human Sciences Press.

Gilliland, B.E., and James, R.K. (1997). *Crisis Intervention Strategies* (3rd edn.). Pacific Grove, CA: Brooks/ Cole.

Golan, N. (1974). Crisis Theory. In Turner, F.J. (Ed.). *Social Work Treatment: Interlocking Theoretical Approaches,* pp420–456. New York: The Free Press.

Golan, N. (1978). *Treatment in Crisis Situations.* London: Free Press.

Haley, J. (1976). *Problem-solving Therapy.* New York: McGraw-Hill.

Hess, H.J., and Ruster, P.L. (1990). Assessment and Crisis Intervention with Clients in a Hospital Emergency Room. In. Roberts, A.R. (Ed.). *Crisis Intervention Handbook: Assessment, Treatment and Research,* pp196–220. Belmont. CA: Wadsworth.

Hoff, L.A. (1995). *People in Crisis: Understanding and Helping* (4th edn.). San Francisco: Jossey-Bass.

Home Office (2000). *Dealing with Disaster* (3rd edn.). Liverpool: Brodie.

Howe, D. (1993). *On Being a Client: Understanding the Process of Counselling and Psychotherapy.* London: Sage.

Howe, D. (1998). Relationship-based Thinking and Practice in Social Work. *Journal of Social Work Practice,* Vol. 12; No. 1: pp45–56.

Janosik, E.H. (1984). *Crisis Counseling: A Contemporary Approach.* Monterey, CA: Wadsworth Health Sciences Division.

Johnson, R. (1979). Recognising People in Crisis. In Robinson, J. (Ed.). *Using Crisis Intervention Wisely,* pp15–24. Horsham, PA: International Communications.

Kilpatrick, D.G., and Veronen, L.J. (1983). Treatment for Rape-related Problems: Crisis Intervention is not Enough. In Cohen, L.H., and Claiborn, W.L., and Specter, G.A. (Eds.). *Crisis Intervention* (2nd edn.), pp165–185. New York: Human Sciences Press.

Langsley, D.G., Pittman, F.S., Machotka, P., and Flomenhaft, K. (1968). Family Crisis Therapy: Results and Implications. *Family Process,* 7: pp753–759.

Lewis, R., Walker, B.A., and Mehr, M. (1990). Counseling

with Adolescent Suicidal Clients and their Families. In Roberts, A.R. (Ed.). *Crisis Intervention Handbook: Assessment, Treatment and Research,* pp44–77. Belmont, CA: Wadsworth.

Lindemann, E. (1965). Symptomatology and Management of Acute Grief. In Parad, H.J. (Ed.). *Crisis Intervention: Selected Readings,* pp7–21. New York: Family Service Association of America.

Marshall, M. (Ed.) (1990). *Working with Dementia.* Birmingham: Venture Press.

McConville, B.J. (1990). Assessment, Crisis Intervention, and Time-limited Cognitive Therapy with Children and Adolescents Grieving the Loss of a Loved One. In Roberts, A.R. (Ed.). *Crisis Intervention Handbook: Assessment, Treatment and Research,* pp21–43. Belmont, CA: Wadsworth.

Mitchell, R. (1993). *Crisis Intervention in Practice.* Aldershot: Avebury.

Monach, J., and Monach, J. (1993). Crisis Intervention: No Panacea—a Voluntary Organisation Perspective. *Practice,* 6(3): pp181–192.

Newburn, T., (Ed.) (1993). *Working with Disaster: Social Welfare Interventions During and After Tragedy.* Harlow: Longman.

Newburn, T. (1996). Social Work after Major Emergencies. In Jackson, S., and Preston-Shoot, M. (Eds.). *Educating Social Workers in a Changing Policy Context,* pp154–170. London: Whiting and Birch.

O'Hagan, K. (1986). *Crisis Intervention in Social Services.* London: Macmillan.

Parad, H.J. (Ed.) (1965). *Crisis Intervention: Selected Readings.* New York: Family Service Association of America.

Parker, J. (1992). Crisis Intervention: A Framework for Social Work with People with Dementia and their Carers. *The Journal of Care and Practice,* 1(4): pp43–57. Elders.

Payne, M. (1997). *Modern Social Work Theory* (2nd edn.). London: Macmillan.

Petretic-Jackson, P., and Jackson, T. (1990). Assessment and Crisis Intervention with Rape and Incest Victims: Strategies, Techniques, and Case Illustrations. In Roberts, A.R. (Ed.). *Crisis Intervention Handbook: Assessment, Treatment and Research,* pp124–152. Belmont, CA: Wadsworth.

Rapoport, L. (1965). The State of Crisis: Some Theoretical Considerations. In Parad, H.J. (Ed.). *Crisis Intervention: Selected Readings,* pp22–31. New York: Family Service Association of America.

Rapoport, L. (1970). Crisis Intervention as a Mode of Treatment. In Roberts, R.W., and Nee, R.H. (Eds.). *Theories of Social Casework,* pp265–311. Chicago: University of Chicago Press.

Roberts, A.R. (1990). An Overview of Crisis Theory and Crisis Intervention. In Roberts, A.R. (Ed.). *Crisis Intervention Handbook: Assessment, Treatment and Research,* pp3–16. Belmont, CA: Wadsworth.

Roberts, A.R. (Ed.) (1991). *Contemporary Perspectives on Crisis Intervention and Prevention.* Englewood Cliffs, NJ: Prentice-Hall.

Roberts, A.R., and Roberts, B.S. (1990). A Comprehensive Model for Crisis Intervention with Battered Women and their Children. In Roberts, A.R. (Ed.). *Crisis Intervention Handbook: Assessment, Treatment and Research*, pp105–123. Belmont, CA: Wadsworth.

Roberts, A.R., and Dziegielewski, S.F. (1995). Foundation Skills and Applications of Crisis Intervention and Cognitive Therapy. In Roberts, A.R. (Ed.). *Crisis Intervention and Time-limited Cognitive Treatment*, pp3–27. Thousand Oaks, CA: Sage.

Robinson, J. (Ed.) (1979). *Using Crisis Intervention Wisely*. Horsham, PA: International Communications.

Rogers, C.R. (1977). *Carl Rogers on Personal Power: Inner Strength and its Revolutionary Impact*. New York: Delacorte.

Sebolt, N. (1972). Crisis Intervention and its Demands on the Crisis Therapist. In Specter, G.A. and Claiborn, W.L. (Eds.). *Crisis Intervention*, pp66–78. New York: Behavioral Publications.

Sharer, P.S. (1979). Supporting Survivors of Unexpected Death. In Robinson, J. (Ed.). *Using Crisis Intervention Wisely*, pp57–70. Horsham, PA: International Communications.

Shneidman, E. (1972). Crisis Intervention: Some Thoughts and Perspectives. In Specter, G.A., and Claiborn, W.L. (Eds.). *Crisis Intervention*, pp9–15. New York: Behavioral Publications.

Smith, C.R. (1982). *Social Work with the Dying and Bereaved*. London: Macmillan.

Specter, G.A., and Claiborn, W.L. (Eds.) (1972). *Crisis Intervention*. New York: Behavioral Publications.

Stephen, M., and Woolfe, R. (1982). *Coping in Crisis: Understanding and Helping People in Need*. London: Harper and Row.

Thompson, N. (1991). *Crisis Intervention Revisited*. Birmingham: PEPAR Publications.

Thorne, B. (1992). *Carl Rogers*. London: Sage.

Turnbull, G. (1997). Understanding Post-traumatic Stress Disorder. *Psychiatry in Practice*, Autumn, pp5–10.

Umana, M.S., Gross, S.J., and McConville, M.T. (1980). *Crisis in the Family: Three Approaches*. New York: Gardner.

Warner, C.G. (1979). Comforting and Caring for the Rape Victim. In Robinson, J. (Ed.). *Using Crisis Intervention Wisely*, pp119–130. Horsham, PA: International Communications.

Young, K.P.H. (1983). *Coping in Crisis*. Hong Kong: Hong Kong University Press.

Young, M.A. (1995). Crisis Response Teams in the Aftermath of Disasters. In Roberts, A.R. (Ed.). *Crisis Intervention and Time-limited Cognitive Treatment*, pp151–187. Thousand Oaks, CA: Sage.

Chapter Seven

Task-centred Practice and Care Management

Peter Ford and Karen Postle

Introduction

The first part of this chapter comprises an outline of the rationale for and operation of task-centred practice. The chapter then moves to draw on research about the work of care managers (Postle, 1999) to consider what could hinder staff from effectively undertaking task-centred practice. Whilst this research related specifically to the community care of older people, its lessons are generalisable to other fields of care management. Where it is not possible to refer to the people with whom care managers worked simply as 'people', they have usually been termed 'clients'. This was the term used by care managers and, while acknowledged as problematic, was seen as no less so than terms such as 'user', 'consumer' or 'customer'.

Perhaps one reason for the enduring popularity of task-centred practice amongst social workers is that, unlike several other practice models, it was developed within and for social work, originating from research into social work practice. It is also one of the major contributions made by the profession and academic discipline of social work to all those who use their interpersonal skills to help others resolve problems, and its elements are widely used (frequently without acknowledgement) in areas ranging from counselling to education. It is a model of practice that not only derives from research, but lends itself to research, insofar as it embodies the setting of goals whose achievement is easily measured. Consequently the model has been developed and refined through numerous empirical studies in the past thirty years.

Task-centred practice is essentially a clear and practical model that can be adapted for use in a wide range of situations. Its two most important characteristics are that it is focused on *problem-solving*, and that it is *short-term and time-limited*. These characteristics help to define the situations in which it may usefully be applied.

A focus on problem-solving

The approach is designed to help in the resolution of difficulties that people experience in interacting with their social situations, where internal feelings of discomfort are associated with events in the external world. These *psychosocial problems* can be very diverse, ranging from relationship difficulties to a lack of material resources. Research into the effectiveness of task-centred practice has indicated that the model is effective when applied to a specific range of problems, characterised by Reid as follows:

- problems of interpersonal conflict (e.g. within families, or work situations)
- dissatisfaction in social relations (e.g. amongst young adults newly alone away from home)
- problems in dealings with formal organisations
- difficulties in role performance (e.g. in becoming partners, parents etc.)
- problems of social transition (in moving from one role or situation to another)
- reactive emotional distress (e.g. illness, bereavement)
- problems in securing adequate material resources
- behavioural problems

The corollary of the model's known effectiveness in addressing problems in these eight specified areas is that it should not be used in situations not listed here.

Time limits

Planned short-term work is one of the defining characteristics of task-centred practice, which originated from some well-known research into the relative benefits of brief and extended casework conducted by William Reid and Ann Shyne in the late 1960s (Reid and Shyne, 1969). This and later studies suggest that the outcomes of short-term time-limited work are at least as good as those of long term open-ended work. For this reason alone task-centred practice soon became popular within Britain's new social services and social work departments when the model was first promulgated in the early 1970s; for agencies inheriting the traditions of psychosocial casework, an approach with fixed time limits to social work involvement offered obvious cost benefits.

There are other benefits to planned short-term work. Client and social worker alike need to put immediate energy into the work, because time is limited. The dangers of social work effectiveness becoming dependent on the worker/client relationship, which may or not work out, are minimised in the short-term. The research of Reid and Shyne and others indicates that when change does occur in the context of interpersonal work, it tends to happen earlier rather than later in the process.

For all these reasons the proponents of task-centred practice advocate a limit of six to twelve sessions. For situations where further work is indicated, a fresh contract for a further round of work can be made; it is important that the time boundaries are not unthinkingly extended.

General characteristics of task-centred practice

In addition to the key features of a focus on problem solving and the use of time limits, the task-centred model is distinguished by:

- The selection of a target problem from the problems presented.
- The use of tasks to address the selected problem.
- Continued review and negotiation between client and social worker.

The model comprises five sequential phases, and typically will entail perhaps six, and certainly no more than twelve meetings between worker and client. The first three phases, **problem exploration**, **the selection and prioritisation of target problems**, and the **goal-setting, task identification and contract-making phase** usually occupy perhaps two interviews, at the end of which some initial tasks will have been set. Work then moves into the fourth phase, **working to implement the tasks**, which includes a review of the outcomes of the initial tasks and the effect they have had on the identified problems. If the original tasks have been successful in addressing the problems, fresh tasks may be agreed; if they have not, then the reasons for this will be discussed. Some difficulties may be resolved easily, others may require tasks in their own right, and still others may demand a wholly new overall task strategy. During the third and fourth phases, the main focus will be on the planning of tasks that clients will perform themselves. The **ending phase** is represented by a final session which lays emphasis on what the client has learned and achieved; all the work is reviewed. In practice the imminence of the ending will have been mentioned several times already, so that the entire process is experienced as time-limited. This chapter will now set out the five phases in more detail.

Phase one: problem exploration

Getting started: initial explanations

Task-centred practice is characterised by mutual clarity; the client should be as clear as the social worker about the processes that will be followed, in order to participate fully in the work. So explanations are important; but this does not mean that task-centred work begins with a lengthy and detailed introduction to the approach. Explanation can be done incrementally, as the first phase develops. It is important that by the end of this first phase, the client is clear that they are participating voluntarily in a time-limited process, with distinct phases, that will engage them as well as the worker in activities that will aim to resolve some, at least, of the problems presented.

The processes of problem exploration and assessment

The next element of the initial phase of task-centred practice is problem exploration. Reid defined problems as 'unmet or unsatisfied wants as perceived by the client' (1978). The problems to be addressed may be established in various ways, the most obvious being their identification by the client. Alternatively, they may emerge in the course of discussion between social worker and client. Less commonly the worker may take the lead in identifying problems; in this situation the worker must take care not to detract from the client's unique expertise in the understanding of their individual situation. But however problems are identified, it may be the task of the worker to formulate them clearly and in an acceptable form.

The process of problem exploration will entail the answering of a series of questions:

- What happens, typically, when this problem occurs?
- How often does it happen?
- How serious is it for the client?
- How did it begin?
- What has the client done to resolve it?
- How well did these efforts work?

Task-centred practice may not succeed unless there are changes in the contextual factors that influence, and are influenced by the problem. So it is also necessary to establish the context in which problems are occurring:

- What causative factors exist in the surrounding context?
- What are the obstacles to problem solving work?
- What resources can be invoked to help?

The answers to these various questions will provide the data for the cognitive process of assessment. Assessment is no longer, as it once was, an activity in which the expert social worker uses professional knowledge to make judgements about others. In contemporary social work, it is a reciprocal process in which social worker and client exchange information in the course of a dialogue; this 'Exchange Model', set out by Smale, Tuson and their colleagues in 1993, is entirely compatible with the framework of task-centred practice.

As a further check on the suitability of task-centred practice for the problems identified, they should be classified against the list of eight problem types set out in the introduction to this chapter; if they cannot be placed within this framework then it is unlikely that the model will be effective. Finally, three useful tests at this point are:

- Does the client acknowledge the problem and wish to work on it?
- Is the client in a position to work on the problem, with the social worker as his or her agent?

- Is the problem framed in specific, limited and explicit behavioural terms?

Phase two: selecting and prioritising target problems

A 'target problem' is one which both worker and client acknowledge, and which they explicitly agree will become the focus of their work together. It will be based on the client's initial wants, but may have changed and developed in the process of problem identification. Commonly there will be a series of problems presented and discussed, and when this happens they will need to be ranked in the order of their importance to the client. This ranking will facilitate the deciding of which problems need to be addressed first. There are several ways in which this can be done. Priestley and McGuire, for example, have advocated the construction of 'problem checklists' using flip-chart sheets (1978). Milner and O'Byrne suggest a 'problem scale' which facilitates exploration of the interconnectedness of various problems (1998).

Phase three: setting goals, identifying tasks and making contracts

Problem statements and setting goals

Following the identification and ranking of target problems, the first problem to be tackled will need to be framed within a 'problem statement'. The way in which a problem is framed and defined is crucial in motivating both client and social worker. It should be stated in a manner which reflects the concerns of the client but does not at the same time make it seem overwhelming and incapable of solution; instead the statement should foster constructive problem solving work, for example by reflecting how the client might behave differently in order to obtain what they want. Goals may be included within the problem statement, if the parties concerned are ready to engage in the goal-setting process.

Tasks

In task-centred work, a task is defined as a 'planned problem-solving action'. There are three broad classes of task, the most important of which comprises tasks undertaken by a client between sessions. Secondly there are tasks undertaken by the worker between sessions, sometimes in partnership with the client. The third class comprises tasks undertaken within a session.

Task-centred practice is designed to enhance the problem solving skills of participants, so it is important that tasks undertaken by clients involve elements of decision making and self-direction. The model can only empower clients if they understand the purpose of the agreed task and how it is likely to affect the target problem. If the work goes well then they will progressively exercise more control over the implementation of tasks, ultimately enhancing their ability to resolve problems independently.

Tasks may be undertaken individually, on a shared basis among two or more people, or reciprocally; reciprocal tasks involve two people in an exchange of tasks.

Generating and choosing task ideas

The generation of new problem solving ideas is a key feature of the task-centred approach; the creativity of this process can simultaneously break through the depressing failure of previous problem solving efforts and motivate the participants with a sense of optimism. Ideas for possible tasks can be elicited through systematic discussion or through methods like brainstorming. Although the worker will usually start the process, all participants will be invited to join in, for example in family work. Ideas may be based on past problem solving attempts. Questions can be used to clarify what might be done.

The notion that practitioners are the primary and expert source of ideas for tasks is unhelpful, and the potential for clients to generate their own suggestions needs to be given plenty of space. Commonly, accounts of successful task-centred practice feature situations where social worker and client have worked together to identify and develop task ideas. Such examples appear to succeed because both parties are strongly motivated from the inception of the process, and are able to reinforce each other's motivation. The determination to address their problems brought by the client at the beginning is built up and encouraged. For this very reason, it is essential that the initial tasks proposed are feasible and offer a reasonable chance of

success. Although the task-centred approach contains mechanisms for recovering and learning from failed tasks, it is most effective when its problem solving methods succeed from the outset. So it is better to start with modest tasks that are achievable than attempt larger tasks where the risk of failure is greater.

The process of task generation may have produced several ideas and possibilities; when this happens the selection of appropriate initial tasks to address the target problem will need some care. The criteria of likely success, relevance to the target problem and participants' motivation should assist this selection process.

Establishing incentives and motivation for task performance

The task-centred model is founded on the notion that the individual's propensity to engage in tasks is motivated by the unsatisfied wants that constitute the problem. In order to undertake a task, the person must want something that they do not have. The task may not, of itself, satisfy the want, but the person must see it as a step in that direction. Such incentives provide the initial motivation for task performance.

If the initial task has a successful outcome and produces movement towards a desired goal, then motivation is reinforced. This feedback provides incentives for the next stage, which may be a similar task or perhaps a more difficult one. Failures can also be motivating. Analysis of what went wrong can generate ideas for new and different tasks. Throughout the work, mutual clarity is essential. The client needs to understand the process, and the social worker needs to understand the client's priorities, goals and motivation. Their confidence should be ascertained, their strengths and abilities identified, and learning from past successes as well as failures should be discussed. Role-played rehearsals may be useful in approaching daunting tasks. Large goals may be reduced to more attainable sub-goals.

Planning the details of task implementation

Most tasks require a degree of detailed planning. Take a task as seemingly simple as 'Bob will call the dentist to make an appointment'. Bob has not been to the dentist for many years. He fears that his acutely painful toothache may be caused by undiagnosed cancer of the mouth, and his consequent anxiety is so great that he has been unable to pick up the telephone. But while he does nothing, he fears that his condition is worsening. He does not know whether he is still registered with the dental practice, and all who work there are strangers to him. He has very little money and fears that his eligibility for free National Health Service treatment may have lapsed, leaving him with a bill he cannot pay. So the necessary planning involves working out, in detail, when he will make the telephone call, what he will say about his toothache and what enquiries he will make about his registration and the costs of treatment. His motivation to address the task needs to be reinforced so that it is greater than his paralysing anxiety. In discussion with his social worker Bob agrees firstly that they will role-play the telephone call together, and secondly that if he is happy with the role-play he will then make the actual call, a few days later, from the social work office with his social worker alongside him. (This is an anonymised real-life example, and was not a situation involving care management; 'Bob' made the call, it wasn't cancer, he got treatment, and his confidence in his own problem solving abilities was increased in direct proportion to the reduction in his overwhelming anxiety.)

Planning involves not only preparing for the task, but also learning the skills of how to plan. It reinforces the importance of the task, increasing the likelihood that the client will remember it and attempt it. The role of the social worker at the task planning stage is to ask questions:

- How will this task be done?

- Who will do what?

- What is needed for this task to be attempted with good prospects of success?

The degree of detail required in planning is a matter of judgement for the worker. In the example just given, an overtly simple task needed breaking down and planning in considerable detail; in other situations this will not be necessary. In all cases the worker should aim to stimulate the client's thinking about the task to be done. At the same time, there should be allowance for the possibility that the client may appropriately modify the task or even substitute a better one; the task-centred model, despite its order and clarity, can be adapted in many ways, and one of the present authors recalls William Reid himself advocating flexibility in its application, at a seminar in the early years of the model's development.

Simulating and rehearsing tasks

Plans of any kind are more likely to succeed if they can be tried out first. Many task plans can be rehearsed beforehand using role-play or other kinds of simulation exercise. The role-play of a simple telephone call was an important element in the case example given above, in which the social worker played the role of dentist's receptionist and the client played himself. This could have been preceded by, for example, the two roles being reversed, enabling the worker to model the task behaviour desired. Different approaches and scenarios can be tried out in this way. The model is explicitly educational, enabling the client to rehearse and learn new problem solving skills.

Anticipating potential obstacles to task performance

In the task-centred approach, obstacles are defined as impediments preventing clients from solving their problems. Obstacles may obstruct specific task plans, or more generally they may impede all kinds of problem solutions. In our example, the obstacle was chronic, intense and growing anxiety, and this was hindering both the specific task plan and more general attempts to improve the situation. An obstacle may itself be a target problem: in which case the chosen strategies would not necessarily differ from those adopted if it were no more than an impedance. In our case, anxiety was not the target problem; nevertheless, the simple task strategy of making a call was designed to reduce some of the anxiety, and achieved this modest aim.

It is good practice to try and anticipate how potential obstacles will be tackled. A useful technique in this regard is to ask 'What if...?' questions. 'What if Bob finds out that he no longer qualifies for free dental treatment?' or even 'What if Bob discovers that he does have a malignant condition?'

The answers to 'What if…?' questions can promote discussion of how to resolve obstacles. An even simpler question is for the social worker to ask the client 'What might go wrong with the tasks?' This 'anti-sabotage' procedure can sometimes uncover potential obstacles that no one had thought of. Or the discussion can invoke the history of previous problem solving efforts, which may be associated with failure and need to be reframed as learning opportunities.

Summarising, task agreement and contracts

Before the planning session ends, the social worker and client together will need to review and summarise the task plan. This is especially important when the plan is complex, when there are several tasks, when several people are involved, or when the task performers are children. Useful techniques at this point include the production of written task plans for all parties, perhaps as part of a written contract, or the worker simply asking the client to present their version of what the plan is; this can, of course, be reciprocal, and the client may ask the worker what he or she will be doing to contribute to the plan.

The end of this phase of task-centred work is often marked by the making of a contract between worker and client. A contract is essentially an agreement to work together in order to resolve the stated problem or problems, and to achieve any specified goals. At this point it is essential that the client agrees explicitly to undertake the task. This should not be omitted amidst all the other matters being discussed, and nor should silence be assumed to imply consent. The actual contract may be verbal or written, and it may include a detailed task plan. Written contracts may be perceived as formal, but have the merit of being easy to review later on.

Phase four: working to implement the tasks

Implementation of tasks between sessions

There is not a great deal to say about this self-evident phase, but that is not to deny its importance. Its success will depend on all the groundwork undertaken in the previous phases of the process. Clients may go away and work on their agreed tasks on their own, or with others. Social workers similarly may work on their agreed tasks; for example, the worker's tasks may include advocacy on behalf of the client. Or both may work together on the tasks. Some of the North American literature on task-centred practice uses the sporting metaphor of 'coaching' to describe the role of the practitioner at this stage, attributing significant expertise to the worker. Whilst this idea may not accord fully with the notion of the client as expert, the image of the 'coach' does embody ideas of encouragement and support which are entirely consistent with good practice. This does not necessarily imply practitioner and client spending considerable time working together; telephone calls can provide useful contacts during this period.

Intermediate review of tasks and problems

The central period of working on planned tasks will be punctuated by regular, planned review meetings. The first purpose of these sessions is to assess progress in the implementation of agreed tasks. This progress will be a measure of any changes achieved, in relation both to the target problems and to the problem solving abilities of the client. Successful task accomplishment, or progress in that direction, will be praised. Failed tasks may be met with an empathic response from the worker. If the agreed tasks were not attempted, then a discussion of the reasons for this will be necessary. Obstacles to task performance may need further consideration. This review of tasks often leads on to the generation of ideas for the next task.

The second function of review sessions is to review changes in target problems. This is likely to involve continuing exploration of the problem, including its frequency and severity, and the client's impression of any changes that are happening as a result of the work, or other factors. Discussion of this area can be assisted by using questions, such as:

- How much change has occurred?
- Is it sufficient—for the client? For the social worker?
- How durable is the change likely to be?
- What factors have caused the change?
- What has the task work contributed to the change?

- Does analysis of the change suggest a shift in the focus of the work?

The analysis of change resulting from task-centred work can assist the empirically-oriented practitioner in evaluating the effectiveness of their practice. Exploration of the changing dynamics of the target problem is a process that began in the first phase of the model, continues through this intermediate stage and will be concluded in the final review.

Following the review of tasks undertaken and changes in target problems, a number of possibilities appear. If it is agreed that enough has been achieved and there are no other problems pressing, then the work may be concluded by moving directly into the final phase. Alternatively, if there has been sufficient change in the prioritised target problem, the work may move on to the next problem, revisiting phase three above. A third possibility is to continue working on the first target problem through new or revised tasks.

Phase five: bringing the work to an end

Concluding session

The ending of the process of task-centred work will have been anticipated in the first sessions, when social worker and client together agreed on time limits for the work. In the intermediate sessions the worker will have reminded the client of the time remaining. The agreed time limits are not absolutely rigid. If the successful completion of a task has led to the successful resolution of a problem, then the work may be concluded early. Alternatively, the participants may agree on an extension of the agreed time limits where further work looks likely to improve the outcome. In such cases they should contract to meet for a small number of additional sessions, usually no more than four.

Final task and problem review

As with the intermediate sessions, the final session begins with a review of task accomplishments, which leads into a review of progress made in addressing the target problems. This final problem review should be made with as much attention to detail as the original problem exploration in phase one; in addition, any progress made will be evaluated. Useful questions at this point may be:

- What was the problem like at the outset?
- What changes have since occurred?

Such questions facilitate an evaluation that is realistic, rather than unduly positive or negative. Written material may also be helpful at this point, for example the records of the social worker or any written contracts made earlier.

Review of accomplishments and problem solving skills

In the final session it is important to acknowledge what clients have accomplished, in order to reflect back and reinforce what they have achieved. In Bob's case, he commented that it had been important that he, rather than his social worker, had called the dentist. Although he had been afraid to make the call, the fact that he had done it increased his confidence in attending the ensuing dental appointment, an event which he had also feared. In this way the review of accomplishments can lead directly into the identification of improved problem solving skills. The worker should help the client to generalise these skills, so that they may be applied to future problems, including problems not addressed in the work just undertaken.

Future plans

As a general rule, the conclusion of social work intervention should be prospective as well as retrospective. Problems may continue to exist, or they may recur. So, finally, worker and client together will consider how the former will address problems in the future, on the basis of positive accomplishment and the learning of improved problem solving skills. If the task-centred model has been employed effectively, both the client and the social worker will emerge from the process with enhanced abilities in their respective situations.

Obstacles to implementing task-centred practice

Care management is by no means the only field of practice in which UK social workers currently operate; but it is one of central importance. This part of the chapter examines some of the obstacles in current care management practice which militate against the use of task-centred practice. It considers: the core nature of the client/worker relationship; the focus on risk; dependence upon individual packages of care as solutions to problems; and the time-limited nature of care management. Finally, the chapter argues the need to deconstruct and reconstruct social work/care management because, in adopting this process, the value of approaches such as task-centred work can be recognised and incorporated into care management practice. Although these arguments could be applied to a wide range of social work practice methods, some of which are explored elsewhere in this book, we suggest that they are particularly pertinent to task-centred practice because its time-limited, planned and contract-based approach appears superficially to fit well with care management; this semblance of 'fit' needs careful examination.

The core nature of the client/worker relationship

Task-centred practice, like any other social work method, cannot be applied on its own and is dependent upon the worker's use of self in the development of a relationship with the person with whom they are working. The use of self, however described, is widely recognised as important and integral to social work (England, 1998; Howe, 1996; Payne, 1996; Sheppard, 1995).

Recent research undertaken with care managers working with older people showed that, although care managers were continuing to use themselves skilfully in their work, they frequently commented on their loss of opportunity for this, feeling that such work was being squeezed out by the increase in bureaucratic tasks which they had to undertake (Postle, 1999). One care manager expressed this change in his work thus, summing up what many of his colleagues expressed:

> The social work bit wants to go out and do what you might perceive as social work, and the care manager's bit is the management of the budget, which is management of care. That sort of thing is one step removed from the clients. You could be a very efficient care manager and not have to see the client at all.

This approach was consistent with many managers' expectations of the care management task, as indicated by the following comments from a team manager:

> There just isn't the time for them to be giving of themselves in the way that they were...I'm not putting down the counselling, but it's got to be seen as something apart from what we do...we should actually be purchasing counselling skills, buying them in from a secondary provider.

In interviews with care managers, they variously referred to 'client-centred stuff', 'counselling', 'listening', 'spending time', 'using yourself', 'therapy', 'support', and work 'beyond the package'. This element of their work, the emotional labour, can be seen as core to the social work task (Camilleri, 1996) and essential to the successful application of any social work method. Yet it was such work which care managers felt under pressure to reduce and which became regarded, as one care manager described it, as 'undercover' work.

Care managers felt forced to adopt a much more cursory approach. For example, a trainer running an in-house course asked whether staff found that people always told them something really important right at the end of a visit or several visits. The students agreed that this was often the case and the trainer's advice, clearly given with the intention of helping the students to reduce their time pressures, was to tell the client to 'Tell me the problem sooner' instead of leaving it until the last five minutes. This comment relies on a bureaucratic, linear and procedural approach to the work, in which the worker can fit the client to her/his schedule rather than working at the client's pace and thus enabling and empowering them to participate on a more equal basis in the work. It contrasts with the use of tacit knowledge and reflection (Eraut, 1994; Schön, 1991). An alternative approach to that suggested by the trainer can be found in the work of Biestek and appears closer to the nature of the practice which the care managers were saying that they now found difficult because of the increasingly bureaucratic nature of their work:

> The function of the caseworker is principally to create an environment in which the client will be comfortable in giving expression to his feelings. The skill to create this environment is much more important

than the skill of asking stimulating questions. In fact, the latter skill will be ineffective without the permissive atmosphere.

(Biestek, 1961: p40)

The function which Biestek describes, while clearly never universally present in social work, is nonetheless a crucial starting point for working with someone to determine the problem issues which could be resolved by use of task-centred practice. However, if this element of developing a relationship is subsumed by market-led process-driven approaches, the resultant tendency will be to look for short-termist quick-fix forms of working, as indicated by the trainer's comment above. Hence there is a risk that, in applying task-centred practice, care managers would not take time to work alongside the client to determine the problem to be addressed or that they may, indeed, see the care management procedure as the sole or predominant task.

The focus on risk

Care managers operate in a prevailing climate of risk, reflecting the heightened sense of risk in the contemporary society in which they work (Beck, 1992; Giddens, 1991). This is a society concerned with the actuarial calculation of risk and its reduction or elimination, and yet one in which the new risks become increasingly difficult to manage (Giddens, 1991; Ginsburg, 1998; Parton, 1996). Much care management work, particularly assessment, focuses on the extent to which someone is at risk and, indeed, this governs the 'eligibility criteria' for a service (Harding, 1997). At the same time, many staff perceived a considerable risk of, at least, complaints and, at worst, litigation against themselves or their local authorities, and their work was increasingly circumscribed by concerns about risks related to health and safety. Concurrently, however, the speed of work throughput did not give care managers time properly to evaluate and monitor risk, or spend time with people or their carers working on ways to reduce it. Such approaches could well include using task-centred practice to enable people to find and use strategies for risk reduction. This was how one team manager summarised her dislike of the current approach:

I don't like the 'quick in and out, do the assessment, do the review, close it' type of approach where you focus on delivery of care…I feel quite strongly that, if someone goes out and does an assessment and identifies a number of risk factors and the person is neutral, or even a bit resistant, about having help, I don't feel we should say, 'There's nothing we can do.' I feel that we plug away.

Hence the focus on risk militates against seeing or hearing and then working with anything which is not an issue of serious risk. In our example given above, were Bob in receipt of community care, his need to visit his dentist might well not have been identified as a problem or, if it was, it may have been seen as something which there was little or no time for his care manager to work with him to resolve. Coupled with the process-driven nature of the work, this emphasis on risk makes it very hard for care managers to work beyond immediate presenting problems.

Dependence upon individual packages of care as solutions to problems

Care managers work within a contemporary society in which universalising notions of consensus have largely collapsed (Harvey, 1989). This contrasts with the collectivism more easily identifiable with the modernist origins of the UK welfare state and with the social democracy of the 'old left' (Giddens, 1998). Although care managers' work reflected both individualism and collectivity, the care management approach described by the SSI Guidance locates the care manager as an expert in a procedural model of assessment which does *not* afford expertise in their situation to the person being assessed (SSI and SWSG, 1991 (a), (b) and (c); Smale et al., 1993; 2000).

Care managers tended to work in individualised ways with people, looking at individual solutions to individual needs, rather than considering the broader picture of what could benefit a community and, in turn, the individual. This individualised approach was exemplified in the observation of a care manager's visit to an elderly woman where the care manager discussed whether the woman's shopping could be done for her by a volunteer. This would be cheaper than the current arrangement where the woman went shopping with a paid carer, which she preferred, because it enabled her to choose goods herself. This was constructed as this woman's problem, rather than one which many elderly people experience and which, with a less individualistic approach, time to think creatively and a less market-driven environment, could be resolved differently.

The flexibility to work in different ways was constrained by the procedural and individual nature of the work, causing care managers to reflect, as this one did:

> *Have I done that contract? Did I send that arrange-ment? Oh! I've got to get this signed, got to do that, have they had a care plan…There's sometimes time for this type (creative/developmental) of work. You can think about other things…there's a bit of time for it.*

Where there is a concentration on the bureaucratic aspects of the job and anxiety about completing these tasks, care managers will have difficulty concentrating on wider aspects of work, encompassing preventative or community-based work or, indeed, on working in any way other than by the provision of individual packages of care. This individualism is compounded by the degree and form of specialisation and fragmentation in care management which presents a response to people's situations and problems which segments and compartmentalises them, militating against opportunities for collective work. The emphasis on assessments of individuals, rather than of individuals in their situations, means that a holistic picture of their environment is not obtained (Smale *et al.*, 1993). The lack of this broader picture curtails enhancement of the client's or their wider network's problem solving capacities, thus making it difficult to use an approach such as task-centred practice which relies on the widest possible exploration of problems, a field from which to generate and choose task ideas and, above all, the person's expertise in their situation in order to correctly identify how their problem solving capacity can be enhanced (Smale *et al.*, 2000).

The time-limited nature of care management

When discussing the focus on risk, it was noted that there was a tendency for the nature of the work to be, as the team manager quoted above

described it, 'quick in and out, do the assessment, do the review, close it'. Her comments fit with notions of dealing with 'core business' only, an approach which had come to dominate the way care managers were working. As the same team manager said:

> *I'm increasingly hearing managers say, 'That's not our job' and, 'We're not going to get involved with **that** because we do **this** and it's sort of setting boundaries around a very small area of work.' The lines of demarcation are being put in quite wrongly, I think.*

Although, of course, social work intervention should always be focused, concentration on core business, together with other public sector management orthodoxies such as decentralisation and devolution, can be very effective in helping organisations to be strategic and to meet goals. The goals may, however, become short-term because these are the easiest ones against which outputs and performance can be measured. Such orthodoxies do not have the capacity to enable organisations or managers to deal with complexity and uncertainty (Clarke and Newman, 1997). Considering that the core business of social work/care management could be defined as dealing with social problems characterised by their complexity and uncertainty, it becomes apparent that the adoption of such orthodoxies might prove problematic. In discussing how care managers might get job satisfaction, another team manager's comments epitomise this change of emphasis from quality to output:

> *Perhaps people need to get their job satisfaction from quantity rather than quality and perhaps you need to think, 'Wow! I helped x number of people' rather than, 'I have helped Mrs. So and so over the last six months' which I think, really, is where we're at.*

The operation of care management meant that the initial worker was unlikely to remain involved and there was little opportunity to develop a relationship, however brief, with the person. One of the care managers described it like this:

> *The ethos is you do the care package for the clients, you do a review and you close. That's the idea anyway, which means that, at that time, you choose the best care agency that you can get and you're happy with the initial thing and you're happy at the review stage, and then it tends to be somebody else's problem when it breaks down more often as not.*

However, because workloads were very high, once cases were closed, reviews of care packages were either very delayed or not done. As one of the team managers described:

> My view would be that you're much safer to say, 'I set up the services. The care management process is that that's what happens and then we review it in six months time.' And that, to some extent, provided those reviews are carried out, unfortunately they're not, but I mean if those reviews were carried out, then to all extents and purposes, we've done the job that we're paid to do.

Although the process was intended to encompass reviews, the volume of work prevented these from being done. Hence the time-limited nature of care management precludes the possibility of the checks on implementation needed for task-centred practice to be effective. The person's case would be likely to have been closed to monitoring/review long before the care manager could ascertain and review their progress with the task.

Deconstructing and reconstructing social work: care management: the opportunity for incorporating task-centred practice

There is a continuum of views on the question of whether care management and social work are dichotomously opposed (Simiç, 1995), or merge and contain degrees of overlap (Sheppard, 1995). Care managers used understandings of social work to frame and describe their views of care management at differing points on this continuum. For example, changes resulting from working within a quasi-market were described as characteristic of care management, not social work. Often care managers' comparisons dichotomously polarised and contrasted social work and care management. For example:

> I suppose that's [contact with people] why you go into social work and that's where the satisfaction comes from…that's diminished, for me, there's very little satisfaction. There are bits, but it comes from when I'm doing social work. This other stuff isn't social work, is it? It's care management, which I think is just a different job.

Care managers' descriptions of 'social work' implied a discrete entity, lost in the transition to care management. They did not mention social work's diverse and contested nature or, for example, allude to debates concerning radical social work (Langan, 1998), patronising and paternalistic aspects of social work exposed by feminist critiques (Orme, 1998), the maintenance/change debate (Davies, 1981), or the contested nature of professionalism (Payne, 1996). In contrasting social work and care management, staff understandably talked about elements of social work which they found rewarding and satisfying but thought had lessened. Such elements as counselling, listening, and support became collapsed into 'social work' as if constituting it unproblematically. However, even brief references to debates and critiques imply that social work has never been a discrete and uncontested entity. Viewing it as such fails to problematise and deconstruct its nature, so that it is not subject to critical examination or scrutiny in a societal context. Social work, in transition to care management, has taken on attributes of contemporary society apparently uncritically. Hence care management evolved as a highly individualistic response to problem solving within a managerialist and market-driven ethos. The possibility of working differently necessitates operating in a manner which challenges this prevailing ethos.

However, the seeds of opportunity for further challenge and change exist in the possibility of a reinvention/reconceptualisation/reconstruction of social work/care management. This begins with deconstructing social work, examining how the meaning behind its diverse elements can be positively used in addressing people's social problems (Camilleri, 1999; Leonard, 1997; Pease and Fook, 1999; Smale *et al.*, 2000). Such deconstruction includes examining the flaws in social work practice, for instance its failure to make alliances with the users of its services and other bodies who work with them, as well as its strengths.

The diverse and eclectic elements of social work practice (Payne, 1996), encompassing the therapeutic and emotional as well as the radical and political, the ability to work with the individual and with wider networks and communities, and a broad and diverse knowledge base, all need to be valued equally, rather than vying for position as the best or only form of practice. Acknowledging the core and unique (albeit contested) nature of the social work relationship, which is in danger of being eroded as the foundation for the work by the bureaucratic and procedural aspects of care management, offers some optimism and could result in the recognition of the value of approaches such as task-centred practice, and their incorporation into care management practice to the benefit of the people it serves. As an example of this and to end our chapter on an optimistic note, the Community Care (Direct Payments) Act 1996 is due to be extended to apply to people over 65 (Department of Health, 1998: para 2.15). Once people have cash in their hands, care managers, rather than designing prescriptive care packages for their clients, could fittingly use task-centred approaches to help them to devise appropriate solutions to their problems.

Postscript

Whilst we were writing this chapter, in July 2000, we were saddened to learn of the death of Professor Gerry Smale, of the National Institute for Social Work. It will be apparent to readers of the chapter that we have a high regard for his work, which continues to influence many people who are committed to the development of a social work that is simultaneously skilled, empowering and refreshing in its approach.

References

Beck, U. (1992). *Risk Society. Towards a New Modernity*. London: Sage.

Biestek, F. (1961). *The Casework Relationship*. London: George Allen and Unwin.

Camilleri, P. (1996). *(Re)Constructing Social Work*. Aldershot: Avebury.

Camilleri, P. (1999). Social Work and its Search for Meaning: Theories, Narratives and Practices. In Pease, B., and Fook, J. (Eds.). *Transforming Social Work Practice: Postmodern Critical Perspectives*. London: Routledge.

Clarke, J., and Newman, J. (1997). *The Managerial State*. London: Sage.

Coulshed, V., and Orme, J. (1998). *Social Work Practice: An Introduction*. Basingstoke: Macmillan.

Davies, M. (1981). *The Essential Social Worker*. London: Heinemann.

Department of Health (1998). *Modernising Social Services: Promoting Independence, Improving Protection, Raising Standards*. London: Department of Health.

Doel, M., and Marsh, P. (1992). *Task Centred Social Work*. London: Ashgate.

England, H. (1998). *Social Work as a Profession: The Naïve Aspiration*. Southampton: CEDR, Department of Social Work Studies, University of Southampton.

Eraut, M. (1994). *Developing Professional Knowledge and Competence*. London: The Falmer Press.

Giddens, A. (1991). *Modernity and Self-identity. Self and Society in the Late Modern Age*. Cambridge: Polity Press.

Giddens, A. (1998). *The Third Way: The Renewal of Social Democracy*. Cambridge: Polity Press.

Ginsburg, N. (1998). Postmodernity and Social Europe. In Carter, J. (Ed.). *Postmodernity and the Fragmentation of Welfare*. London: Routledge.

Harding, T. (1997). *A Life Worth Living: The Independence and Inclusion of Older People*. London: Help the Aged.

Harvey, D. (1989). *The Condition of Postmodernity: An Enquiry into the Origins of Social Change*. Oxford: Blackwell.

Howe, D. (1996). Surface and Depth in Social Work Practice. In Parton, N. (Ed.). *Social Theory, Social Change and Social Work*. London: Routledge.

Langan, M. (1998). Radical Social Work. In Adams, R., Dominelli, L., and Payne, M. (Eds.). *Social Work: Themes, Issues and Critical Debates*. Basingstoke: Macmillan.

Leonard, P. (1997). *Postmodern Welfare: Reconstructing an Emancipatory Project*. London: Sage.

Milner, J., and O'Byrne, P. (1998). *Assessment in Social Work*. Basingstoke: Macmillan.

Orme, J. (1998). Feminist Social Work. In Adams, R., Dominelli, L., and Payne, M. (Eds.). *Social Work: Themes, Issues and Critical Debates*. Basingstoke: Macmillan.

Parton, N. (1996). Social Work, Risk and the Blaming System. In Parton, N. (Ed.). *Social Theory, Social Change and Social Work*. London: Routledge.

Payne, M. (1996). *What is Professional Social Work?* Birmingham: Venture Press.

Pease, B., and Fook, J. (1999). Postmodern Critical Theory and Emancipatory Social Work Practice. In Pease, B., and Fook, J. (Eds.). *Transforming Social Work Practice: Postmodern Critical Perspectives*. London: Routledge.

Postle, K. (1999). Care Managers' Responses to Working Under Conditions of Postmodernity, PhD thesis, University of Southampton.

Priestley, J., and McGuire, P. (1978). *Social Skills and Personal Problem-solving*. London: Tavistock.

Reid, W.J. (1978). *The Task-centred System*. New York: Columbia University Press.

Reid, W.J. (1992). *Task Strategies*. New York: Columbia University Press.

Reid, W.J., and Shyne, A.W., (1969). *Brief and Extended Casework*. New York: Columbia University Press.

Schön, D. (1991). *The Reflective Practitioner. How Professionals Think in Action*. New York: Basic Books.

Sheppard, M. (1995). *Care Management and the New Social Work: A Critical Analysis.* London: Whiting and Birch Ltd.

Simiç, P. (1995). What's in a Word? From Social 'Worker' to Care 'Manager'. *Practice*, 7: pp5–18.

Smale, G., Tuson, G., and Statham, D. (2000). *Social Work and Social Problems: Working Towards Social Inclusion and Social Change.* Basingstoke: Macmillan.

Smale, G., Tuson, G., with Biehal, N., and Marsh, P. (1993). *Empowerment, Assessment, Care Management and the Skilled Worker.* London: HMSO.

SSI and SWSG (1991a). *Care Management and Assessment—Practitioners' Guide.* London: HMSO.

SSI and SWSG (1991b). *Care Management and Assessment—Summary of Practice Guidance.* London: HMSO.

SSI and SWSG (1991c). *Care Management and Assessment. Managers' Guide.* London: HMSO.

Chapter Eight

Cognitive Behavioural Methods in Social Care: A Look at the Evidence
Brian Sheldon

Choosing an approach

This is a book providing different perspectives on the tasks of staff working in the personal social services, within which committed advocates are invited to make a case that a given model or approach has much to offer. I cannot escape the charge of commitment myself, and in any case this is usually seen as a 'good thing' in our discipline. However, I have long been suspicious of method, approach, or theory-led explanations as to how troublesome social circumstances or behaviour arise in the first place, and what should be done about them (see Sheldon, 1978). My misgivings are as follows:

1. Epistemology (the study of knowledge and its development) is replete with examples of large-scale theorising (Marxism, psychoanalysis, feminism: I have nothing against the latter stance, but something against the research methods typically employed). These products purport to be able to explain virtually *everything*, but tend also to require that our critical faculties be disengaged, the better to tune into broader waveband insights derivable from emotion and values. Living in anxious circumstances as we do, we have tended in the past to prefer these, but at a price I would say.

2. Developing 'crushes' on favoured theories or approaches sometimes induces us to dis-attend to both inconsistencies *within* them (why should only some kinds of trauma be hard to recover from memory, when most people who have suffered bad experiences have great trouble forgetting the fact? see Webster, 1996), or to logical inconsistencies *between* them and other theories. The inescapable problem is, however, that if Bowlby and Erikson are right about major influences on child development (I don't think they are) then Klein, Freud and Piaget must be wrong; if

Skinner is right (he is only somewhat right) then Piaget, and Vygotsky are wrong: the significant events, the discernible stages and the timescales proposed are all different. Thus, ideas which contradict each other should not be (but often are) plonked down next to each other on 'salad bar' training courses. This is usually referred to as 'eclecticism': another allegedly 'good thing'.

3. The standard approach to such problems within social work has been to adopt a relativist position; ensuring that words like right, wrong, or science are accompanied by 'don't really mean this literally but can't think of another word to reveal the complexity behind what I'm trying to argue' inverted commas. Post-modernism (I think the term post-rationalism more accurate) has given a further boost to this idea of no fixed position from which to evaluate either theories, or results derived from empirical research. To challenge this idea Sokal and Brincmont (1998) published a spoof post-modernist view of relativity theory which was full of accurate physics but philosophical nonsense. It was taken very seriously and much debated in top French philosophical journals. The attempts at cognitive-dissonance reduction and face-saving which followed disclosure provide us with a wonderful, negative image template of the skills necessary for critical thinking when evaluating evidence (see Gambrill, 1997; Macdonald and Sheldon, 1998). Nor is this only a game for physical scientists and philosophers. Some time ago, a colleague and I published an April Fools day spoof in *Community Care*. It advertised a course based on a new American theory directly relevant to social work. The course details were full of quasi-biological references about 'semi-permeable membranes surrounding the client's motivational system' etc. Interest

was considerable; requests for block-booking reductions were received, and we were forced to leg it with quiet dignity. Couldn't happen today of course. Last April's proposals for a National Flipchart Archive received a stern rebuff.

These are not remarks about gullibility, but do point to a rather naïve appetite for the novel and for the all explanatory synthesis. But human beings are very complicated, we have been studying each other for a long time, and so such things are (necessarily) hard to come by.

Well no, there isn't any fixed or privileged position from which to observe, and we do indeed always influence what we are trying to measure. People react to knowledge of observation, and we have a strong tendency to find what we expect or have been told to find; as the following chastening example from another field shows. There was once much controversy about the precise number of human chromosome pairs per cell in the human body. Most 11-year-olds can now tell you that it is 23, but in the 1920s staining and microscope slide preparation techniques left the matter in some doubt. In 1923, the eminent American zoologist, Theophilus Painter, pronounced that there were 24 pairs. This authoritative conclusion was repeated in textbooks over the next thirty years alongside photographs clearly showing (had anyone bothered to count) only 23 pairs. The power of argument from authority; the power of routine 'givens', and the power of peer-group pressure are all revealed in this case and we have many equivalent examples in our own field (see Sheldon, 1987; Sheldon and Macdonald, 1999).

I do not think I am contradicting myself in the paragraphs above, because it is scientific method that has induced us to become constructively paranoid about trusting unaided judgement, and because science (without the little inverted commas) is our best hope if we are to allow for, compensate for, and control out as far as possible, this set of well-understood human tendencies to jump to conclusions and stick to them; readily to countenance what accords with our existing views, and not what does not.

Therefore, the logical starting point for any consideration of how best to select a remedial approach to any given set of problems is to consider (a) what it presumes about the aetiology (the growth and development pattern) of the problem and whether there is robust research to support this view; and (b) to consider what is known, at what level of methodological rigour, about previous attempts to help *via* the application of given methods. In other words, we must learn to review the evidence for what we do before we do it, and not just to respond routinely or reflexively and justify it later. Therefore, I make use of and teach cognitive behavioural approaches to personal and social problems because of the extent and the quality of the evidence, including evidence of limited effect in some areas, and not just because I am used to it. Because I used to be used to some very different methods, implanted by a training course which seemed positively to favour the unlikely and the bizarre—the experience is still to be had, I think.

The above prescription takes us on to the idea of evidence-based practice as a unifying concept for all the foregoing. Evidence-based approaches have the following aims:

- Optimal bias reduction regarding our preferential use of research in practice, on the '*what* is known depends on *how* it is known' principle formulated by Bacon in 1604. 'Studies and theories are not created equal' about sums up this point (see Sackett *et al.*, 1996; Sheldon, 1978).

- The explicit selection of methods based upon 'current best evidence'.

- A responsibility requiring practitioners to debate with clients why a particular approach looks like a good bet, and then to monitor progress and evaluate results as rigorously as possible. Not a new idea, but one which is gathering force within our discipline and more importantly, is taking root within social service organisations (see CEBSS, 1999).

The proposition before us, then, is that would-be helpers should be more discerning in their selection of research and theory for use in practice, and learn to prefer findings from 'studies of good quality' (DoH, 1994). What exactly does this mean? Before trying to answer this question let me enter the proviso that there is no single methodological approach that is always better than others, it all depends on what we are trying to find out. In short, some methodological approaches give us more secure results in some fields. All empirical investigations can make a contribution providing what is being claimed in the way of results and practical implications is plausibly attributable to what was done to produce a hoped-for change, and could not equally, be due to collateral influences. Thus, one does not need, (nor could one ethically set up) a randomised controlled trial (RCT) to find out what it is like to be a child within the public care system. In-depth, largely qualitative interviews with children and carers is the most revealing approach. Such methodologies are all the more suitable if based on a random, stratified sample of respondents (because children come into care for different reasons, have different problems, and are placed in different circumstances). However, if on the basis of signposts from qualitative research we decide to take a particular course of action to try to find our way towards better outcomes, we probably do need an RCT or two if we can get them. Despite much debate in academic circles about whether experiments are the only fruit or not, they are, in the British social care field, as rare as blue oranges.

Thus, regarding *intervention* research, there is a very definite hierarchy (not just a continuum) of methods which produce higher or lower levels of *attributive confidence* (i.e., address through their procedures the question: are these differences due to that programme within the boundaries of a five in a hundred or a one in a hundred statistical chance($p<0.05$; $p>0.01$) that they are not?). Here is what this methodological hierarchy looks like:

Figure 1: Attributive confidence in intervention research studies

Methodology	Procedure	Attributive Confidence
Systematic review of randomised controlled trials or meta-analysis of controlled trials: These look at effect sizes from comparisons of one approach with another standard or routine intervention, or with nothing, across many studies of the same type.	The pre-publication of a search strategy (usually involving both electronic databases and the hand-searching of journals) against specific inclusion and exclusion criteria. These cover issues regarding relevance and methodological sufficiency. Exhaustive search of data-sources; an unvarnished presentation of results and implications, and regular up-dating are other hallmarks.	These studies maximise bias reduction, so much so that almost always the effect size (degree of comparative benefit) against hard outcome indicators is reduced in comparison with other methodologies. If well conducted they provide our most secure results. If producing negative outcomes, then they are still very valuable in advising what *not* to do.
Single experiments: Comparing the effects of an intervention with an attention, placebo control, or other-treated group, since attention and belief in the expertise of helpers also have strong, effects. Best of all, (but rare) are studies	Random allocation to two groups (within which good-sized samples iron out differences between recipients). One group then receives an as consistent as possible exposure to the intervention under test. The other receives non-specific	Maximal bias reduction, but single studies can sometimes be errant (either positively or negatively). Standardising (that is making as uniform as possible) the intervention 'ingredients' poses problems, but large

Figure 1: cont.

Methodology	Procedure	Attributive Confidence
with three conditions compared: no intervention, standard intervention and test intervention.	attention or another service. Outcomes are assessed against specific quantitative outcome indicators (e.g. re-admission to hospital, recidivism). Such findings can be backed up by standardised qualitative tests.	samples help to average out intervention differences. Sub-analysis of service-provider variations can also help to reduce this problem. Differential drop-out rates require particular attention.
Single experiments with a non-intervention control group:	Random allocation of subjects; some get an as consistent as possible exposure to a given approach and others are left to their own devices.	Very substantial bias reduction properties, but does not tell us how far any differences between groups are due to specific approaches under test or non-specific attention factors. Replications or even concordant findings from quasi-experimental or pre-post studies (see below) increase plausibility.
Narrative reviews: These are not usually as exhaustive as systematic reviews and tend to have lower inclusion and exclusion criteria. Can also contain research using different methodologies. In such cases findings should be 'layered' i.e., it should be possible to see what results come in what proportion from which methodologies.	Authors draw up a list of topics which they wish to search e.g., 'social work in general hospitals'; 'supported housing for learning disabled people' and then track down likely sources and look for emergent trends and implications.	Suffers from the problem of 'convenience samples' i.e., sources readily available to the authors, and from a higher possibility of selective perception than where a very tight, pre-published protocol is in place. Nevertheless, very worthwhile and convenient summaries, sometimes coming close to later, more systematic reviews in their conclusions for less cost and labour. A good starting point for something more rigorous.
Quasi-experimental studies:	These are comparison studies but without random allocation, therefore we can never be sure that we are	An underused investigative method since it compares the results (usually pre and post) between areas where

Figure 1: cont.

Methodology	Procedure	Attributive Confidence
Quasi-experimental studies (cont.)	comparing like with like, though case-matching helps moderately to increase confidence.	an approach is in use with a comparable area where it is not. Very useful for use in social services where different services are routinely introduced in one area and not in another.
Pre-post tests: Sometimes known as time-series designs, these procedures compare problems and gains on a before and after basis in a single sample.	Baseline, i.e. pre-intervention (preferably standardised) measures are taken in key problem areas prior to service (see Fischer and Corcoran, 1994 for an accessible manual). They are then repeated at the end of the programme for comparison purposes.	Most evaluations in social services are post-only (see below) and so it is difficult to calculate the value-added. This approach takes 'snapshots' of functioning on a before and after basis. Nevertheless it cannot determine the extent to which any improvements which occur are due to the mere passage of time (maturational factors) or to other collateral factors unconnected with the intervention.
Post test-only: measures: This approach reviews outcomes only, without benefit of specific pre-intervention (baseline) measures.	A sample is chosen against criteria of need, type and extent of problem(s). The intervention is made, and then measures of outcomes are made.	Since most social services approaches and projects are still not evaluated at all, this is better than nothing. It can be improved by standardised referral criteria being in place at the outset.
Client-opinion studies: Largely qualitative studies (occasionally with quantitative elements such as scales). Usually post-only, but there is no reason why pre-post qualitative measures should not be taken (there are, however, few examples of this happening).	A sample of clients receiving a particular service, or those with a particular set of problems receiving a range of interventions from social services are interviewed for their opinions on the effects of services and, usually, on the *way* in which they were provided.	These studies are rich in qualitative detail about what it is like to be on the receiving end of services. However, a common problem is representativeness. Do the respondents in the sample reflect the range of service-user and problem character-istics? Random sampling of populations, helps here. Should be routine in social services as part of the service-planning process.

Figure 1: cont.

Methodology	Procedure	Attributive Confidence
Single case designs: Largely quantitative measures (though there is no reason why standardised qualitative measures should not be included) applied to single cases.	Measures are taken on a before and after (a.b. design) or before/after/follow-up basis (ABA designs) or even in experimental form (ABAB designs) where interventions are baselined, the intervention made, then withdrawn, then reinstated and differences noted. Mainly used in behaviour therapy, though there is no reason why this should be so, providing that case-specific behavioural change in line with the aims of a given approach are pre-specified.	Should be more widely used by practitioners whatever the intervention method in use. Enables staff and clients to assess progress and adjust accordingly.

How well therefore does the range of techniques known collectively as cognitive behavioural therapy (CBT) match up to these standards? Well, a very curious thing happened recently in this field. The editor of one of its most prestigious journals seemed to be arguing for *less* research. When academics call for less we should really sit up and take notice! The argument ran: 'we really have no further need of further experimental work on the effectiveness of cognitive behavioural therapy'. He is right: the multidisciplinary literature contains over 4000 empirical examples, the vast majority producing significantly positive results against comparisons with either no intervention or with other commonly employed methods. These results add up to the fact that, within this literature, in respect of a wide range of demanding problems, virtually no other approach ever does better (Benton and Schroeder, 1990; Bergin and Garfield, 1994; Gould *et al.*, 1997; Jones *et al.*, 1998; Sweet and Loizeaux, 1991; Van Etten and Taylor, 1998). This is true on a smaller scale in our own field (see Reid and Hanrahan, 1981; Sheldon, 1986;

Macdonald and Sheldon, 1992; Macdonald and Winkley, 2000). The editor went on to observe that further training and dissemination work ought now to be our priority. To which sensible view I would only wish to add the rider that these approaches are sometimes used by psychologists and American clinical social workers against rather discrete problems in somewhat protected settings. There are some examples to the contrary (see Scott, 1989; Sheldon, 1995; Hudson and Macdonald, 1988) but extending the use of CBT to routine settings (where things are a whole lot messier) is undoubtedly the next challenge for this discipline.

However, looking at where we are now. How well does the approach meet the criteria for evidence-based practice outlined above? Here are some arguments that it does so very well:

1. There is a very large body of empirical research on how problems arise in the first place as a result of maladaptive learning or through learning deficits (see Bandura, 1969; Sheldon, 1995).

2. There is a close 'logical fit' (the best predictor of a positive outcome in effectiveness research) between these 'nature of' studies and the body of techniques which constitute the CBT approach. In other words, there are no general purpose approaches based loosely on theoretical assumptions in this field, rather specific methods are indicated as a result of empirical investigations of the causes of problems.

3. Research on 'nature of' and 'what to do about' questions relies much more on experimental and quasi-experimental methods (as we have seen, the strictest tests of professional good intent) than is typical across the helping professions (see Gough, 1993).

4. Users of CBT approaches are trained to be explicit about what they are trying to achieve, and help is offered in a contractual way, based upon informed consent (see BABCP, Code of Ethics). If anything, having favoured quantitative rigor for so long, we now lack good, representative, qualitative research on the experience of being a client with whom these approaches are being tried. However, where we have such findings, the findings are rather positive. Indeed, looking at the comparative research regarding other approaches, a fair conclusion would be that although clients are willing to consider all sorts of arguments (from the plausible to the fanciful) about the origins of their difficulties, they turn into behavioural fellow travellers when it comes to the evaluation of outcomes (Sheldon, 1989). Is there more or less aggression? Can they do useful things that would have been very unlikely prior to intervention? Do the children now regularly go to school? Has deliberate self harm reduced or disappeared—wherever such problems originally came from?

5. Any idea that CBT might be useful for a few minor, easy to target problems must simply be abandoned in the light of the empirical evidence. There are now reviews and compilations of evidence based largely on experimental studies showing successful application in fields such as depression (Gloaguen *et al.*, 1998); schizophrenia (Jones *et al.*, 1998; Falloon, Boyd and McGill, 1984); challenging behaviour with children (Sheldon, 1995; Macdonald and Winkley, 2000); learning disabilities (Bennett and Gibbons, 2000); in post-traumatic stress disorder (Van Etten and Taylor, 1998) and with the multi-faceted problems which generally come the way of social care staff (Scott, 1989; Cigno and Bourne, 1999).

6. Central to this form of practice is the use of single-case experimentation (see Sheldon, 1983). That is, of employing quantitative alongside qualitative measures of change against which progress, or its absence, can be monitored. In short, a rigorous form of case management, making use of hard outcome indicators, is firmly in place (see Figure 3 for an example).

7. The idea that CBT approaches rob therapeutic encounters of their humanity is a common myth. The cognitive and the behavioural literatures are full of discussions of relationship skills, motivation building approaches and so forth (see Sheldon, 1995, Ch.1). Moreover, a number of studies suggest that clients positively prefer an explicit 'recipe' to follow where help is on hand to cook it (see Stein and Gambrill, 1976). However, although such process factors deserve our close attention, they do not always constitute a sufficient condition for change. There is always the possibility, as so often reported upon in the early effectiveness studies of social work (see Gibbons *et al.*, 1978), that however well-regarded we may be for our settee-side manner, we sometimes do little manifestly to affect problems. An ethical as well as a technical issue, surely?

If any readers have been harbouring 'get on with it Sheldon' thoughts during the foregoing discussions, then I am unrepentant, since I consider that *all* proposals as to what busy practitioners should do more or less of should be accompanied by a review of the evidence to back up the advice. Put another way, should not authors and teachers have to (as maths teachers used always to urge) 'show their working out'?

This work done, we are now free to look at research on learning and how it might be applied to interventions.

Classical conditioning and its therapeutic derivatives

I.P. Pavlov won his Nobel Prize for his work on the *physiological* processes of digestion. Interestingly, the word in italics is often presented in publishers' proofs as *psychological*—a good example of higher-order classical conditioning at work—since Pavlov is now associated above all with his contributions to psychology. He and his colleagues embarked upon a project to map the range and the effects of conditioned reflexes from a sense of frustration, because no matter how great the care they took to control the circumstances in which they conducted their experiments, certain psychological phenomena always interfered. In other words, the laboratory animals developed associations and anticipations about food, as they do in ordinary domestic life. These effects fascinated Pavlov, who saw them as a challenge to scientific method.

Pavlov's procedure (the right pictures will probably be in your head as a result of classical conditioning) was to collect saliva directly from the cheek gland of a dog held in place by a harness, in a sound-proofed laboratory. Now, and I will say this only once, the purpose of presenting animal experiments is to get the 'psychological grammar' right. There is nothing in this chapter that does not apply equally well to human beings (see further on).

Here is the sequence:

1. A tone is sounded (*Neutral Stimulus: NS*) no salivary response occurs.

2. The tone is sounded and meat powder is deposited into a dish in front of the animal or directly into it's mouth (an *unconditional stimulus: UCS*) in that it produces salivary flow as a matter of innate reflex. This procedure is repeated several times.

3. The tone (CS) is presented without the meat powder (UCS) and salivary flow occurs to this stimulus alone—the dog has learned a new response.

4. Stimuli resembling the CS will tend to produce a similar reaction.

Classical conditioning is then, a pattern of *stimulus association* learning. Stimuli impinge in *clusters*, there are spatial and temporal connections (features of place, circumstances and time) which throughout evolutionary history it has been useful for animals (and humans) to respond to interchangeably since one, or one class, might predict the likelihood of the other. Thus anything that might reliably signal the possibility of satisfaction of a basic drive, or the avoidance of danger, and so prepares us for what may ensue, conveys an advantage on 'better-safe-than-sorry' principle literally: vital in evolution. In the case of salivation this operates by ensuring that the elapsed time between first prospect and food energy being available for use is shortened, as is the feeding episode during which we would once have been vulnerable to predation.

In the case of learned fear-reactions the advantages operate through the fight/flight mechanism of the body changes in muscle tone, heart rate, blood pressure and blood-clotting speed, sweating, breathing rate, pupil size, and so forth, all of which prepare us for more effective escape or for combat.

However, while it is useful to remind ourselves of the power of fierce drives and emotions, it is a mistake to forget the powerfully pleasurable feelings which (through the limbic system in the brain) exert a telling influence on our behaviour and thinking. Praise from an admired friend or mentor can, for example, produce such warm feelings that all our day-to-day doubts and worries are washed away. It has long been known that the brain contains dedicated centres for pleasure as well as for pain (Olds, 1956). The biochemistry of all this is not our particular concern but the environmental effects most certainly are, since decision making, our own and that of our clients, is not the desiccated intellectual process represented in some textbooks on cognition. It is powerfully influenced by emotion; by chains of conditioned predispositions, and by intrusive memories of past successes and failures. (see, Damasio, 1994).

Let us turn now to a human experiment in this field, that of Watson and Rayner (1920). These pioneers were keen to see whether Pavlov's results applied in cases of unreasonable fear and anxiety. 'Little Albert' as the study was called in parody of Freud's celebrated 'Little Hans' case of alleged castration anxiety. Sorry, but I can't resist this: Little Hans was analysed by post using his father as intermediary, and Freud's interpretation of the fear was basically Oedipal—the animal representing strong and possibly dangerous masculinity, pawing the ground between the boy and his mother. This interpretation ignores two interesting facts (a) that most horses in nineteenth-century Vienna would be mares or geldings, and (b) that Hans' fear began after a large brewer's dray horse collapsed and died in the shafts next to him (too simple to be considered significant). The procedure, which would nowadays have gotten everyone concerned into trouble under the Children Act, was as follows. The six-month-old Albert was placed in a play pen and introduced to a tame white rat (NS)—no reaction beyond curiosity occurred. A gong was then struck loudly (UCS) every time the animal was introduced. Next the animal (CS) was repeatedly released *without* the accompanying noise, but it still gave rise to fear and avoidance reactions. The child had learned a new fear (a conditioned response, CR) purpose-built in the laboratory.

Two clinically important phenomena were demonstrated in Watson and Rayner's work. The first is *generalisation*. Pavlov noted from his experiments that anything resembling the CS would eventually, in chain-like fashion, come to produce the same CR. Little Albert came proportionately to fear a whole range of similarly furry objects bearing decreasing resemblance to the original CS.

But, sauce for the goose, something interesting has happened in later discussions of the experimental procedure:

- The extent of the generalisation has been exaggerated to include fur coats.

- The fact that the stimulus conditions had to be reinstated as L.A. began naturally to desensitise is rarely mentioned.

- Albert never was treated for his artificially induced fear, his mother took him away (see Harris, 1979).

The temptations of the nice story; not very threatening to the main findings, but interesting in a 'post modern' sort of way.

We see this phenomenon of stimulus generalisation in our own cases, where clients have had a bad experience in one setting but adverse responses spread to a wide range of vaguely similar circumstances. This is a notable feature of post-traumatic stress disorder (see Joseph *et al.*, 1995;) and of social phobias, leading to increasing withdrawal.

Moving out of the laboratory, here is a case example from my own practice (Sheldon, 1995). Mrs Wood, aged 40, was referred to the social services department for 'support' by her somewhat exasperated family doctor. In his view Mrs Wood suffered from agoraphobia, a 'dependent personality', and a number of other poorly specified 'psychiatric difficulties'. Knowing how to motivate social workers, the doctor also said that he had some worries about Mrs Wood's young son, because not only had she barely left the house in the previous three years, but very little had been seen of this child. Stimulus conditions reliably associated with being grilled before a child abuse inquiry ('UCS').

Mrs Wood described herself as always having been 'a nervous person'. She recounted stories about dismounting from her bicycle as a child whenever a car came up behind her, going some distance out of her way to avoid a dog, feeling very shy and conspicuous as a teenager, and so forth—a range of normal enough fears, but noteworthy in their combination and extent. She reported a strong and persistent fear of hospitals and of all medical encounters, probably stemming from her mother's bloodcurdling accounts of the birth of her younger sister.

Mrs Wood became pregnant 'by accident', comparatively late in life. In order to persuade her to have the baby in hospital, the doctor had played up the dangers of a home confinement, raising her already high level of anxiety about the birth.

One hot summer's day, when she was seven months pregnant, Mrs Wood had fainted while crossing a footbridge spanning a small river near her home. 'I was sure I was going to fall in, and when I came round, people said an ambulance was on the way and I panicked. People were trying to hold me down, covering me with clothing.' She fought to get free: 'I knew I had to get away, I got very upset, and eventually I persuaded someone to take me home. When I got in I was shaking all over. I shut and bolted the doors, back and front…I was sure that the ambulance was going to call at the house…I hid out of sight of the windows…and eventually (it took about an hour) I calmed down, and sat waiting for my husband to come home from work.'

'Catastrophic' or even 'paranoid' thoughts of this type are an important feature of panic reactions.

Mrs Wood had her baby at home, against medical advice, painfully, but without serious complication. She tried to go out several times after that but never got further than the front garden, or if at night, as far as the front gate. She reported the following feelings at each attempt: 'Shivering, awful feelings in the pit of my stomach; pounding heart; light-headedness.' In the daytime everywhere seemed 'very bright and stark'. She felt conspicuous out in the open, 'almost as if I might be struck down'. Her breathing felt loud in her ears and her biggest fear was that she would collapse again.

If we examine this case in the light of classical conditioning theory, the following pattern emerges:

- Mrs Wood may have possessed a predisposing personality for strong fear reactions (see Claridge, 1985); certainly her accounts of her earlier life showed her to be eminently conditionable to a range of not objectively threatening circumstances.

- Against a background of heightened anxiety about pregnancy, dreading the thought of the possibility of having to go into hospital, Mrs Wood experienced a traumatic incident (UCS) which aroused in here a powerful fear reaction (UCR).

- This incident, when paired with the previously neutral stimulus of the footbridge and other stimuli associated with being out of doors (CSs), produced a conditioned response to these stimuli. Even after the incident itself had passed, the pregnancy was over, she was perfectly well, and the crowd no longer in sight, she still experienced fears associated with this context.

- Mrs Wood reported that her panic state was made worse by the attempts of would-be helpers to restrain her until the ambulance came. Natural escape behaviour was prevented, thus intensifying her fear.

- This conditioned fear response quickly generalised to virtually all outdoor circumstances, even though objectively they barely resembled the circumstances of her collapse. Furthermore, every time Mrs Wood tried to go out of doors she was punished for the attempt by her powerful emotions (setting up a 'fear of fear' reaction): even though she saw such feelings as annoying and irrational.

- Cognitive factors played a part in maintaining Mrs Woods avoidant reactions. Her strong emotions influenced her thought patterns, and vice-versa. When asked about what she thought would happen if she tried to confront her fears, she responded with typically 'catastrophic' views: 'I'd die and then my child would be on his own' etc. Thus, these hypotheses were never tested out, and avoidance reactions continued to predominate.

Intervention methods: slow exposure and systematic desensitisation

The applicable evidence in such cases strongly favours exposure therapy and systematic desensitisation (slow exposure). Such approaches are also useful in cases where strong and unreasonable fears which do not amount to full-scale phobias, but which nevertheless seriously interfere with life satisfaction, are concerned. Current estimates suggest that such problems are experienced by one in 12 of the population as a whole, and are further concentrated in social services caseloads. Here is an outline of the approach (systematic desensitisation) used with Mrs Wood.

There are two kinds of systematic desensitisation: *in vivo* (live practice); and *imaginal*, a cognitive approach using the same principles but employing imagination rather than direct exposure. Both forms have the same three therapeutic ingredients:

1. A graded hierarchy of anxiety-producing stimuli (see Figure 2).

2. A relatively slow rate of progression through the stages of this hierarchy, the pace being dictated by the need for a lowering of anxiety to occur before the next item is approached.

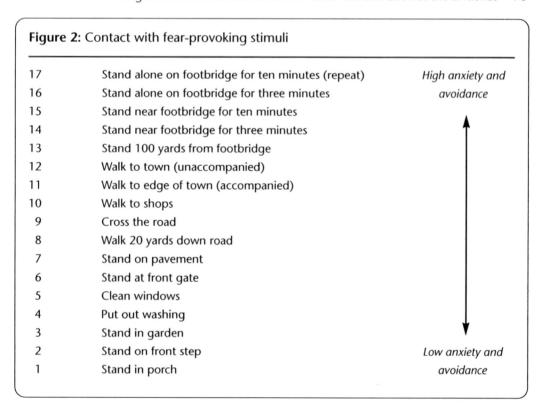

Figure 2: Contact with fear-provoking stimuli

17	Stand alone on footbridge for ten minutes (repeat)	*High anxiety and*
16	Stand alone on footbridge for three minutes	*avoidance*
15	Stand near footbridge for ten minutes	
14	Stand near footbridge for three minutes	
13	Stand 100 yards from footbridge	
12	Walk to town (unaccompanied)	
11	Walk to edge of town (accompanied)	
10	Walk to shops	
9	Cross the road	
8	Walk 20 yards down road	
7	Stand on pavement	
6	Stand at front gate	
5	Clean windows	
4	Put out washing	
3	Stand in garden	
2	Stand on front step	*Low anxiety and*
1	Stand in porch	*avoidance*

3. A counter-conditioning element in the form of deep muscle relaxation. This was always an effective technique (Bandura, 1969; Bergin and Garfield, 1994) and rapid exposure methods are only coming to supersede it on the grounds that they are more efficient—if one can persuade clients to co-operate.

Mrs Wood was taught progressive relaxation and deep breathing *in situ* during the assignments contained in Figure 2. Sometimes she was accompanied by a student social worker, and sometimes deliberately not. If the next step looked too large, the progression from one to the other could be bridged by spending longer completing the earlier task. The procedure was labour intensive but short-term, and in fact this client never did make it across the footbridge during the course of the programme. She said firmly that she could easily go to town another way, so that it was not a real problem. However, she reported at follow-up that she had at last conquered this fear. Following a row with her husband, she had felt particularly determined about the

issue and had marched to the bridge and stood trembling on it for ten minutes: amateur counter-conditioning, but effective, and wonderful solace for family therapists.

Operant conditioning

The more we learn about child development, the more we are forced to abandon the environmental determinism of the 1960s and acknowledge the active, experimenting, contribution of children themselves. Much of child development 'unfolds' from within. Very young babies show signs of a strong urge to explore, to *operate upon,* (hence the word 'operant;' not a fancy new term, it's in *Hamlet,* Act III) and to manipulate their environments (see Donaldson, 1978). Such activities rapidly attract consequences of a positive, an aversive, or a relief-producing kind. Some of these consequences just happen, e.g. reaching out and touching something hot; some we deliberately organise, e.g. in withdrawing attention from bad behaviour. Thus, from the earliest years, by accident and by design, human beings are exposed to sets of *contingencies* (if you…, then…) which experiences amount to a sub-Darwinian process of the natural (and unnatural) selection of behaviour patterns. Some sequences are 'stamped in', others 'stamped out' (Thorndike, 1898). Nothing new here, and once again the contribution of behavioural psychology has taken the form of carefully charting the dynamics of this way of acquiring new responses.

The towering contribution is that of the American psychologist B.F. Skinner (1953; 1971) whose project was to develop an entire psychology without reference to interior goings on. Lets start with Skinner's animal experiments just to get the sequence clear. He gave his name to a glass-sided box equipped with a food dispenser and a release lever or disc which the animal (usually rats or pigeons: never both) could operate from the inside. All other factors are under the control of the experimenter. Here is a summary of Skinner's procedures:

- A hungry rat is placed in a glass-sided box with a food release lever, and engages in exploratory (operant) behaviour, eventually bumping into the lever and hitting the jackpot. The rat tries this again and clumsy initial operation quickly gives way to expert tapping. The rat's unlikely behaviour (for a rat) has been *positively reinforced* and so it is repeated, or rather the other way around. It has learned a new pattern of behaviour. Thus, a positive reinforcer is a stimulus which strengthens, amplifies, or increases the rate of a behavioural sequence that it follows.

- Next imagine a Skinner box with a wire-grid for a floor, capable of delivering an irritating and continuous level of shock *until* an encounter with the lever turns this off for a period. As in the previous case the rat spends a lot of time operating the respite lever. This process is called *negative reinforcement*. It also leads to an *increase* in new behaviour, but with the object of *removing* an aversive set of conditions. Thus a negative reinforcer is a stimulus the contingent removal of which strengthens, amplifies or increases the frequency of the behaviour pattern which led to it.

- Next consider a situation where depressing the lever in the Skinner box leads every time to a loud noise. Such

behaviour is decreased, probably extinguished, under these conditions. The animal quickly learns an avoidant reaction. Thus a *punishing* stimulus *decreases* or extinguishes a behaviour pattern which it follows.

Here are a couple of case vignettes which show reinforcement contingencies at work:

- A lonely man with a serious drink problem who had learned that brushes with the police after altercations in public houses usually resulted in his daughter coming to stay with him until he was 'better'.

- A 12-year-old boy who felt that his needs came a poor second to his parents' troubles, discovered, by accident (operantly), that a random, peer-inspired episode of fire-setting leading to a visit from the police had the effect of jerking his father out of the depressed state he had been in since a serious industrial accident, and produced some concern for *him*. More fires broke out.

Intervention methods: contingency management

Evidence suggests that the most effective methods in such cases of maladaptive learning are based on *contingency management*, i.e. changing reinforcement patterns to ensure that useful, pro-social behaviour attracts reinforcement, and that negative, self-defeating, anti-social behaviour does not. In case these terms seem a little Orwellian, giving rise to 'who is to decide about these things' feelings, well, at a political level, I agree. But in most day-to-day cases the distinction is obvious. There is, after all, nothing admirably rebellious about setting fire to neighbours' property to attract the attention of your depressed father, and there is nothing dissidently incorrigible about getting plastered and attacking people so that your daughter will abandon her own family to come and look after you; there are simply better ways to live. So, these issues remain, awkwardly, matters of informed judgement and debate.

Here is an example of the application of contingency management (sometimes called differential reinforcement) techniques to a problem.

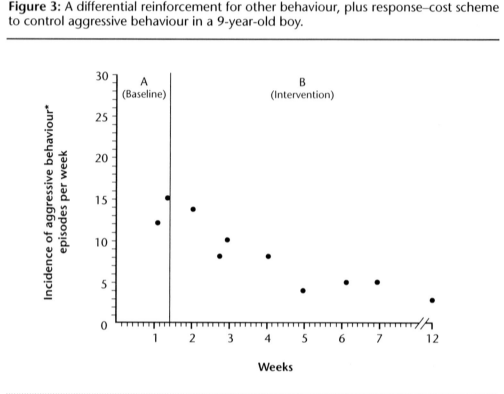

Figure 3: A differential reinforcement for other behaviour, plus response–cost scheme to control aggressive behaviour in a 9-year-old boy.

*Operationally defined as: shouting at mother or passers by in the street; threatening mother or members of the public; swearing, pushing or throwing objects.

From the age of six onwards Kenneth's behaviour had been a cause for concern to his mother and his teachers. He was aggressive to other pupils, swore foully at his mother, and on a few occasions when shopping had run through the supermarket pushing trolleys into people. His general demeanour was aggressive and he liked to dress in combat gear and have his hair cropped in military style. Following the departure of his father, from whom he got most of this behaviour, Kenneth's mother made a determined effort to change his conduct. At the time of the referral to a child guidance clinic she recounted that she had spoken to him at length about her embarrassment at his behaviour, tried to bribe him, and, as a last resort, used physical punishment: all to no avail.

The approach of the social worker in this challenging case emphasised the need for consistency. Most of what had been tried before had been tried for short periods, the mother giving up and moving on to something new if an approach proved ineffective in the short-term. The differential reinforcement programme used in this case contained the following features:

1. The identification of, and positive reinforcement of, low-probability behaviours somewhat incompatible with shouting, swearing and aggressive or embarrassing behaviour in the street while away from school. Those chosen were improved school attendance; small-scale domestic tasks; regular attendance without incident at an after-school club. The reinforcers used were stars and street-credible stickers signifying a build-up of credit towards significant purchases, e.g. training shoes, a construction set, football

kit, plus collateral reinforcement in the form of praise.

2. An ultra-reliable set of sanctions for adverse behaviour, based on deprivation punishments, e.g. staying indoors; time-out for 15-minute intervals—terminatable by a believable apology after five; loss of television privileges.

3. Basic assertion training for, and rehearsal of typical incidents with, mother—the key part of the programme as it turned out.

Progress came fairly rapidly once the mother grasped the idea of consistency and had learned to respond to current behaviour rather than memories of yesterday's. The child remained at home, which was once an outcome in serious doubt.

Vicarious learning and modelling

Probably the most distinctive feature of CBT is that its practitioners do not rely upon verbal influence alone, but seek to *demonstrate* more adaptive, more skilful, and one hopes, more effective approaches to problems. Many of the difficulties which come our way are due to *learning deficits*, that is, to serious gaps in the behavioural repertoires of individuals. For example: how to manage difficult behaviour from a child; how to negotiate about rather than fight over conflicts of interest; how to cope with living again in the community after a period in a psychiatric unit; how to be calmly and rationally assertive when put upon. Solutions to these problems are largely a matter of social skills, which may not have been acquired naturally. Vicarious learning can account for the following patterns of change:

1. The second-hand acquisition of completely new *sequences* of behaviour. Remember adolescence when, being stalled somewhere between childhood and adulthood most of us experimented cavalierly with strange new ways of walking, dressing, talking, and so forth, mostly gathered from others or from images in the media. Such behavioural symbols of changing identity are tried on, kept, adapted, or discarded according to the internal and external emotional pay-offs they produce. The problem is that sometimes there are no suitable models

available (e.g. of how to walk away from trouble without loss of face) and so learning deficits accrue which threaten further development.

2. Emotional reactions can also be learned vicariously. As children we learn what to fear by watching others behave fearfully, or how to cope by watching others approach threatening circumstances with *sang froid*.

3. Thought patterns, more particularly problem solving styles, can be acquired by watching how others deal with challenges and then inferring (not always accurately) what processes of mental computation and interpretation led them to a given course of action.

Case illustrations

A man in a fairly serious state of depression who had been made redundant three times in two years, had worked out a survival plan based upon observations of others not made redundant. His chosen models had allegedly 'kept their heads down' and survived. Yet on every occasion of loss of employment the reasons given to him were that he appeared to lack initiative, made only a minimal contribution to the team to which he belonged, and was more concerned with the inconsequential details of his own tasks rather than co-operation with colleagues. The approach used, with some success in that he has been off Prozac for over 12 months and is increasingly well-regarded at work, was based upon the modelling and rehearsal of a more pro-active, assertive approach in situations identified by him as threatening.

Such modelling and social-skill training programmes should be organised according to the following common stages:

1. Identifying specific problems resulting from gaps in the client's behavioural repertoire, and deciding what new patterns of behaviour could be developed to fill these.

2. Dividing the target responses into their component parts (for example, coming into a room full of people; deciding who to stand next to and what to say; introducing oneself; getting in on the conversation, and so forth).

3. Identifying with clients any patterns in their thinking (images and inner speech) which may encourage misinterpretation of the motives of others or avoidance responses, e.g. 'people are looking at me, they can tell I don't belong here'.

4. Demonstrating to clients what a competent performance might look like; rehearsing any problematic parts of the sequence or going through it slowly and deliberately, emphasising options and decision points.

5. Developing more complex performances by chaining together different sequences.

6. Gradually introducing difficulties likely to be found in real life as the client becomes more able to cope with its vicissitudes (for instance, not getting an immediate answer when trying to make friends; meeting increased persistence after saying no to something).

7. Supervising practical assignments on which clients report back (Sheldon, 1999).

A group approach

The transfer of clients from psychiatric units back into the community is fraught with difficulties. In my experience, the fears and worries of clients are handled individually. However, many of these sources of trepidation are held in common by them. I was once involved in running a group for about-to-be discharged patients who were encouraged first to identify their worries, then to discuss the extent to which they might be over-reacting to fears and neglecting sources of support, and then to rehearse ways of approaching difficult situations *via* role-play, sometimes with video feedback. This project had both cognitive, modelling, and live practice desensitisation elements, and was thought very useful by participants at the evaluation stage.

Outcome studies in this field point to modelling as an effective technique providing that it focuses on explicitly defined behavioural deficits. The results from more general purpose programmes are less good.

Cognitive factors and methods

Here are the factors and their associated approaches to which the cognitive therapy literature suggests that we should attend in cases where we suspect that negative thinking is impeding attempts to improve functioning:

- *Selective Perception.* Perception is no camera-like activity in which sense data is recorded, then later 'developed' and looked at on a screen in the head. It is an active, constructive process strongly influenced from the outset by our brains overriding raw sensory data, and is strongly influenced by past experience. Thus we are all capable of not attending to things which later look obviously important (see any child abuse inquiry report) or of over-concentrating on negative stimuli and favouring pessimistic interpretations. This is a particular problem in cases of depression; low morale; in anxiety states, and regarding challenging behaviour in children. The approach used in CBT constitutes a friendly, persistent, but logical, evidential challenge to such distortions, and encourages clients to test out more optimistic ideas in a controlled way.

- *Attributions.* Human beings search actively for meaning when confronted by complex stimuli. We seek to attribute causality (sometimes making mistakes) as we try, like amateur scientists, to evaluate potential threats, rewards, or sources of relief. Attributive cognitions fall into two main patterns: the external (circumstantial) and the internal (dispositional). The typical direction of causal attribution tends to vary with personality, with experience, with regularly encountered contingencies, and according to emotional state. It may be that some of us are statistically more likely to look to our environments for explanations of our failures; some of us are more likely to blame ourselves. The same can be said of our successes. Generally speaking, women are statistically more likely to look outwards for explanations of success and inwards for explanations of failure. As you might have guessed, the situation is reversed for men (Brown, 1986, Ch. 9).

Social workers often encounter individuals whose patterns of self-blaming or self-excusing cognitions seem implausibly uni-directional. Here are a couple of case examples:

- A young woman, worried and preoccupied by memories of persistent sexual abuse in childhood, who felt that she 'must have' done 'something' to encourage her stepfather.

- A client with a string of different psychiatric diagnoses to her name, living in a hostel, who attributed the sound of nearby laughter to cruel jokes being made at her expense, and silence in the house to a wish by her critics that they should not be overheard when discussing her failings. Thus she could never win.

- *Dichotomous Thinking*. Clients with a string of bad experiences behind them sometimes seek the security of completely good versus completely bad views of their problems and present non-negotiable alternatives to staff trying to help them. For example: 'He's just like his father and he'll never change, but if he doesn't then…' In such cases exponents of CBT try to establish the idea of a *continuum* of possibilities, along which small down payments of change against a more realistic plan might become acceptable if little experiments begin to show useful gains.

   In the research literatures of psychotherapy, social work and clinical psychology, two strong trends have been visible for some time:

1. That the elements of a focused, fairly intensive, task-centred, quasi-behavioural approach, within which due regard is paid to the problem of translating new understandings into behavioural change, are strongly associated with positive outcomes (see Reid and Hanrahan, 1981; Macdonald and Sheldon, 1992; Bergin and Garfield, 1994; Macdonald and Winkley, 2000).

2. That problems which have behavioural components (virtually all do) but which are also strongly rooted in, or maintained by, internal factors such as mood and thought patterns, respond well to approaches which seek to analyse, make clear, and test out in reality the perceptions, beliefs and any patterns of negative, self-defeating cognition which lead to avoidance, disengagement and, eventually, alienation.

Obstacles to the use of cognitive behavioural approaches by social services staff

The primary function of the Centre for Evidence-based Social Services (of which I am Director) is dissemination of existing research and its implications for practice and service development. It was thus a rational conclusion that as part of our output, staff should receive training in CBT. This view was supported by findings from a large questionnaire exercise (N=1226) conducted by the Centre (Sheldon and Chilvers, 2000) within which respondents gave high priority to items regarding initiatives that would improve their 'knowledge of effective intervention methods'. Accordingly, we have now conducted eight three-day courses including case-project work, a follow-up day, and some on-site support in the interim for staff from 16 social services departments. This project has involved 274 professional grade staff, and given that every phase was subject to evaluation (*via* anonymous questionnaires) is a training research project in its own right. Here are our findings from the exercise:

- All courses were substantially over-subscribed. The high point was 217 applications for 40 places within seven days of advertising, with other courses attracting potential applicants on an average 4:1 ratio for the places available— which means something.

- Questions as to prior knowledge of cognitive behavioural methods revealed the following:
  - although virtually all participants had *heard* of the approach only a small minority had received any training on their qualifying courses
  - subsequent departmental training courses never touched the subject.

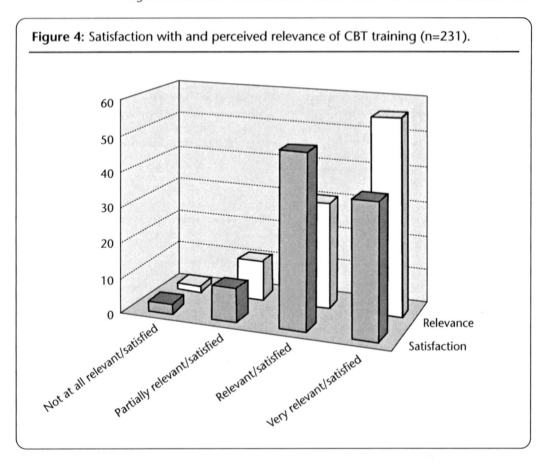

Figure 4: Satisfaction with and perceived relevance of CBT training (n=231).

Therefore, we find ourselves in a position where possibly the most effective approaches to a wide range of problems within the remit of social services were, hitherto, less likely to be taught than other approaches with a less substantial record of effectiveness. But let us turn now to what happens when staff do get training in these methods.

If we take as our quality standard the last two columns on the right of Figure 4, then we have an 87.7 per cent rating of satisfaction and an 87.2 per cent level for relevance.

As indicated earlier, these courses also contained a project phase, in which staff were asked to apply what they had learned to a case and produce assessment and evaluation data on this work. However, of the 274 staff involved, only 85 (31 per cent) came back with case material showing that they had been able to apply these methods. The course tutors issued an amnesty on this at the end of the training, inviting people who might not have an opportunity to use the approach to attend anyway and to tell us why this was so.

These staff identified the following obstacles to implementation (in rank order):

1. Pressure of work—but then one has to ask what was being done instead? The answer appeared to be increasing amounts of risk-management work (child care workers) and accountability exercises (all).

2. That therapeutic work is discouraged in some authorities, which have regimes which determine that even qualified staff spend most of their time assessing cases and then trying to find external providers who might provide limited help on a tight budget.

3. CBT work usually requires short-term but intensive involvement with clients and their families; this, we are told is also discouraged by present conventions,

within which clients either receive glancing, problem containing contact when crises occur, or longer term 'drip-fed' support if their needs are largely practical and foreseeable (which many are not). Inadequacy of resources is at the heart of this problem. However, the point remains that if we do not intervene in timely fashion, using effective approaches, then we only get these cases later, in direr circumstances, when most therapeutic possibilities have evaporated.

More recent experiments, providing greater contact with staff during the project phase appear to be bearing fruit.

Conclusions

I have tried in this chapter to bring together arguments about the need for the principles of evidence-based practice to inform our selection of approaches. We have also examined together the research track record of CBT methods, and, *via* case examples and references to other research, looked at their relevance to parts of the social care field. My main conclusion is, therefore, that here is a body of knowledge and techniques, directly applicable to mainstream practitioners in our field with an unrivalled record of effectiveness, which have been rather self-defeatingly neglected. Further, and to my continuing amazement, most qualifying courses do not teach these approaches to their students. If we look for reasons as to why this is the case, then the prime contenders are the so-called reforms of the 1980s, which pushed anything but high-eligibility-threshold, problem containment off the agenda (a very expensive way to run a service, by the way) and the dumbing down of social work education during the same period (see Macdonald and Sheldon, 1998). However, if we look at recent political developments, in child care, mental health, and rehabilitation services for elderly people, then it is obvious that new opportunities for something more rational and more effective are now there for the taking. Will we?

Acknowledgements

Sincere thanks are due to Sue Bosley (secretary at the Centre for Evidence-based Social Services) and Alice Caldwell (Research Assistant at CEBSS) for their help in the preparation of this chapter and Professor Geraldine Macdonald (University of Bristol) for her support in this project.

References

BABCP *Code of Ethics*, British Association for Behavioural and Cognitive Psychotherapies. Cambridge University Press.

Bandura, A. (1969). *Principles of Behavior Modification*. New York: Holt, Rinehart and Winston.

Bennett, D.S., and Gibbons, T.A. (2000). Efficacy of Child Cognitive-behavioral Interventions for Anti-social Behavior: A Meta Analysis. *Child and Family Behavior Therapy*, 22(1): pp1–15.

Benton, M.K., and Schroeder, H.E. (1990). Social Skills Training with Schizophrenics: A Meta-analytic Evaluation. *Journal of Consulting and Clinical Psychology*, 58(6): pp741–747.

Bergin, A.E., and Garfield, S.L. (Eds.) (1994). *Handbook of Psychotherapy and Behavior Change* (4th edn.). Chichester: John Wiley and Sons, Inc.

Brown, R. (1986). *Social Psychology*. New York. Free Press.

CEBSS (Centre for Evidence-based Social Services) (1999). *Annual Report*. University of Exeter.

Cigno, K., and Bourne, D. (1999). *Cognitive Behavioural Social Work in Practice*. Aldershot: Arena.

Claridge, G. (1985). *Origins of Mental Illness*. Oxford: Blackwell.

Damasio, A.R. (1994). *Descartes; Error: Emotion, Reason and the Human Brain*. New York: Grosset Putnam.

DoH, (1994). *A Wider Strategy for Research in the Personal Social Services*. London: HMSO.

Donaldson, M. (1978). *Children's Minds*. London: Fontana Press.

Falloon, I.R.H., Boyd, J.L., and McGill, C.W. (1984). *Family Care of Schizophrenia*. New York: Guilford Press.

Fischer, J., and Corcoran, K. (1994). *Measures for Clinical Practice: A Sourcebook, Vols. 1 and 2* (2nd edn.). New York: The Free Press.

Gambrill, E. (1997). *Social Work Practice: A Critical Thinker's Guide*. Oxford: Oxford University Press

Gibbons, J.S., Butler, J., Urwin, P., and Gibbons, J.L. (1978) Evaluation of a Social Work Service for Self-poisoning Patients. *British Journal of Psychiatry*, 133: pp111–118.

Gloaguen, V., Cottraux, J., Cucherat, M., Blackburn, I.M. (1998). A Meta-analysis of the Effects of Cognitive Therapy in Depressed Patients. *Journal of Affective Disorders*, 49(1): pp59–72.

Gough, R. (1993). *Child Abuse Interventions*. London: HMSO.

Gould, R.A., Otto, M.W., Pollack, M.H., Yap, L. (1997). Cognitive Behavioral and Pharmacological Treatment of Generalised Anxiety Disorder: A Preliminary Meta-analysis. *Behavior Therapy*, 28: pp285–305.

Harris, B. (1979). Whatever Happened to Little Albert? *American Psychologist*, 34: pp151–160.

Hudson, B.L., and Macdonald, G.M. (1988). *Behavioural Social Work*. London: Macmillan.

Jehu, D. (1967). *Learning Theory and Social Work*. London: Routledge and Keagan Paul.

Jones, C., Cormac, I., Mota, J., Campbell, C. (1998). Cognitive Behaviour Therapy for Schizophrenia (Cochrane Review). In *The Cochrane Library*, Issue 1, 2000. Oxford: Update Software.

Joseph, S., Williams, R., and Yule, W. (1995). Psycho-social Perspectives on Post-traumatic Stress. *Clinical Psychology Review*, 15: pp515–544.

Macdonald, G.M. (2000). *What Works in Child Protection?* Basingstoke: Barnardos.

Macdonald, G.M., and Sheldon (1992). Contemporary Studies of the Effectiveness of Social Work. *British Journal of Social Work*, 22(6): pp615–643.

Macdonald, G.M., and Sheldon, B. (1999). Changing One's Mind: The Final Frontier? *Issues in Social Work Education*, 18(1): pp3–25.

Macdonald, G.M. and Winkley, A. (2000). *What Works in Child Protection?* Barkingside: Barnardo's.

Olds, J. (1956). Pleasure Centre in the Brain. *Scientific American*, 195: pp105–116.

Reid, W.J., and Hanrahan, P. (1981). The Effectiveness of Social Work: Recent Evidence, in Globerg, E.M., and Connolly, N. (Eds.). *Evaluative Research in Social Care*. London: Heinemann Educational Books.

Sackett, D.L., Rosenberg, W.M., Gray, J.H.M., Haynes, R.B., Richardson, W.S. (1996). Evidence-based Practice: What it is and What it isn't. *British Medical Journal*, 312(7203): pp71–72.

Scott, M. (1989). *A Cognitive Behavioural Approach to Clients' Problems*. London: Tavistock.

Sheldon, B., and Chilvers, R. (2000). *Evidence-based Social Services: Prospects and Problems*. Lyme Regis: Russell House Publishing.

Sheldon, B., and Macdonald, G.M. (1999). *Research and Practice in Social Care: Mind the Gap*. Centre for Evidence-based Social Services, University of Exeter.

Sheldon, B. (1978). Theory and Practice in Social Work: A Re-examination of a Tenuous Relationship. *British Journal of Social Work*, 8(1): pp1–22.

Sheldon, B. (1983). The Use of Single Case Experimental Designs in the Evaluation of Social Work. *British Journal of Social Work*, 2(1).

Sheldon, B. (1986). Social Work Effectiveness Experiments: Review and Implications. *British Journal of Social Work*, 16: pp223–242.

Sheldon, B. (1987). The Psychology of Incompetence. In Drewry, G., Martin, B., and Sheldon B. (Eds.). *After Beckford: Essays on Child Abuse*. Egham, Surrey: Royal Holloway and Bedford New College.

Sheldon, B. (1989). *Studies of the Effectiveness of Social Work*. PhD Thesis, University of Leicester.

Sheldon, B. (1995). *Cognitive Behavioural Therapy: Research, Practice and Philosophy*. London: Routledge.

Skinner, B.F. (1953). *Science and Human Behaviour*. New York: Macmillan.

Skinner, B.F. (1971). *About Behaviourism*. Eaglewood Cliffs, NJ: Prentice Hall.

Sokal, A., and Brincmont, J. (1998). *Intellectual Impostures*. London: Profile Books.

Stein, T.J., and Gambrill, E.D. (1976). Behavioral Techniques in Foster Care. *Social Work*, 21(1): pp34–39.

Sweet, A.A., and Loizeaux, A.L. (1991). Behavioral and Cognitive Treatment Methods—A Critical Comparative Review. *Journal of Behavior Therapy and Experimental Psychiatry*, 22(3): pp159–185.

Thorndike, E.L. (1898). Animal Intelligence: An Experimental Study of the Associative Processes in Animals. *Psychological Review*, Monograph 2.

Van Etten, M.L., and Taylor, S. (1998). Comparative Efficacy of Treatments for Post-traumatic Stress Disorder: A Meta-analysis. *Clinical Psychology and Psychotherapy*, 5: pp124–126.

Watson, J.B., and Rayner, R. (1920). Conditional Emotional Reactions. *Journal of Experimental Psychology*, 3: pp1–14.

Webster, R. (1996). *Why Freud was Wrong: Sin, Science and Psychoanalysis*. London: Fontana Press.

Chapter Nine

Counselling and Contemporary Social Work

Frances Fleet

…we grew together,
Like to a double cherry, seeming parted,
But yet an union in partition;
Two lovely berries moulded on one stem…
(Shakespeare, *A Midsummer Night's Dream*,
III:II pp208–211)

Writing about counselling in a book on social work theories, models and methods poses some basic difficulties. On the one hand there appears to be some confusion about whether social workers can or indeed should practice 'counselling' in contemporary practice (Valios, 2000). Brown (1998) refers to a growing 'timidity' among social workers towards exercising counselling skills. The author of this chapter has been aware of experienced social work staff often regretting a perceived loss of the counselling element from their role in the wake of recent changes, while students express concerns that they are not given 'counselling training' on many DipSW programmes and so will be ill-equipped to deal with feelings and emotional problems in practice. On the other hand the social work literature repeatedly affirms the vital importance of counselling skills (Brearley, 1995; Brown, 1998; Coulshed and Orme, 1998; Payne, 1995; Seden, 1999.)

It may help initially to take a brief foray into our history. Both social work and counselling have a common ancestry. Brearley (1995) traces the development of both services from the nineteenth century and deals much more comprehensively than this single chapter can do with the links between the two. Both social work and counselling have their roots in the social casework described by such authors as Perlman (1957), Ferard and Hunnybun (1962), and Hollis (1964). Casework's objective was to engage the client in a re-evaluation of the person in his or her situation (Hollis, 1964). The worker sought to assist the client to a better adaptation to his/her circumstances and to enhanced coping skills. It drew predominantly on psychodynamic theory and was criticised and eventually superseded in the 1970s because it was felt that the emphasis on the individual often resulted in a pathologising of the client without sufficient critical focus on social and structural factors (Barber, 1991; Kenny and Kenny, this volume). Social work moved on to be invested with ever increasing legal responsibilities and to develop methods such as those explored in the other chapters of this volume. Counselling developed from a similar background, coupled with the early counselling services of marriage guidance (Jacobs, 1982). Its progress has however retained the central emphasis on the individual's adjustment and sense of emotional well-being.

Because of its shared history it is hardly surprising that the social work and counselling professions share many core skills and values. This historical link however calls into question whether it is correct to talk about social workers using 'counselling skills' or utilising 'counselling approaches' as if they were borrowing these from a profession that has a prior right to them. It may be more helpful to think in terms of a discrete 'social work practice' approach which utilises similar skills to our closely related colleagues but does so in the furtherance of our distinctly different objectives and responsibilities.

So what precisely do we mean by 'counselling' and what are the difficulties with using it directly as a social work intervention? On the one hand a degree of mystique has gathered around the term which hints at an esoteric body of knowledge and skills set apart for those who practice as 'counsellors'. At the same time however we have seen an explosion in 'counselling' covering areas such as careers, debt, even personal 'style' or home decor, much of which clearly does not take the practitioner into intensely fragile areas of the psyche. The counselling literature recognises a distinction between those practitioners who are 'counsellors' and those who provide counselling in the context of a relationship which is 'primarily focused on other, non-counselling concerns' (McLeod, 1998: p4).

McLeod cites nurses and teachers as examples of this but the definition would be equally applicable to social workers.

There are numerous definitions of counselling and a huge volume of literature. What is clear is that counselling is a method of working which draws on a variety of disciplines, including philosophy as well as psychology (McLeod, 1998) and incorporates a wide range of theories and applications. McLeod refers to over four hundred different modalities having been identified. This just adds to the confusion for any social work practitioner considering using counselling as a method of intervention. How many modalities should be studied? Which should be applied in what contexts? How do you know if you are 'doing counselling' right? What damage will you do the client if you get lost in this vast landscape?

In 1965, just at the point when the two professions were beginning to diverge Halmos wrote:

> ...all counselling procedures share a method: they are all 'talking cures', semantic exercises, they all attempt treatment through clarification of subjective experiences and meanings.
>
> (Halmos, 1965: p3)

Within counselling this objective survives largely intact as we see from the British Association for Counselling's 1984 definition which is still being cited in current texts:

> The task of counselling is to give the 'client' an opportunity to explore, discover and clarify ways of living more satisfyingly and resourcefully.
>
> (BAC, 1984 cited in McLeod, 1998: p3)

Counselling involves communication between two or more people with the sole objective of enabling the client to make progress in terms of growth and change. In most instances this will be change in personally selected directions. It is not usually the counsellor's role to define or impose the objectives, although it should be acknowledged that increasingly counsellors are becoming involved in the work of agencies where there is a clear agenda for social control, such as statutory drug services.

The emphasis on non-directive practice suggests possible limitations and conflicts in using counselling as a primary method of intervention for most social workers, since much of our statutory work is about clearly defined issues of management of risks or difficulties of practical functioning. The needs and situations which bring most people to the attention of social workers today can rarely be resolved by talking alone (Cordon and Preston-Shoot, 1987). If these would suffice, if 'counselling' is what is needed then it could be argued that it would be more appropriate to refer the client to a specialist agency such as Cruse or Relate or to a general facility such as the counsellors now employed by some GP surgeries. This would protect the client from the stigma sometimes attached to social work involvement (Feltham and Dryden, 1993) and would free up valuable social worker time.

A later definition by the British Association for Counselling highlights another potential conflict:

> People become engaged in counselling when a person occupying regularly or temporarily the role of counsellor, offers or agrees explicitly to offer time, attention and respect to another person or persons temporarily in the role of client.
>
> (BAC, 1985: p1)

This emphasis on explicit offering or agreeing is deliberate, as it is seen by the BAC as 'the dividing line between the counselling task and ad hoc counselling and is the major safeguard of the rights of the consumer' (BAC, 1985: p2).

Brearley (1995) rightly identifies how this distinction could be very difficult to maintain when the worker occupies more than one role in relation to the client, such as gate-keeper as well as provider of services, or has potentially conflicting responsibilities. In a child protection situation for instance, it is difficult to see how one worker could offer a pure counselling role of this kind to a parent and simultaneously maintain the statutory responsibilities for the child's safety; sufficiently difficult indeed to raise questions of appropriateness and integrity in the attempt.

Other ethical questions are also raised by the prospect of counselling in a context of social work practice. Even counselling that targets what appear to be fairly 'safe' objectives and intends intervention at a relatively superficial level has a habit, by the nature of the processes involved, to move quite swiftly on to more sensitive material. For this reason, as emphasised in the BAC definition above, it is important for there to be an element of mutual consent to the work and the methods. In statutory social work, even the most carefully negotiated mandates take place in a context of constraint and unequal balance of power, which may call into question the degree of consent that is possible, or the reality of the client's capacity to terminate the counselling or limit its boundaries without at the very least being assessed as 'unmotivated' or 'resistant'.

Social work practice also needs to be able to meet the needs of all service users. Much counselling practice has developed in the private sector. Even when the resource is made available, it remains, in Halmos' phrase, primarily a 'talking cure' which may not be truly accessible to clients with limited cognitive skills or capacity for verbal expression. There are further issues about the appropriateness of counselling, with its essentially Euro-centric origins and values, for clients from all cultural backgrounds (Brearley, 1995). There are also issues about choice of worker. Most users of social work services have little choice over who is allocated to them, even in terms of gender or ethnic background. These factors can be crucial in counselling practice (d'Ardenne and Mahtani, 1989). Finally Payne (1995) draws our attention to the fact that counselling may be inadequate for oppressed groups, who need the broader approach of social work.

There are then a number of question marks about social workers working directly as 'counsellors' with their clients. It is, however, often the case that the benefits of the provision of resources or the effectiveness of interventions to protect will be greatly reduced or even fail completely if Halmos' 'subjective experiences and meanings' are not acknowledged, explored and taken into account. Writing of care management in 1995 Michael Sheppard observed:

> If I, as care manager, am to work with and for a consumer it is important that I know their purposes (which in due course I may influence) and their perspectives on their situation.
>
> (Sheppard, 1995: p220)

This has always been recognised. In 1982 the Barclay Report saw 'counselling' as a parallel activity with 'social care planning'; the two functions being 'different but interlocking' (Brearley, 1995). Then came the Griffiths Report and the community care legislation. Malcolm

Payne says of care planning that it is '…not a management activity…It is rather a human interaction…' (Payne, 1995: p111) and he offers a tri-partite model in which care management, community social work and counselling are shown as distinct but overlapping processes. It is what are generally called 'counselling skills' then that help us to take clients with us, to engage them in the process, to exercise control without alienating, to challenge, motivate and empower. It is this kind of skilled interpersonal practice that I am suggesting should be seen as fundamentally characterising social work intervention, rather than being an 'add on tool' that we feel we are borrowing from another discipline whenever we encounter the need. Sheppard calls such skills the 'oil which lubricates the engine of care management' (Sheppard ,1995: p231).

Research supports this view (Pilling, 1991). Macdonald and Sheldon identified that 43 per cent of their sample of users of community care services for people with mental health problems cited emotional support and reassurance as the most helpful services provided, as against 32 per cent preferring practical help. The authors note:

> This important aspect of service provision has been shown to be one that needs protection within current organisation changes towards a purchaser/provider split and privatisation.

They also identified that:

> Nearly three quarters of respondents made positive comments about the quality of the working relationship which they enjoyed with staff. In social work the 'medium is the message' to a greater extent than in other professions. If clients do not trust their would-be helpers they will not confide, and if they do not confide the risk of a crisis due to unresolved pressures is increased.
>
> (Macdonald and Sheldon, 1997: p46)

In this excerpt we can see very clearly ways in which the judicious use of skills similar to those of counselling enhance the achievement of the clear objectives of modern social work, such as the avoidance of crises which might have repercussions in terms of public protection or might result in unnecessary hospital admissions.

It is therefore important that we achieve a competent level of understanding and expertise in using these powerful and effective methods. We also need, however, to confront honestly the power which such methods bestow and the inherent responsibility to use them with integrity. We therefore have much of value to learn from the rich vein of counselling literature but we may need to adapt some of its theory to the context of social work practice. This is what I propose to attempt to do in the second half of this chapter.

The worker–client relationship

We will start with the pivotal concept of the use of relationship. Raiff and Shore (1993) tell us that social workers need to pay constant attention to the relationship with the client. It is a view shared by many writers in the social work field (Kadushin, 1990; Lishman, 1994; Payne, 1995). This emphasis on relationship in fact dates back to the mutual roots of social work and counselling referred to above. Two seminal works for the development of both professions were Biestek's *The Casework Relationship* (1957) and Ferard and Hunnybun's *The Caseworker's Use of Relationship* (1962). Writing from about the same time up until 1990, initially in the field of psychotherapy, Carl Rogers produced numerous texts leading to the development of 'person-centred counselling' which has also been profoundly influential on social work. These early works drew largely on the psychodynamic understanding of what happened in the contacts between client and worker. They saw the relationship as the primary 'tool', using the dynamic between worker and client as indicative of past relationships and unconscious processes as well as a way of identifying and developing constructive changes.

> *The casework relationship is the dynamic interaction of attitudes and emotions between the caseworker and the client, with the purpose of helping the client achieve a better adjustment between himself and his environment.*
>
> (Biestek, 1957: p12)

These are themes which are explored at much greater length in the chapter by Kenny and Kenny in this volume.

Today the relationship between worker and client is still seen as pivotal but the emphasis now is on relationship as an aid to intervention rather than a primary tool in its own right. Sheldon for instance cites it as the essential 'packaging' for cognitive behavioural methods (Sheldon, 1995). Davis emphasises that 'the quality of risk work is linked directly to the establishment of relationships of trust and empathy.' (Davis, 1995: p117). Our understanding of the components of the relationship however still owes much to those early works. Biestek's 'principles' are less quoted now, but Carl Rogers' three essential components of genuineness, unconditional positive regard and empathic understanding still exercise a profound influence over both professions. In particular Kadushin (1990) and Lishman (1994) both offer in-depth exploration in the social work context.

Genuineness

Mearns and Thorne (1988) describe the impact of this as:

> *The more the counsellor is able to be him/herself in the relationship without putting up a professional front or a personal facade the greater will be the chance of the client changing and developing in a positive and constructive manner.*
>
> (Mearns and Thorne, 1988: p14)

Is this applicable to social work? Lishman defines genuineness as 'being oneself' (Lishman, 1994: p46) and it is certain that we are ourselves the medium through which interventions are delivered. Our use of self, that is how we are with people, is therefore likely to have a powerful influence on whether or not clients, carers or other professionals respond positively. In particular, it is likely to influence the level of trust which is achieved and without this it is unlikely that anyone will be able to respond with either positive motivation or confidence.

Unconditional positive regard

In the social work literature unconditional positive regard is more often referred to as 'acceptance'. For social workers, as for counsellors, this has to be achieved without any suggestion of condoning behaviour or attitudes which contravene either our responsibilities or our professional values (Lishman, 1994). Kadushin maintains:

> *Although acceptance does not necessarily mean agreeing with or condoning the client's frame of reference, his point of view, and his concept of reality, it involves granting their validity. It implies interpreting others in terms of themselves.*
>
> (Kadushin, 1990: pp48–49)

Acceptance therefore requires a separation of the person, of intrinsic worth as a unique individual, from the behaviour and conveying this clearly and unambiguously in all forms of communication.

Empathy

Empathy is a key concept in counselling and social work but one which because of its subtlety is difficult to define.

Gerard Egan defines it as *'getting in contact with another's world'* (Egan, 1994: p106). We can expand this to say that it means understanding the *significance* for the other person of their situation; what it means practically, what interpretation they put on it and what expectations this leads to, how it meshes or conflicts with their values or their self image, what feelings are triggered, what past events are echoed and old emotions re-awakened. Clearly, this is a tall order. Egan acknowledges that it may be 'metaphysically impossible' to achieve fully but he suggests it can be approximated and 'even an approximation is a very useful way of helping' (Egan, 1994: p106).

It might be worth pausing here to ask why it is so useful? Howe's 1993 research identified that:

> The broad message from the consumers of therapy and counselling is that it is therapeutic and comforting to believe that another person understands what you are feeling...
>
> (Howe, 1993: p63)

Mearns and Thorne (1988) tell us that receiving empathy builds self-esteem as the client realises that they are 'understandable' and that someone (the counsellor) believes they are sufficiently important to try to understand them. They also suggest that empathy is a powerful influence when working with resistance:

> ...for it is almost impossible to maintain an alienated position in the face of someone who is showing you profound understanding at a very personal level.
>
> (Mearns and Thorne, 1988: p46)

The same writers draw attention to the process by which empathy exerts its influence. In their view it enables a client to become more aware of feelings and awareness of feelings is the first step to taking responsibility for them.

Understanding is, however, of limited use unless it can be communicated to the client. Kadushin refers to the responses, which do not, of course, have to be verbal, needing to have an 'I am with you' quality (Kadushin, 1990: p51). Egan (1994) sees the impact of empathic responses resting in the interviewer's ability to filter out and feed back themes and core messages in the client's communication. Mearns and Thorne call this working on the 'edge of awareness' (Mearns and Thorne, 1988: p44).

But does social work in the current context which is set out in the introduction to this book require such delicacy of technique? If social workers are indeed now operating in an environment in which 'the language of the market has become the new currency of exchange' what room is there left for such profoundly personal skills? The answer rests in the immediacy of the interpersonal task, where the individual social worker still encounters the same confusions, ambivalence, loss of direction and desperation that characterised similar encounters when social caseworkers first developed such concepts as aids to communication and change. The role may have changed, that is the objectives and responsibilities required of the social worker and the context may have become more concerned with the three 'E's of effectiveness, economy and efficiency (Stepney, this volume), but face to face it still takes what Kadushin calls 'entering imaginatively into someone else's life' for the worker to have sufficiently accurate comprehension to decide how to proceed (Kadushin, 1990: p51). It is also not hard to see how a method that enhances the possibility of change and acceptance of responsibility can have very direct application to social work's intervention with abusers and offenders as well as those for whom guilt, regret or anxiety may underlie presenting problems.

Consideration of empathy prompts a recognition that constructive relationships between workers and clients do not just happen. As Kenny and Kenny (this volume) show, they are dependant on both values and skills. In both these respects counselling and social work practice have much in common, but in neither area can concepts be exported whole.

Values

The basic value of respect for the individual is undoubtedly shared by both professions, and major disagreements over this are rarely discernible either in practice or professional literature. Some of the other counselling values may however need different interpretation or application in the social work field. Social workers have quite different responsibilities to counsellors. This is not to say that counsellors do not sometimes face major ethical dilemmas relating to similar issues (McLeod, 1998), but their statutory obligations are different, their mandates more limited, in the sense of being more tightly defined and the values with which they operate quite rightly reflect this. Client self-determination for instance, which is absolutely central to most counselling contracts, may be less easy to apply in social work, where the nature of the professional intervention may require the exercise of a degree of control or modification of certain behaviours, or where choices of resources may be limited by budgets or agency policy. Similarly, the statutory social work agencies are unlikely to be able to guarantee the same level of confidentiality which private counsellors and to a lesser extent voluntary agencies may provide. There are also major issues for social workers around the value of being 'non-judgemental'. This needs very careful qualifying for social workers in order to differentiate between being non-judgemental as opposed to suspending all capacity to make judgements, as much of our work involves making massive judgements about the conflicting needs of child and parent, victim and perpetrator, carer and dependant or about the risks posed by individuals or their circumstances (Milner and O'Byrne, 1998).

Skills for social work practice

Communication skills such as listening, responding, facilitating and challenging are articulately addressed in the work of Egan (1994) and Nelson-Jones (1993) in the counselling field and Lishman (1994), Kadushin (1990) and Seden (1999) for social work. This chapter can only touch briefly on these but it will do so by seeking to explore how they translate into an effective social work practice in relation to the cycle of assessment, planning, intervention, review and endings (Taylor and Devine, 1993).

Assessment

The quality of an assessment clearly depends on the accuracy of the information obtained. The major source of information will inevitably be clients and those who surround them. This calls for listening skills of the highest order (Kadushin, 1990; Lishman, 1994). It is vital for instance that we can hear what Rogers called 'sensing meanings of which the client is scarcely aware' (Rogers, 1980: p142) as well as being able to 'hear' with all our senses, not just our ears. We also need to exercise the skills of questioning and exploring so that we can seek clarification of often intensely complex situations and we may need to be able to challenge constructively in order to help clients recognise the part they play in the situation they face.

It is also vital that we have the capacity to develop, sometimes very quickly or in very adverse circumstances, the kind of constructive relationships which we have referred to above. The information social workers need from clients is often intensely personal, emotive, embarrassing and in psychodynamic terms, well defended. If people are to be able to share such information there needs to be a high degree of trust, sense of acceptance and belief that they are understood.

Coulshed and Orme (1998) remind us that it is essential that we take account of emotional factors as well as practical ones. This is true even in the apparently most straightforward assessments which seem to call for only material resources. Without attention to the emotional implications of factors such as deteriorating mobility, isolation or depression, assessment is unlikely to translate successfully into the next stage.

Planning and decision making

Issues of motivation and engaging the client in the process are of key importance here. Without these two elements the best of plans will never translate into successful outcomes and any initial progress will not be sustained. Sheppard sees the relationship as again crucial:

The central task of the practitioner is to establish a climate of trust and warmth…in which the consumer feels safe and is able to face up to the consequences of his or her actions or make difficult decisions about the future.

(Sheppard, 1995: p232)

High quality planning will enable the social worker to begin identifying appropriate goals with the client and selecting strategies to achieve these which mesh with the client's aspirations and values while addressing any risk issues. While the preferred intervention will be based on empowerment and client self-determination, agency objectives and priorities may impose limitations. There may also be conflicts resulting from differing aspirations and needs of clients, carers or families. The skill for the social worker is to negotiate the ensuing dilemmas to achieve the best available outcome for all concerned. The foundations of a constructive professional relationship and well developed empathic skills of negotiation, empowerment and facilitation undoubtedly increase the chances of this occurring.

Implementation

The skills required in the implementation phase depend on the nature and length of the contact. In some instances social work contacts are very long term. In others the involvement is brief and relatively functional. In either situation, especially when major life changes or traumas are involved, it is likely that social workers will at times either initiate or find themselves undertaking what appears to be a 'counselling' role of listening to distress or supporting someone striving to make personal sense of emotional conflicts (Cordon and Preston-Shoot, 1988). This chapter is suggesting that this does not involve straying from our role into 'becoming a counsellor' but is a privileged and necessary part of the social work task.

This is not to say that there are not times when social workers do assume a more formal counselling role. Some social workers, particularly in specialist provider settings such as therapeutic intervention with children or adult victims, or addiction agencies, clearly are providing a counselling intervention with their clients. Brown (1998) is of the opinion however that even in these units it is not 'pure'

counselling as by definition the work will be located in the context of a wider intervention such as child protection or family support.

Similarly, social workers in field teams may consciously seek training in specific counselling modalities for particular purposes. Motivational Interviewing (Miller and Rollnick, 1991) for instance may be of considerable value to any staff whose work involves facilitating behavioural change and there are counselling approaches corresponding to many of the social work theories and models explored in this volume. Much of the counselling literature addresses work with specific client groups or dilemmas. So for instance we can usefully consult books such as those by Trower, Casey, and Dryden (1988) for cognitive behavioural counselling, Drauker (1992) for counselling survivors of childhood sexual abuse or the many chapters in a major text such as that by Palmer, Dainow and Milner (1996) for a wide range of applications.

Evaluation and endings

Evaluation and endings are areas that do not receive as much attention as they deserve in many of the texts on either social work or counselling. It is probably true to say, however, that they are of critical importance for consolidating the work and enabling the client to move on either into the next phase of implementation or to 'go it alone'.

With the development of evidence-based practice in social work and other professions (Sheldon and Macdonald, 1999) evaluation is no longer viewed as an optional extra. Evaluation provides the opportunity to review what has occurred and to note the outcomes. It is a unique vehicle for powerful intervention in that it provides real evidence of the consequences, positive or disastrous, of what has been done and therefore offers fruitful ground for potent challenge, affirmation or learning.

All the above is also true of endings and a final evaluation needs to be part of the conclusion of the work. Endings also, however, need to take particular account of the emotional responses of both the client and the worker if they are to avoid negative reactions relating to feelings of loss or rejection. This is well summed up by Petruska Clarkson:

Every goodbye which is well done in the present can retrospectively help heal incomplete goodbyes of the past. In addition it is of educative value in that it can help clients learn how better to negotiate life's many natural and unnatural endings in the future.

(Clarkson, 1989: p134)

For the social worker endings need to be handled in ways that are empowering and facilitating with the long term objective, for the best of motives, of the client not coming back!

Conclusion

This chapter has attempted to argue that what are often referred to as 'counselling skills' are as much a part of our inheritance as that of our colleagues who define themselves as counsellors. In particular social workers need to establish constructive professional relationships with their clients, based on the core components first identified by 'casework', but refined to harmonise with the legal, political and administrative frameworks and restraints under which contemporary agencies function. Workers also need high levels of interpersonal skills, both communication skills and methods of intervention, many of which have been primarily explored and refined within the counselling profession.

Although we may often work with people in similar situations, social workers have different responsibilities and objectives to counsellors and there are real difficulties if we allow role confusion to creep in. It is important therefore for social workers to be clear that they are not able to offer 'counselling' in the purest technical sense to their clients, although there will be times when their social work practice will utilise very similar skills and methods, particularly when they are addressing the emotional components of their clients' situations.

Finally, it is my hope that by considering social work and counselling as Shakespeare's 'double cherry', that is, distinct professions linked by their common origins, we can avoid giving precedence to either but can acknowledge the differing responsibilities, objectives and expertise of each.

Counselling on the whole is probably better at claiming recognition of its knowledge base and skills. It also generally gains a better press, although ironically, many of the practitioners

involved in high profile instances of provision of 'counselling', such as in the wake of major disasters, will in fact be social workers.

Social work, on the other hand, has many detractors and generally appears to be less ready to assert its own expertise and excellence. This chapter does not intend to replicate this. It hopefully carries the message that far from needing to borrow from other professions, social work has its own long and impressive history of uniquely tailored, highly skilled interpersonal interventions which form a foundation for its complex and multi-faceted practice. It is these fundamental skills which enable the fulfilment of social work's specific roles and responsibilities with some of the most disadvantaged and difficult client groups.

References

Barber, J.C. (1991). *Beyond Casework*. London: Macmillan.

Biestek, F.P. (1957). *The Casework Relationship*. London: Unwin Hyman.

Brearley, J. (1995). *Counselling and Social Work*. Buckingham: Open University Press.

British Association for Counselling (1984). *Code of Ethics and Practice for Counsellors*. Rugby: BAC.

British Association for Counselling (1985). *Counselling: Definition of Terms in Use with Expansion and Rationale*. Rugby: BAC

Brown, H.C. (1998). Counselling. In Adams, R., Dominelli, L., and Payne, M. *Social Work: Themes, Issues and Critical Debates*. London: Macmillan.

Clarkson, P. (1989). *Gestalt Counselling in Action*. London: Sage.

Cordon, J., and Preston-Shoot, M. (1987). *Contracts in Social Work*. Aldershot: Gower.

Coulshed, V., and Orme, J. (1998). *Social Work Practice: An Introduction*. London: Macmillan.

d'Ardenne, P., and Mahtani, A. (1989). *Transcultural Counselling in Action*. London: Sage.

Davis, A. (1996). Risk Work and Mental Health. In Kemshall, H., and Pritchard, J. (Eds.). *Good Practice in Risk Assessment and Risk Management*. London: Jessica Kingsley.

Drauker, C.B. (1992). *Counselling Survivors of Childhood Sexual Abuse*. London: Sage.

Egan, G. (1994). *The Skilled Helper* (5th edn.). Pacific Grove, CA: Brooks/Cole.

Feltham, C., and Dryden, W. (1993). *Dictionary of Counselling*. London: Whurr.

Ferard, M., and Hunnybun, N.K. (1962). *The Caseworker's Use of Relationship*. London: Tavistock.

Halmos, P. (1965). *The Faith of the Counsellors*. London: Constable.

Hollis, F. (1964). *Casework: A Psychological Therapy.* New York: Random House.

Howe, D. (1993). *On Being a Client.* London: Sage.

Howe, D. (1998). Relationship-based Thinking and Practice in Social Work. *Journal of Social Work Practice*, Vol. 12(1): pp45–56.

Jacobs, M. (1982). *Still Small Voice: An Introduction to Pastoral Counselling.* London: SPCK.

Jacobs, M. (1988). *Psychodynamic Counselling in Action.* London: Sage.

Kadushin, A. (1990). *The Social Work Interview: A Guide for Human Service Professionals* (3rd edn.). New York: Columbia University Press.

Lishman, J. (1994). *Communication in Social Work.* London: Macmillan.

Macdonald, G., and Sheldon, B. (1997). Community Care Services for the Mentally Ill: Consumers' Views. *International Journal of Social Psychiatry*, Vol. 43(1): pp35–55.

McLeod, J. (1998). *An Introduction to Counselling* (2nd edn.). Buckingham: Open University Press.

Mearns, D., and Thorne, B. (1988). *Person-centred Counselling in Action.* London: Sage.

Miller, W., and Rollnick, S. (1991). *Motivational Interviewing: Preparing People to Change.* New York: Guilford Press.

Milner, J., and O'Byrne, P. (1998). *Assessment in Social Work.* London: Macmillan.

Nelson-Jones. R. (1993). *Practical Counselling and Helping Skills: How to Use the Lifeskills Helping Model* (3rd edn.). London: Cassell.

Palmer, S., Dainow, S., and Milner, P. (1996). *Counselling: The BAC Counselling Reader.* London: Sage.

Payne, M. (1991). *Modern Social Work Theory.* London: Macmillan.

Payne, M. (1995). *Social Work and Community Care.* London: Macmillan.

Perlman, H. (1957). *Social Casework: a Problem Solving Process.* University of Chicago Press; Cambridge University Press.

Pilling, S. (1991). *Rehabilitation and Community Care.* London: Routledge.

Raiff, N., and Shore, B. (1993). *Advanced Case Management: New Strategies for the Nineties.* London: Sage.

Rogers, K. (1980). *A Way of Being.* Boston: Houghton Mifflin.

Seden, J. (1999). *Counselling Skills in Social Work Practice.* Buckingham: Open University Press.

Sheldon, B. (1995). *Cognitive-behavioural Therapy: Research, Practice and Philosophy.* London: Routledge.

Sheldon, B., and Macdonald, G. (1999). *Research and Practice in Social Care: Mind the Gap.* CEBSS/Exeter University.

Sheppard, M. (1995). *Care Management and the New Social Work—A Critical Analysis.* London: Whiting and Birch.

Taylor, B.J., and Devine, T. (1993). *Assessing Needs and Planning Care in Social Work.* Aldershot: Arena.

Trower, P., Casey, A., and Dryden, W. (1988). *Cognitive-behavioural Counselling in Action.* London: Sage.

Valios, N. (2000). Vanishing Act. *Community Care*, March 15th: pp20–21.

Chapter Ten

Ecological Social Work: The Application of a Systems Model of Development in Context

Gordon Jack and Delia Jack

Introduction

Students undertaking qualifying training and practitioners studying for post-qualifying awards are frequently required to reflect upon the theories, models, and methods that inform their practice. A significant proportion of the assignments and portfolios submitted for assessment make references to 'systems theory' and 'systemic thinking'. Systems approaches appear to have wide appeal and utility for social workers trying to make sense of the complex array of individual, group, community, and organisational circumstances confronting them. This holds true for a wide range of practice settings and user groups.

It is somewhat surprising to find, therefore, that recent texts dealing with the theories and methods of social work often virtually ignore systems approaches to practice (Adams, 1996; Hill and Tisdale, 1997; Brandon et al., 1998; Adams, Dominelli and Payne, 1998). Those texts that do devote space to systems approaches tend to adopt a highly critical stance, usually centred on the undoubted shortcomings of one particular model, known as the 'unitary approach' (Jordan, 1977). This model was developed during the 1970s in the United States (Goldstein, 1973; Pincus and Minahan, 1973). It crossed the Atlantic at the same time that Social Services Departments came into existence in England and Wales, and it was presented as a general theory of social work that could unify the profession, enabling different methods of practice to be integrated within one overarching framework (Payne, C., 1994). However, the 'unitary approach' was couched in technical language and often led to rather impersonal and bureaucratic practice. It also failed to incorporate a sufficient analysis of the political and structural causes of personal distress, placing an emphasis, instead, on individual adaptation to the existing social order (Payne, M., 1997; Payne, C., 1994).

Unfortunately there has been insufficient differentiation between systems theory in general, and the 'unitary approach', as one flawed model, which has led some writers to virtually consign the whole systems perspective to a historical footnote in the development of social work practice. (e.g. Adams, 1996; Lorenz, 1994; Payne, M., 1997). The only consistently cited positive references to the application of systems theory in contemporary practice tend to be restricted to family therapy (e.g. Burnham, 1986; Gorrell Barnes, 1998), although this method of practice is itself subject to highly critical debates in the field of social work (Seligman, 1994). In particular, feminist critiques of family therapy have condemned this approach for a preoccupation with nuclear families, ignoring wider social support networks, and a failure to address the discrimination that women experience within nuclear families (Coulshed, 1991). There has also been a fairly widespread adoption of systems thinking in the responses that have developed in relation to the management of young offenders and child protection (Cavadino and Dignan, 1992; Department of Health, 1995). However, these 'systems management' approaches to social work can be criticised on the same grounds as the 'unitary approach', in that they fail to address issues of structural inequalities within society, focusing instead on how best to process the casualties of those inequalities.

This chapter presents a different application of systems theory that has wide contemporary relevance to social work practice and avoids many of the shortcomings of other applications of systems theory outlined above. In particular, the ecological approach that will be outlined incorporates appropriate analysis of the structural causes of disadvantage and includes full consideration of the wider social support networks that exist beyond the nuclear family. Furthermore, it points the way to forms of practice that are empowering for individuals, groups and communities, seeking to maximise informal sources of help with the active support of statutory and voluntary welfare agencies. Although the particular examples of the model provided here are taken from social work with children and families, the approach has equal utility for a wide range of practice with different user groups.

An outline of the ecological model

As a result of growing public awareness about the environmental impact of various forms of human activity, most people are now familiar with the general principles of ecology. Within this framework, the planet is understood to consist of a number of systems and sub-systems, involving plants, animals, people and their physical surroundings. These different systems are involved in constant processes of mutual interaction with one another. A delicate ecological balance has evolved, in which changes in one system can have significant consequences for another system, and vice-versa. The development of all living things is therefore inextricably bound up with the characteristics of the environments that they inhabit (Dent-Read and Zukow-Golding, 1997).

There are a variety of different mechanisms of interaction that can occur between different systems. Sometimes the interaction is *cumulative*, with different factors acting together to reinforce one another. For example, research consistently demonstrates the way in which single environmental risk factors often have minimal impact on human development but combinations of risk factors can multiply the potential harm dramatically (Rutter, 1979; Garmezy, 1994). Other interactions demonstrate *moderating* or *mediating* mechanisms, in which the effect of factor A on factor C depends upon the characteristics of an intermediate factor B. For example, the existence of a supportive relationship with a spouse has been shown to moderate the negative influence of parents' own adverse family backgrounds on their ability to provide nurturant parenting themselves (Quinton et al., 1984; see Luster and Okagaki, 1993, for other mechanisms).

The ecological model is a holistic, dynamic-interactional systems approach, based on human ecology (Bronfenbrenner, 1979; Jack, 1997). It can be visualised as a nested arrangement of interacting systems, rather like a set of Russian dolls, with the individual located at the centre (Bronfenbrenner, 1979; see Figure 1).

Briefly, the immediate settings in which individuals develop are called *micro-systems*. Interactions between these settings constitute

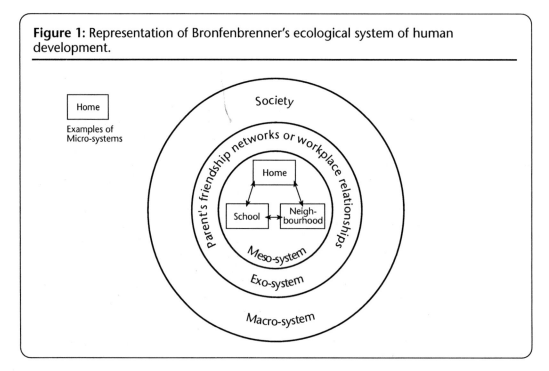

Figure 1: Representation of Bronfenbrenner's ecological system of human development.

what is known as the *meso-system*. Moving further outwards, settings that influence an individual's development, but in which they are not directly involved, are called *exo-systems*, and the final level of influence, which consists of the cultural and societal environments in which all other systems are embedded, is known as the *macro-system* (Bronfenbrenner, 1979; Garbarino, 1990).

Within this model, a developing child can be seen to be part of a number of micro-systems, starting with their immediate family and going on to include extended family networks, school, and neighbourhood settings. As an adult, further micro-systems are added, which might include the workplace and various social, cultural or political groupings. All of these micro-systems can play a significant role in shaping the health, well-being and development of the individuals involved. The child's relationships with their parents and siblings, and the parents' relationship with one another will have lasting effects, throughout the rest of the child's lifetime, helping to influence the environments they will inhabit, and the way that they are likely to behave within those environments.

The interactions between micro-systems make up what is called the meso-system. The social worker applying the ecological approach to their practice will therefore not only be interested in the nature and quality of relationships within different micro-systems, but also in the interconnections between them: for example, the nature of the connections between a young person's peer-group and their family and whether or not the parents of a child are in touch with teachers at the child's school. Or, for adults, whether or not their extended family and their neighbourhood circle of friends, have any contact with one another. This might become a significant element in the assessment of, for instance, a frail, elderly person, living on their own.

Many of a parent's micro-systems, such as their friendship networks and workplace settings, will also constitute a child's exo-systems. For example, aspects of a parent's workplace, including their levels of pay, conditions of employment and hours of work will all have an influence on the child's development, even though the child is not directly participating in that system. However, other exo-systems influencing the child are likely to be independent of their parents, such as their school's board of governors or the management committees of local youth and leisure services.

The final element of the ecological model are the macro-systems, in which all else is embedded. These are the cultural, political, legal and religious contexts of the society in which children and adults are developing. Here, the social worker will be interested in a society's attitudes towards, for example, its older people, the roles it promotes for men and women, the extent of any inequalities of income, the existence of discrimination against certain minority groups and the nature of the relationship between the state and the family. These, and many other factors, will have profound effects on different groups, depending on such factors as age, class, race, disability and religion. To give just one example, societies like Britain that sanction the physical punishment of children by their parents, tend to have higher levels of physical abuse of children than countries like Sweden and Japan, where such punishment is either legally or morally prohibited.

At first sight, the terminology used in describing the ecological model, which has been adapted from the biological sciences, can be rather off-putting to social workers. However, the model conveys some important messages for contemporary practice. The ecological model makes it clear that individuals and their environments can never be understood separately from one another. Although human development is often presented in terms of the separate contributions of nature and nurture, the ecological approach makes it clear that human development is best understood as the product of an indivisible mix of nature *and* nurture (Garbarino, 1990). The social worker adopting this approach will be interested in the interactions that occur between factors at different ecological levels of influence, and the way that these factors shape both the behaviour of individuals and the environments that they inhabit.

Within the ecological model, social workers will also want to place a strong emphasis on a phenomenological approach, in which an individual's own perceptions of their circumstances will be a central feature of the assessment and will inform any further action that may be required. This is where the social worker's capacity for accurate communication and empathy have to be allied to a broader appreciation of the way that environments impact on different individuals and groups. The social worker can make an important contribution to a developing understanding of the balances that exist between stressful and supportive elements at individual, group and community levels, any or all of which may be identified as targets for action. Social work also has an important role to play in developing, maintaining or strengthening supportive systems and reducing, challenging or replacing stressful systems. In particular, social workers are likely to find themselves trying to influence the *social support networks* available to individuals and groups and the *social capital* available within communities. These topics are the subject of the next section.

The importance of social support and social capital

The main components of social support can be grouped together under three general headings—emotional support, practical help and information/advice (Cutrona and Russell, 1990). Research has consistently demonstrated the influence that social support can have upon personal development and behaviour (Dunst *et al.*, 1988). The availability of social support is associated with a whole range of both psychological and physical health benefits (Gottlieb, 1981; Wills, 1985; Cohen and Syme, 1985). Conversely, social isolation is repeatedly found to be associated with poorer personal health and family functioning (Blaxter, 1990; Coohey, 1996). Social support that is both desired and actually provided has beneficial effects for all recipients. However, even the perception that social support will be available, if it is needed, can have significant benefits, particularly for those living in disadvantaged circumstances (Hashima and Amato, 1994).

The structure of different social support networks varies according to the total number of members included, their relationships to one another (e.g. relatives, friends, neighbours) and their geographical spread. Relationships within networks can be more or less supportive, and they also vary according to such things as frequency of contact, reliability, and the nature

and extent of the help that they can provide (Jack, 1997). To a large degree, social networks also tend to reflect people's general position in the social structure of the society in which they live (Cochran, 1993). Adults with higher levels of income and education tend to have larger social networks, providing more supportive relationships with members spread over a wider geographical area. By contrast, those at the lower end of the socio-economic scale, and members of minority ethnic groups, tend to have access to more restricted social networks, being more reliant on local relatives and having fewer friends in their networks (Fischer, 1982; Cross, 1990; Werner, 1995). Networks also vary according to such factors as gender, social class, marital status, and culture. For example, women generally have more stable and confiding relationships than men (Leavy, 1983) and middle-class married mothers report larger networks than both their working class counterparts and single mothers (Bell and Ribbens, 1994).

This brief description of variations in social support networks provides a perfect illustration of the importance of adopting an ecological approach to social work. Whilst some of the variation in the social support available to different individuals (and the use that they make of that support) can be attributed to personal characteristics (Crittenden, 1985; Polansky *et al.*, 1985; Seagull, 1987), socio-economic and other community level or societal influences are also crucially important. This is illustrated when we go on to consider social capital, which includes the relationships and exchanges between all members of a neighbourhood or a society. The level of social capital in a community has a significant impact on individual health and behaviour (Garbarino and Kostelny, 1992; Kawachi *et al.*, 1997). However, as with personal social networks, relative disadvantage and discrimination seriously undermine social capital, leaving those potentially in the greatest need of the protection it can provide, least likely to benefit from it (Jack and Jordan, 1999). This is well illustrated in a study carried out in Chicago into variations in violent crime rates between over three hundred neighbourhoods. The researchers found that 'collective efficacy', which is a measure of social capital (incorporating mutual trust and informal social control in the community), was seriously undermined by levels of poverty, unemployment and residential stability. Neighbourhoods with the highest collective efficacy scores had rates of violent crime 40 per cent lower than those with the lowest scores (Sampson *et al.*, 1997). This is where the community development skills of social workers utilising the ecological approach are called upon. With an awareness of the interactions between social capital, socio-economic disadvantage and personal development and behaviour, the social worker can play an important role, along with other welfare professionals and voluntary organisations and groups, in assisting disadvantaged communities to enhance the social capital of their environments.

Having provided a general introduction to the ecological model, the final two sections of this chapter will go on to look at the application of this approach to different areas of practice with children and families. The first illustration contrasts an ecological approach with the more well-known systems management response to young offenders. This is followed by a more detailed consideration of the way in which the ecological model can be used with children with disabilities and their families.

Contrasting systems management and ecological approaches to young offenders

The English criminal justice system is composed of a number of separate agencies with very different perspectives and responsibilities, including the police, the criminal courts, and probation and social services. However, these different agencies are, in many respects, mutually dependent upon one another in the processes of decision making about young offenders (Cavadino and Dignan, 1992). A *systems management* approach to young offenders, initiated by a group of academics at Lancaster University, was developed during the 1980s (Thorpe *et al.*, 1980) and continues into the present day. It involves an attempt by social workers to influence decision making by others, with the aim of diverting young offenders away from prosecution and custody. It is based on labelling theory (Becker, 1974) which highlights the tendency of official interventions to

confirm young people in 'delinquent' identities, so reinforcing (rather than reducing) their chances of re-offending. A strategy of minimal welfare intervention is also promoted, because of the increased risk of custody which follows repeat offending, when welfare measures are deemed to have 'failed' (Smith, 1998; Haines and Drakeford, 1998).

On the surface, this approach might appear to be very successful. During the 1980s, for example, custodial sentences for juveniles fell by 80 per cent (from 7,500 to 1,500), the use of care orders as a response to offending behaviour almost disappeared, and the total number of juvenile prosecutions dropped by almost two-thirds (NACRO, 1992). However, on closer examination, these changes cannot simply be attributed to systems management. A 25 per cent fall in the overall juvenile population during the same period is probably more significant and a fall in police detection rates must also be added to the equation. In fact, offending rates, per head of the juvenile population, probably rose during the 1980s, by as much as 50 per cent (Utting *et al.*, 1993). Self-report surveys also consistently reveal that the vast majority of crimes committed are never even reported to the police and only about 3 per cent of all offences committed result in any official action by the criminal justice system (Audit Commission, 1996). Clearly, the systems management approach, on its own, has a number of serious shortcomings as a response to juvenile offending. It does nothing to address the causes of offending, or the contexts within which most offending arises, and uses a lot of public money in processing the small minority of young offenders who are brought to official attention.

This brings us to a consideration of the ways in which the ecological model might help to provide a more effective, preventive approach. Research has consistently demonstrated that a range of factors, at individual, family and community levels, are implicated in offending by juveniles. The most important factors identified include:

(a) Child Factors

- peer relationships with other offenders
- school problems, including behaviour, attainment, truancy and exclusion
- unemployment
- abuse of alcohol and drugs

(b) Family Factors

- parental conflict
- poor parental supervision
- inconsistent or harsh parental discipline
- parental history of criminality
- poor parent-child attachments

(c) Community Factors

- economic disadvantage
- lack of social cohesion

(Utting et al., 1993; Home Office, 1995;
Audit Commission, 1996; Sampson et al., 1997;
Rutter et al., 1998)

Any serious attempt to prevent, or significantly reduce, juvenile crime will need to address *all* of these factors *and* the interactions between them. It is also helpful to consider the *resilience* of some young people, who manage to stay clear of persistent or serious offending despite sharing many of the risk factors identified above. Again, research studies have consistently identified a number of characteristics of resilience, including:

(a) Child Factors

- higher IQ
- avoidance of delinquent peers
- supportive relationship with an adult outside of the family

(b) Family Factors

- parental involvement in child's schooling
- close parental supervision of child's activities/friendships

(c) Community Factors

- 'urban sanctuaries', providing positive out-of-school activities
- 'social efficacy', providing informal social controls on young people's behaviour in the community

(Kolvin et al., 1988;
Sampson and Groves, 1989; McLaughlin et al., 1994;
Rutter et al., 1998).

It is this analysis of the balance between risk factors and protective factors which is one of the distinctive features of the ecological approach.

Social workers applying this model will assess the range of factors that either support or undermine personal health and development, aiming to maintain and enhance features associated with resilience and change or challenge known risk factors, at individual, family, and community levels. This approach is likely to gain greater influence in social work now that it has been incorporated as one of the fundamental principles underpinning the Department of Health's guidance for the assessment of children in need and their families (Department of Health, 2000a; Jack, 2000). The final section considers the way in which this approach can be utilised in work with children with disabilities and their families.

Children with disabilities and their families

There are some 360,000 children under sixteen years of age with disabilities in England and Wales, representing 32 per 1,000 of that population (Department of Health, 2000b). Multiple disability is common, with disabled children, on average, having between two and three different conditions, often including behaviour problems. The overwhelming majority of children with disabilities (over 90 per cent) live at home with their parents (Social Services Inspectorate, 1998; Joseph Rowntree Foundation, 1999).

The families of children with disabilities tend to experience a number of socio-economic disadvantages. They have significantly lower financial resources on average, than similar families with non-disabled children. This is due to the extra costs of bringing up a child with a disability (three times greater, on average, than the cost of bringing up a non-disabled child), as well as restrictions on parents' employment opportunities and earning potential, and benefit levels which fall well short of meeting even the minimum essential costs involved (Social Services Inspectorate, 1998; Joseph Rowntree Foundation, 1999). Black and minority ethnic families of children with disabilities are particularly likely to experience economic disadvantage, due to higher than average levels of unemployment and lower take-up of welfare benefits (Kumar, 1993; Caesar *et al.*, 1993; Shah, 1995; Smaje, 1995).

Economic inequalities of this kind have consistently been shown to increase the levels of stress experienced by parents in general, and those with children with disabilities in particular (Quine and Pahl, 1991; Sloper *et al.*, 1991; Sloper and Turner, 1993). This means that social work with disabled children and their families should be built on an understanding of both the economic pressures likely to be present and the way in which such pressures tend to undermine parental well-being and family functioning (Blackburn, 1991; Bywaters and McLeod, 1996; Beresford *et al.*, 1996).

Parents of children with disabilities are also faced with extra caring and emotional demands. The most widely available service designed to support parents with pre-school children with disabilities in their own homes is Portage. This is a home-visiting programme in which trained staff work with parents to set educational and developmental goals for their children and to devise step-by-step methods of achieving the goals set. Evaluations of this approach indicate that it is valued by parents (Beresford, 1994) and produces short-term gains for children. However, longer term gains are harder to identify (Cunningham, 1986; Sloper *et al.*, 1986), in line with evaluations of other early intervention programmes for a range of children and families (Kirkham, 1993; Crnic and Stormshak, 1997). Although such findings are disappointing, they are all that can be expected in the absence of both ongoing support services and effective strategies for tackling the other disadvantages faced by children with disabilities and their families in their wider community and societal contexts. One of the most imaginative schemes for providing the necessary ongoing support involves allocating a set number of hours of a support worker's time for the family to use flexibly throughout the year, as and when they require it. The support worker can assist in the home, with domiciliary tasks and child care, as well as providing emotional support and help with trips out of the home (Morris, 1998). This sort of service can be a very useful supplement to the social support that is available to families with a disabled child through their own networks and communities.

Unfortunately, research clearly indicates that families of children with disabilities tend to have access to more restricted sources of support than similar families with non-disabled children (Baldwin and Carlisle, 1994; Beresford, 1995; Lawton, 1997). This is

especially true for black and minority ethnic families, who are more likely to have unmet needs and less likely to have support from their extended families than similar white families (Joseph Rowntree Foundation, 1999). These difficulties are often compounded by the barriers that can exist in accessing integrated mainstream services, such as child care, education and leisure facilities. These barriers tend to reduce opportunities for natural breaks from caring and increase the potential for social exclusion. For example, a study of young people with learning disabilities found that most of them led rather quiet, solitary lives, involving limited personal relationships within largely segregated special schools and placements (Flynn and Hirst, 1992). Even the specialist, segregated provision directed at children with disabilities and their families may not reach them. For example, the most common service offered by social services is respite care, but the majority of families with a disabled child still do not use this service, either due to lack of information, or lack of suitability to meet their needs. Often older children, or those with more severe disabilities or behaviour problems, are not catered for at all, and there may also be a shortage of culturally appropriate carers (Singh, 1992; Trivette *et al.*, 1997: Joseph Rowntree Foundation, 1999; DoH/Council for Disabled Children, 1999).

An ecological approach can help to highlight issues relating to social support, social capital and socio-economic disadvantage that are important for the social worker to incorporate into their everyday practice. Children with disabilities and their parents need access to information and advice about local services, parenting support and financial issues. They are also likely to need a range of practical assistance, including help with child care, breaks from caring responsibilities and domiciliary services. In addition, there are also a wide range of issues that may need attention within the wider community and society contexts that they inhabit. These include access to improved transport, employment opportunities and material resources and better co-ordinated, and preferably inclusive, recreational, health, education and social services (Audit Commission, 1994; Tozer, 1996; Beresford *et al.*, 1996; Trivette *et al.*, 1997). The ecological approach therefore requires that social workers use their organisational positions to influence policies, procedures, and the allocation of resources, in ways that help to challenge social exclusion and discrimination against children with disabilities and their families, as well as other disadvantaged groups.

A number of environmental changes can be achieved by *community-building* strategies, that aim to enhance or extend the capacity of local people and neighbourhood organisations to provide supportive responses to children and their families (Kretzmann and McKnight, 1993; Coulton, 1996; Weil, 1996; Jack and Jordan, 1999). This is the approach promoted by social workers and other agencies operating in one area of Devon, from which the following examples have been taken.

The first example illustrates the importance of the *way* in which respite services are arranged. It concerns a seven-year-old boy with autism, moderate learning difficulties and behaviour problems, who is the oldest of five children in the family. His parents were very reluctant to use traditionally-arranged respite care services. However, the organiser of the local parent support group knew of a couple interested in befriending a child with special needs. The social worker involved encouraged the parents to allow their son to meet this couple at the local Saturday club that he attends along with other children with special needs. A successful relationship was established, and the boy went on to visit their home, where he enjoyed the peace and quiet and the individual attention he received. This contrasted with his own family circumstances, which he often found very difficult to cope with. The rest of his family enjoyed these breaks from caring and the arrangement eventually developed into a pattern of overnight stays. This focus on the importance of the way in which services are arranged is reinforced by an American study of respite care. Traditionally arranged care, with the family making a request to a project worker, who identifies a suitable provider and schedules a service, was found to be much less successful than what was termed a 'resource-based' approach. In this latter model, the project worker collaborates with the parents to identify and extend existing child care networks in the local area (babysitters, playgroups, child-minders and family centres).

Evaluation over a twelve-month period showed that parents involved in the resource-based approach had increased both the number of carers in their social networks and the frequency of provision of care. They also increased their level of perceived control over the arrangements and showed higher levels of overall satisfaction with the care provided than the service-based recipients of respite care (Trivette *et al.*, 1997).

The next three examples illustrate the way in which the provision of *one-to-one support, by local people*, can facilitate the participation of children with disabilities in mainstream activities. The first example concerns a young person, aged sixteen, with Down's syndrome, autism and severe learning difficulties, who also has two siblings with disabilities. He attends a special school and has no verbal communication, so greatly restricting his opportunities to interact with people in his local community. However, as he particularly enjoys swimming, it was arranged for a local volunteer befriender to provide one-to-one assistance, to enable him to attend the swimming baths in his home town once a week, so reducing his social exclusion. The other two examples concern the difficulties that can be faced by children with disabilities living in small rural villages. The first concerns a girl, aged six, with Down's syndrome, living in a village ten miles from the nearest town. She attends the village school, with the help of a classroom assistant provided by the local education authority but she couldn't attend the local summer playscheme. The solution involved social services arranging to pay her existing classroom assistant to support her in attending what then became an 'integrated' playscheme, providing for both disabled and non-disabled children together. After the first year of this arrangement, the playscheme were keen to assume more direct responsibility for this girl and obtained their own grant funding to pay the carer. The second rural example involves a boy of ten, also with Down's syndrome, attending his local school with a one-to-one classroom assistant. He wanted to join the local cub pack, along with his school friends. However, although the cub leader was happy to include him, his parents were reluctant to allow this without extra support. On this occasion, the social worker involved was able to arrange funding for a local domiciliary care worker, who had previously only ever worked with elderly people, to provide the support the boy's parents wanted. The arrangement not only extended the boy's own contacts with his school friends but also provided an opportunity for him to develop some degree of independence from his parents and to enhance his self-esteem.

The final example illustrates the *extension of integrated provision*. It focuses on a project for young people, aged 13–25 years, called the GTI group (Getting Teenagers Involved), which was established in a seaside town that had a number of young people with disabilities attending special schools outside of the area. Few of these children met their friends out of school or college and virtually none of them had contact with their peers in the local community. The local community college had an existing youth programme for its own students. With the involvement of parents, the local social services, youth services, and the college, an additional *integrated* youth club was established. Leadership is now provided by paid staff, but the majority of the extra support needed by the children with disabilities who attend the club is provided by young people from the community college. Some of these young people are working towards their Duke of Edinburgh award but many of them provide any assistance required as a normal part of their attendance at the group. The group now has plans to run a befriending scheme, which will build on the relationships established at the weekly youth club, enabling the young people with disabilities to extend their engagement with the local community.

Conclusions

In the examples cited above, the role of the social worker using an ecological approach was often crucial in extending the capacity of local people and local organisations to meet the needs of children with disabilities and their families in ways which increased their social networks and reduced their social exclusion. On their own, these examples do not provide all of the answers to the problems faced by many children with disabilities and their families, or any other disadvantaged groups or individuals. However, the ecological model

does help to emphasise the attention that needs to be paid to a wide range of factors at individual, family, community, and societal levels, often simultaneously. The social worker adopting this approach will also be alerted to the interactions between various factors which serve to reinforce one another on some occasions while, on other occasions, revealing important protective factors or aspects of resilience, that can be nurtured. By helping individuals to increase or strengthen their networks of both informal and formal support, social workers are also contributing towards the development of social capital, helping to strengthen communities in ways that will have positive benefits for all their residents. This reduces the need to provide direct, professionally organised support and segregated services, both of which can undermine effective informal sources of support and increase stigma and social exclusion.

The ecological model presented here, unlike other applications of systems theory, incorporates an anti-discriminatory perspective that can help to identify the structural causes of oppression and point up appropriate strategies for action to address these issues (Payne, C., 1994). It also embraces the wider social networks of relationships, beyond the nuclear family, that are often crucial in supporting oppressed individuals and groups, and it leads to social work practice that is essentially empowering and personal. This is in stark contrast to the systems management and care management approaches that have dominated social work practice in the UK over the past two decades.

References

Adams, R. (1996). *The Personal Social Services: Clients, Consumers or Citizens?* Harlow: Longman.

Adams, R., Dominelli, L., and Payne, M. (1998). *Social Work: Themes, Issues and Critical Debates.* Basingstoke: Macmillan.

Audit Commission (1994). *Seen But Not Heard: Co-ordinating Community Child Health and Social Services for Children in Need.* London: HMSO.

Audit Commission (1996). *Misspent Youth: Young People and Crime.* London: HMSO.

Baldwin, S., and Carlisle, J. (1994). *Social Support for Disabled Children and their Families: A Review of the Literature.* Edinburgh: HMSO.

Becker, H.S. (1974). Labelling Theory Reconsidered. In Rock, P., and McIntosh, M. (Eds.). *Deviance and Social Control*. London: Tavistock.

Bell, L., and Ribbens, J. (1994). Isolated Housewives and Complex Maternal Worlds: The Significance of Social Contacts Between Women with Young Children in Industrial Societies. *Sociological Review*, 42(2): pp227–262.

Beresford, B. (1994). *Positively Parents: Caring for a Disabled Child*. London: HMSO.

Beresford, B. (1995). *Expert Opinions: A Survey of Parents Caring for a Severely Disabled Child*. Bristol: The Policy Press.

Beresford, B., Sloper, P., Baldwin, S., and Newman, T. (1996). *What Works in Services for Families with a Disabled Child?* Barkingside: Barnardo's.

Blackburn, C. (1991). *Poverty and Health: Working with Families*. Buckingham: Open University Press.

Blaxter, M. (1990). *Health and Lifestyles*. London; Routledge.

Brandon, M., Schofield, G., and Trinder, L. (1998). *Social Work with Children*. Basingstoke: Macmillan.

Bronfenbrenner, U. (1979). *The Ecology of Human Development*. Cambridge, MA: Harvard University Press.

Burnham, J. (1986). *Family Therapy: First Steps Towards a Systemic Approach*. London: Routledge.

Bywaters, P., and McLeod, E. (Eds.) (1996). *Working for Equality in Health*. London: Routledge.

Caesar, G., Parchment, M., and Berridge, D. (1993). *Black Perspectives on Services for Children and Young People in Need and their Families*. London: NCB/Barnardo's.

Cavadino, M., and Dignan, J. (1992). *The Penal System: An Introduction*. London: Sage.

Cochran, M. (1993). Parenting and Personal Social Networks. In Luster, T., and Okagaki, L. (Eds.). *Parenting: An Ecological Perspective*. Hillsdale, NJ: Lawrence Erlbaum Associates.

Cohen, S., and Syme, S.L. (1985). Issues in the Study and Application of Social Support. In Cohen, S., and Syme, S.L. (Eds.). *Social Support and Health*. Orlando, FL: Academic Press.

Coohey, C. (1996). Child Maltreatment: Testing the Social Isolation Hypothesis. *Child Abuse and Neglect*, 20(3): pp241–254.

Coulshed, V. (1991). *Social Work Practice: An Introduction*. Basingstoke: Macmillan.

Coulton, C.J. (1996). Poverty, Work and Community: A Research Agenda for an Era of Diminishing Federal Responsibility. *Social Work*, 41(5): pp509–520.

Crittenden, P.M. (1985). Social Networks, Quality of Child Rearing and Child Development. *Child Development*, 56: pp1299–1313.

Crnic, K.A., and Stormshak, E. (1997). The Effectiveness of Providing Social Support for Families of Children at Risk. In Guralnick, M.J. (Ed.). *The Effectiveness of Early Intervention*. Baltimore: Paul. H. Brookes.

Cross, W. (1990). Race and Ethnicity: Effects on Social Networks. In Cochran, M., Larner, M., Riley, D., Gunnarson, L., and Henderson, C. Jr (Eds.). *Extending Families: The Social Networks of Parents and their Children*. London: Cambridge University Press.

Cunningham, C. (1986). Early Intervention: Some Findings from the Manchester Cohort of Children with Down's Syndrome. In Bishop, M., Copley, M., and Porter, J. (Eds.). *Portage: More Than a Teaching Programme?* Windsor: NFER-Nelson.

Cutrona, C.E., and Russell, D.W. (1990). Type of Social Support and Specific Stress: Towards a Theory of Optimal Matching. In Sarason, B.R., Pierce G.R., and Sarason, I.G. (Eds.). *Social Support: An Interactional View*. New York: Wiley.

Dent-Read, C., and Zukow-Golding, P. (1997). Introduction: Ecological Realism, Dynamic Systems, and Epigenetic Systems Approaches to Development. In Dent-Read, C., and Zukow-Golding, P. (Eds.). *Evolving Explanations of Development: Ecological Approaches to Organism-environment Systems*. Washington, DC: American Psychological Association.

Department of Health (1995). *Child Protection: Messages from Research*. London: HMSO.

Department of Health (2000a). *Framework for the Assessment of Children in Need and their Families*. London: The Stationery Office.

Department of Health (2000b). *Children Act Report 1995–1999*. London: the Stationery Office.

Department of Health/Council for Disabled Children (1999). *Quality Protects: First Analysis of Management Action Plans with Reference to Disabled Children and Families*. London: Department of Health.

Dunst, C., Trivette, C., and Deal, A. (1988). *Enabling and Empowering Families: Principles and Guidelines for Practice*. Cambridge, MA: Brookline Books.

Fischer, C. (1982). *To Dwell Among Friends: Personal Networks in Town and City*. Chicago: Chicago University Press.

Flynn, M., and Hirst, M. (1992). *This Year, Next Year, Sometime…? Learning Disability and Adulthood*. London: National Development Team.

Garbarino, J. (1990). The Human Ecology of Early Risk. In Meisels, S.J., and Shankoff, J.P. (Eds.). *Handbook of Early Childhood Intervention*. New York: Cambridge University Press.

Garbarino, J., and Kostelny, K. (1992). Child Maltreatment as a Community Problem. *Child Abuse and Neglect*, 16: pp455–464.

Garmezy, N. (1994). Reflections and Commentary on Risk, Resilience and Development. In Haggerty, R.J., Sherrod, L.R. Garmezy, N., and Rutter, M. (Eds.). *Stress, Risk and Resilience in Children and Adolescents*. Cambridge: Cambridge University Press.

Goldstein, H. (1973). *Social Work Practice: A Unitary Approach*. Columbia: University of South Carolina Press.

Gorrell Barnes, G. (1998). *Family Therapy in Changing Times*. Basingstoke: Macmillan.

Gottlieb, B.H. (1981). Social Networks and Social Support in Community Mental Health. In Gottlieb, B.H. (Ed.). *Social Networks and Social Support*. Beverley Hills, CA: Sage.

Haines, K., and Drakeford, M. (1998). *Young People and Youth Justice*. Basingstoke: Macmillan.

Hashima, P.Y., and Amato, P.R. (1994). Poverty, Social Support and Parental Behaviour. *Child Development*, 65: pp394–403.

Hill, M., and Tisdale, K. (1997). *Children and Society*. Harlow: Longman.

Home Office (1995). *Young People and Crime*. London: HMSO.

Jack, G. (1997). An Ecological Approach to Social Work with Children and Families. *Child and Family Social Work*, 2: pp109–120.

Jack, G. (2000). Ecological Perspectives in Assessing Children and Families. In *Department of Health the Child's World: The Reader*. London: The Stationery Office.

Jack, G., and Jordan, B. (1999). Social Capital and Child Welfare. *Children and Society*, 13: pp242–256.

Jordan, B. (1977). Against the Unitary Approach to Social Work. *New Society*, June.

Joseph Rowntree Foundation (1999). *Supporting Disabled Children and their Families*. York: JRF.

Kawachi, I., Kennedy, B.P., Lochner, K., and Prothrow-Stith, D. (1997). Social Capital, Income Inequality and Mortality. *American Journal of Public Health*, 87: pp1491–1498.

Kirkham, M. (1993). Two Year Follow-up of Skills Training with Mothers of Children with Disabilities. *American Journal of Mental Retardation*, 97: pp509–520.

Kolvin, I., Miller, F.J.W., Fleeting, M., and Kolvin, P.A. (1988). Risk/Protective Factors for Offending with Particular Reference to Deprivation. In Rutter, M. (Ed.). *Studies of Psychosocial Risk: The Power of Longitudinal Data*. Cambridge: Cambridge University Press.

Kretzmann, J., and McKnight, J. (1993). *Building Community from the Inside Out*. Evanston, Il: North-Western University Center for Urban Affairs and Policy Research.

Kumar, V. (1993). *Poverty and Inequality in the UK: The Effects on Children*. London: National Children's Bureau.

Lawton, D. (1997). *Family Fund Trust's Statistical Analysis to 31.3.97*. York: Family Fund Trust.

Leavy, R.L. (1983). Social Support and Psychological Disorder: A Review. *Journal of Community Psychology*, 11: pp3–21.

Lorenz, W. (1994). *Social Work in a Changing Europe*. London: Routledge.

Luster, T., and Okagaki, L. (1993). Multiple Influences on Parenting: Ecological and Life-course Perspectives. In Luster, T., and Okagaki, L. (Eds.). *Parenting: An Ecological Perspective*. Hillsdale, NJ: Lawrence Erlbaum Associates.

McLaughlin, M.W., Irby, M.A., and Langman, J. (1994). *Urban Sanctuaries: Neighbourhood Organisations in the Lives and Futures of Inner-city Youth*. San Francisco: Jossey-Bass.

Morris, J. (1998). *Still Missing? Vol. 2: Disabled Children and the Children Act*. London: The Who Cares? Trust.

NACRO (1992). *Criminal Justice Act 1991: Young People and the Youth Court*. London; NACRO.

Payne, C. (1994). the Systems Approach. In Hanvey, C., and Philpot, T. (Eds.). *Practising Social Work*. London: Routledge.

Payne, M. (1997). *Modern Social Work Theory* (2nd edn.). Basingstoke: Macmillan.

Pincus, A., and Minahan, A. (1973). *Social Work Practice: Model and Method*. Itasca, IL: F.E. Peacock Publishers Inc.

Platt, L., and Noble, M. (1999). *Race, Place and Poverty: Ethnic Groups and Low Income Distributions*. York: Joseph Rowntree Foundation (Findings, February).

Polansky, N.A., Gaudin, J.M., Ammons, P.W., and David, K.B. (1985). The Psychological Ecology of the Neglectful Mother. *Child Abuse and Neglect*, 9: pp265–275.

Quine, L., and Pahl, J. (1991). Stress and Coping in Mother's Caring for a Child with Severe Learning Difficulties: A Test of Lazarus' Transaction Model of Coping. *Journal of Community and Applied Social Psychology*, 1: pp57–70.

Quinton, D., Rutter, M., and Liddle, C. (1984). Institutional Rearing, Parenting Difficulties and Marital Support. *Psychological Medicine*, 14: pp107–124.

Rutter, M. (1979). Protective Factors in Children's Responses to Stress and Disadvantage. In Kent, M.W., and Rolf, J.E. (Eds.). *Primary Prevention of Psychopathology* (Vol. 3). Hanover, NH: University Press of New England.

Rutter, M., Giller, H., and Hagell, A. (1998). *Antisocial Behaviour by Young People*. Cambridge: Cambridge University Press.

Sampson, R.J., and Groves, W.B. (1989). Community Structure and Crime: Testing Social Disorganisation Theory. *American Journal of Sociology*, 94: pp774–802.

Sampson, R.J., Raudenbush, S.W., and Earls, F. (1997). Neighborhoods and Violent Crime: A Multi-level Study of Collective Efficacy. *Science*, 277: pp1–7.

Seagull, E.A.W. (1987). Social Support and Child Maltreatment: A Review of the Evidence. *Child Abuse and Neglect*, 11: pp41–52.

Seligman, P. (1994). Family Therapy. In Hanvey, C., and Philpot, T. (Eds.). *Practising Social Work*. London: Routledge.

Shah, R. (1995). *The Silent Minority: Children with Disabilities in Asian Families* (2nd edn.). London: National Children's Bureau.

Singh, J. (1992). *Black Families and Respite Care*. Barkingside: Barnardo's.

Sloper, P., Glenn, S., and Cunningham, C. (1986). The Effects of Intensity of Training on Sensori-motor Development in Infants with Down's Syndrome. *Journal of Mental Deficiency Research*, 30: pp149–162.

Sloper, P., Knussen, C., Turner, S., and Cunningham, C. (1991). Factors Related to Stress and Satisfaction with Life in Families of Children with Down's Syndrome. *Journal of Child Psychology and Psychiatry*, 32: pp655–676.

Sloper, P., and Turner, S. (1993). Risk and Resistance Factors in the Adaptation of Parents of Children with Severe Disability. *Journal of Child Psychology and Psychiatry*, 34(2): pp167–188.

Smaje, C. (1995). *Health, 'Race' and Ethnicity: Making Sense of the Evidence*. London: King's Fund Institute.

Smith, D. (1998). Social Work with Offenders. In Adams, R., Dominelli, L., and Payne, M. (Eds.). *Social Work: Themes, Issues and Critical Debates*. Basingstoke: Macmillan.

Social Services Inspectorate (1998). *Disabled Children: Directories for their Future Care*. London: Department of Health.

Thompson, R.A. (1995). *Preventing Child Maltreatment Through Social Support*. Thousand Oaks, CA: Sage.

Thorpe, D.H., Smith, D., Green, C.J., and Paley, J.H. (1980). *Out of Care: The Community Support of Juvenile Offenders*. London: Allen and Unwin.

Tozer, R. (1996). My Brother's Keeper? Sustaining Sibling Support. *Health and Social Care in the Community*, 4: pp172–185.

Trivette, C.M., Dunst, C.J., and Deal, A.G. (1997). Resource-based Approach to Early Intervention. In Thurman, S.K., Cornwell, J.R., and Gottwald, S.R. (Eds.). *Contexts of Early Intervention: Systems and Settings*. Baltimore, Maryland: Paul H. Brookes.

Utting, D., Bright, J., and Henricson, C. (1993). *Crime and the Family*. London: Family Policy Studies Centre.

Weil, M.O. (1996). Community Building: Building Community Practice. *Social Work*, 41(5): pp481–500.

Werner, E. (1995). Resilience in Development, Current Directions in Psychological Science. *American Psychological Society*, 4(5): pp81–85.

Wills, T.A. (1985). Supportive Functions of Inter-personal Relationships, in Cohen, S., and Syme, S.L. (Eds.). *Social Support and Health*. Orlando, FL: Academic Press.

Chapter Eleven

Community Social Work: Towards an Integrative Model of Practice

Paul Stepney and David Evans

... as a community worker one needs the capacity to operate in a variety of different contexts and at different levels, sometimes quietly, sometimes noisily, helping to draw attention to the apparent existence of need, injustice, or inequality.

(Sawdon, 1986: p33)

Introduction

There is something of a paradox in discussing the possibilities for re-establishing community social work at a time when the profession is facing up to the challenge of globalisation and people's lives are increasingly shaped by wider socio-economic forces rather than the community in which they live (Midgley, 1997). The creation of a more marketised and conditional welfare state and the residualisation of public services has led to the development of more technocratic and mechanistic forms of practice, alongside new patterns of exclusion and a greater reliance on informal care (Walker, 1997; Dominelli and Hoogvelt, 1996). In the UK the system of care management reveals this very clearly. But the debate also highlights the way possibilities associated with the 'community approach' and social inclusion create new opportunities as well as new dangers and contradictions (Mayo, 1998; Jordan, 2000). Here feminist research reminds us that patriarchal assumptions have informed welfare policy since the 1970s (Graham, 1997) and for many service users and carers 'care in the community' has become 'care by the community' (Finch and Groves, 1980). This chapter will explore the possibilities and dilemmas associated with developing a more integrative and empowering model of practice.

The policy context

Against a backdrop of economic globalisation the social policy context is shaped by New Labour's welfare reforms and a plethora of recent initiatives including New Deals to tackle exclusion (DSS, 1998; Stepney *et al.*, 1999);

Modernising the Social Services (DoH, 1998a); *Partnerships in Action* (DoH, 1998b) and *Improving Local Services Through Best Value* (DETR, 1998). Overall, this represents a policy paradigm of partnership, prevention and 'best value' to promote more inclusive citizenship, with an emphasis on social responsibility, economic efficiency and community cohesion (Jordan, 2000): see Chapter One for a more elaborate discussion of these trends.

In theory such a policy context provides considerable scope for social workers to promote inclusion by developing more preventive and participatory local services (Hadley and Leidy, 1996; Itzhaky and York, 1994). However, in a practice shaped by care management this may prove quite difficult unless practitioners rediscover 'community' and develop a more integrative and inclusive approach to their work (Holman, 1993).

In the early 1980s the Barclay Report recommended that community social work should become a central feature of social services provision and social workers should seek to integrate formal services with informal networks of support (Barclay, 1982). However, subsequent research has suggested that those in greatest need frequently have inadequate or non-existent informal networks of support (Abrams *et al.*, 1989; Oakley and Rajan, 1991). It is therefore essential that practitioners do not uncritically embrace the rhetoric of community care and make over-optimistic assumptions about the nature of 'community', but appreciate the difficulty of integrating formal services with informal resources at the local level.

The ambiguous concept of 'community'

Some of the confusion about this approach relates inevitably to the problem of using the concept of 'Community' in any kind of precise way as it frequently evokes many diverse and contradictory ideas. It has become a highly contested concept but nonetheless remains a key notion in the social sciences. In the social work literature it is often used quite loosely reflecting its representation in everyday speech.

Raymond Williams reminds us that the word 'community' has been in use in the English language since the 14th Century (when it was used to denote the commons or common people) and has subsequently come to have a number of meanings and uses, most of which are positive. It is a 'warmly persuasive word' (Williams, 1983) which is probably why it is so popular with politicians. However, it is important to be aware that such positive representations may conceal many deep seated divisions and conflicts based upon class, race, gender, age, disability and sexual orientation: for example, members of supportive working class communities may have conflicting gender interests as women may experience their community as a source of friendships but also as oppressive and restrictive (Williams, 1997); similarly there may be various divisions of interest and identity within 'the gay community' (Weeks, 1996); whilst 'the black community' is likely to comprise of people with diverse national and cultural identities (Gilroy, 1987).

In the sociological literature Hillery (1955) identified 94 different definitions of community, and found that the one common denominator was that they were all concerned with people. This ambiguity has led some to argue that the term should be slowly evicted from academic debate because it is devoid of precise meaning (Abrams *et al.*, 1989). However, there is little evidence of this happening and the ambiguity of the concept provides a clue to its seductiveness and popularity (Hughes and Mooney, 1998).

The Barclay committee defined the term as 'a network of informal relationships between people connected by kinship, common interests, geographical proximity, friendship, occupation, the giving and receiving of services, or various combinations of these' (Barclay, 1982). Pereira *et al.* identify three different meanings from the sociological literature which are consistent with Barclay's definition:

- Community defined by a geographical or spatial boundary.

- Community based on identity which cuts across different boundaries.

- Community as a basis for personal relationships and support.

(see Pereira *et al.*, 1998: p29)

Mayo (1998) suggests that the first two meanings have particular relevance for social work: 'community' as shared locality, a neighbourhood, suburban housing estate, village and so on, and 'community' as the basis for shared interests based upon cultural identity, or 'common identifications of particular needs' which cut across geographical boundaries. The third usage of the term might also be significant here because 'community does not necessarily refer just to the fact of people living in the same place (or sharing the same interests). It refers also to their feelings or sentiments and to social networks and patterns of behaviour' (Willmott, 1984: p5).

Two competing discourses associated with 'community' can be identified which link policy to practice (Hughes and Mooney, 1998). The first is moral communitarianism epitomised by Tony Blair's crusade in the dark estates designed to create a new consensus around social inclusion. The emphasis is on duties and obligations rather than rights as a basis for promoting responsible citizenship (Etzioni, 1995). This discourse provides a moral solution to the crisis of solidarity in modern society, but one which fails to acknowledge the need for redistribution and political action to tackle structural oppression.

An alternative discourse might be termed 'radical left pluralism' which begins by recognising the importance of political struggles against oppression in shaping the experience of marginalised groups (Hughes and Mooney, 1998). This discourse moves the debate beyond the idea of 'community' to the collective struggle for communities, which are characterised by diversity and difference. Radical left pluralism implies a strategy of inclusion and the re-democratisation of civil society to tackle oppression at the local level. According to Hughes and Mooney (1998) these competing discourses on community 'are part of a struggle for a new moral economy' (p99) which is reflected in policy debates as well as research.

Representing 'community' in research

The work of Tönnies (1957), first published in 1887, is often used as a benchmark for contemporary research. Tönnies identified the twin concepts of Gemeinschaft (community) and Gesellschaft (society) which have been used to denote the move away from relationships based on intimacy, loyalty and hierarchy (so much a feature of rural life in the 19th Century dominated by squire, church and harsh conditions) to something more impersonal, diffuse and anonymous which reflects contemporary urban life (Bell and Newby, 1971).

This also raises a point about 'community' as an idealised reference point which people refer to as something that has been lost. The loss of community is then said to be a consequence of rapid social change, urban development and economic globalisation. This creates a crisis of solidarity in modern communities which may be experienced as alienating, hostile, oppressive and essentially beyond control. The major problem with this kind of analysis is that there is evidence that the past was experienced as being just as oppressive as the present (Pearson, 1983). Moreover, the golden age of community (children playing safely on the village green, simple rural life free of conflicts, ample 'community spirit' based around family and church) is largely a myth but one which reconstructs an imagined past whilst simultaneously expressing dissatisfaction with the contemporary world (Lee and Newby, 1983).

In practice, issues of loss may become more complicated than this as the following case example illustrates:

Practice Focus One

In April, 1999, Mrs Peggy Lyle, 84, and her daughter, Ruth, 53, moved from their home in the North East of England to Ex-city. Mrs Lyle suffers from a chronic heart condition which has severely reduced her mobility, and she is registered blind. Ruth has a long history of anxiety and depression, which has included hospital admissions. Both Peggy and Ruth see themselves as each other's carer and have a conscientious sense of the obligations the roles entail. They have moved to Ex-city to be near another of Peggy Lyle's daughters, Sarah, who has lived there since she married about twelve years ago. The idea behind the move has been for Ruth to share with her sister some of the support their mother needs.

Soon after the move Peggy became despondent, tearful and overwhelmed with feelings of helplessness. Ruth feels that she is failing her mother and is surprised to be overtaken with unmanageable feelings of inferiority and inadequacy brought on by living so close to Sarah, her capable sister, who has a part-time professional job. Ruth had to give up her nursing career five years ago on health grounds.

A referral for an assessment was made by the GP. On going out to meet Peggy and Ruth for the first time the social worker was struck by the presentation of dignified bewilderment experienced by Peggy and her daughter in their comfortable flat. It was evidently very painful for Peggy, helped by Ruth, to begin to tell their story. The basis of their account was that they had made a terrible mistake leaving their home town in the North East to come to live in Ex-city. Peggy was tearful as she explained how much she felt disconnected in so many areas of her life. With restricted vision she found it impossible to find her way about the new flat. When she 'looked' out of the window (for she could distinguish light from dark) it was into a townscape she could not picture. She had no conception of what the city she was living in looked like.

Both felt cut off from being able to perform the tasks of a carer (a role that had come naturally to Peggy despite her poor sight), and so felt useless and guilty. No friends or neighbours came to call, nor could they in turn call on any of them. They had no involvement in local community activities. Sarah was busier than either Peggy or Ruth had imagined and could not assist. In her home town Peggy had not required any form of social care but now an extensive package of support might be required.

It seems clear that what Peggy and her daughter had done was abandon a whole active community with all the sustaining power that this provides. It was not until they had removed themselves to another city, far away, that the full significance of how this community had sustained them in a whole variety of informal ways became evident. Hence whilst research may predict the loss of community, the practice example above illustrates the way vulnerable people may make important decisions without reference to community support, and come to realise the true significance of what has been lost.

During the 1950s and 1960s a number of community studies were undertaken, including Young and Willmott's classic study of Bethnal Green in London. At the time this study challenged the conventional wisdom of the day by showing that a universal shift to a pattern of nuclear families was inaccurate. In Bethnal Green, the extended family survived dominated by mother-daughter relations. Young and Willmott also identified a close-knit network of friends, relatives, neighbours reflecting values of mutual aid and a strong sense of local identity and belonging (Young and Willmott, 1957). Forty years on a recent study has found that many structural changes have occurred to the community which is now characterised by fragmentation and difference. A large Bengali community lives there whose major concerns are about social isolation, racial harassment and gender discrimination (Pereira *et al.*, 1998).

Other research supports a picture of the urban community as contested space which may be experienced as hostile and divided. Abrams *et al.* (1989) found that in three northern cities 'not only has the traditional model of working class neighbouring vanished, but the world has turned upside down'. Today it is more accurate to speak of middle-class neighbouring. The reasons for this are largely structural, relating to increased geographical mobility, changes in the labour market, greater fragmentation, rising divorce rates and the privatisation of family life (Snaith, 1997).

Research concerning the way class and gender divisions interact and impact on informal care, found that 'those women in greatest need of support may also be those for whom informal support is least available'

(Oakley and Rajan, 1991: p51). Clearly the picture which emerges challenges the dominant view of policy makers, notably that informal networks of support are universally available and that professionals should tap into them to mobilise community resources (Barclay, 1982). Whilst this might be possible in middle-class areas, in other more disadvantaged neighbourhoods informal networks may not exist outside the family. Where they do exist, they are likely to be quite fragile and marked by complex relationships based on mutuality, attachment and reciprocity. The task, then, might be to help nurture, support and empower informal carers at a time of severe resource constraints.

The construction of community social work (CSW) post Barclay

Although community-based interventions had their origins in the nineteenth century settlement movement, CSW as it emerged following the publication of the Barclay Report, contained a number of key features but also a degree of ambiguity. The confusion concerning the concept may be reduced if some boundaries are established. Firstly, CSW is not a panacea for tackling local problems or indeed injecting some street wise credibility into the profession at a time when technicist models have distanced the practitioner from their clientele. Secondly, CSW is not something which can be left to the individual social workers to do, in between their care management work or at the end of the day, which can be bolted on to an otherwise highly centralised structure (Henderson and Thomas, 1983). Thirdly, it is an approach which should inform the practice of the whole team and command appropriate commitment as well as resources and support from managers and politicians alike (Vickery, 1983).

In moving towards a working definition comparisons are sometimes made with community work, as both appear to share common theoretical assumptions and core skills. Here it is worth acknowledging a fundamental difference in orientation. Whilst community work is concerned with tackling injustice and inequality by organising people and promoting policy change at the local level, all of which finds expression in collective action (Jones and Mayo, 1974; Twelvetrees,

1991), community social work is concerned with developing more accessible and effective local services (Smale, 1988). It is also about finding alternative ways of meeting the needs of individual service users. Both approaches, of course, seek to build on indigenous skills and utilise local resources rather than import them (see also Popple, 1995; Mayo, 1998).

Principally, as the Barclay committee recognised, the vast majority of care in this country is provided informally and much of this support, about 70 per cent according to survey data (OPCS, 1992), is reliant upon the unpaid domestic labour of women. Consequently, gender discrimination and the associated division of labour need careful analysis to avoid promoting a form of practice which reinforces traditional gender roles and patriarchal models of care in the community alongside other forms of oppression.

The Barclay committee advocated new partnerships and collaboration between formal service providers and the community in the provision of care, but underestimated the need for basic community development (Batten, 1967; York, 1984). However, these ideas have always been contested. At the time the committee was fraught with tensions between Robert Pinker, who was very sceptical and dismissive of CSW, and Roger Hadley, who argued that it didn't go far enough in terms of devolving responsibility and power (Barclay, 1982).

The essential difference between these two visions is captured in Table 1 below:

Table 1: A comparison of traditional and community-oriented approaches to social work

Characteristics of traditional approach	Characteristics of community approach	Changes required for community approach
Reactive Practitioner reacts to demands for service made when the situation has deteriorated and the user's network can no longer cope.	*Preventive/proactive* Practitioner intervenes before a service is demanded and before the situation has deteriorated and the user's network can no longer cope.	1. Reduction of reactive responses, replaced by proactive intervention. 2. Reduction of case-by-case approach based on work of individual professional 3. Close interaction with the local community.
Services at arm's length Professional practice is influenced by bureaucratic and institutional norms, is often predefined by department programmes, and is completely monopolised by numerous and pressing demands of individual clients	*Services close to the community* Professional practice is defined by the living conditions and environmental situation of users and their social surroundings	1. Variability and flexibility in the method of conceiving, realising and evaluating local programmes. 2. Individuals are considered in the round, not compartmentalised by programme. 3 Recognise importance of informal networks. 4. Sharing of professional responsibilities.
Based on professional responsibility The practitioner is entirely	*Based on shared responsibility* The practitioner shares	Practitioners replace, in part, their direct responsibilities by activities

Table 1: cont.

Characteristics of traditional approach	Characteristics of community approach	Changes required for community approach
and exclusively responsible for the solution to the user's problems.	responsibility with citizens and/or natural helpers.	supporting others who assume part of these responsibilities.
Centred on the individual client The only target of intervention is the individual client. Evaluation is directed mainly at his/her internal problems and the degree of pathology.	*Centred on the social network* The target of intervention is the social network, including the client's. Evaluation centres on the distribution of responsibility and capacities to adapt.	The practitioner needs to develop skills to evaluate the weight of responsibility experienced by the principal carers, to support them and to identify and elicit the support of potential users and non-users.

Translated and adapted from training documents prepared by Professor Jerôme Guay, Université Laval, Quebec.
Source: Hadley *et al.*, 1987: pp8–9.

As Hadley, Holman and others have noted CSW as it developed during the 1980s was a broad church of different interest groups which took many different forms. However, the above table reveals that CSW has some common organisational features such as a stress on working with people to develop their informal networks; emphasis on early intervention; a concern with preventive action; the desire to utilise and enhance local resources; and ultimately the empowerment of community members for the common good (Hadley *et al.*, 1987; Smale, 1988; Holman, 1993).

During the 1980s CSW policies included decentralising services into small 'patch' teams, developing more integrative services and promoting community (and user) participation which advanced alongside more traditional approaches. One way of implementing this approach has been to adopt a patch system of locally based staff serving relatively small populations of 10–15,000 people. Various patch models emerged during the 1980s in Normanton, East Sussex, Islington, Humberside, (see Cooper, 1983; Beresford and Croft, 1986; Smale *et al.*, 1988). Staff were likely to include

two or three social workers, community care workers, occupational therapists as well as local people employed in a paid and unpaid capacity, e.g., as carers, street wardens, home helps, etc.

Research evidence concerning the effectiveness of CSW

Many CSW initiatives by definition were small scale and localised. However, research by Hadley and others suggested that if properly resourced the outcomes could be highly promising if not impressive. For instance the Normanton patch team was investigated and compared with a traditional team in Featherstone. It was found that crisis work, including the use of emergency protection orders, reduced significantly during the second and third years of the project. In Normanton 40 per cent of clients officially referred were known to the team as opposed to three per cent in Featherstone (Hadley and McGrath, 1984). Working with older people, using local residents as street wardens or home helps, resulted in a lower proportion entering residential care, increased satisfaction with the services and improved life expectancy: a finding which corresponds with research by Challis and Davies in Kent (Davies and Challis, 1986).

According to Holman (1993) partnerships based on availability, local knowledge and joint action are the essence of community social work. Social workers need to find ways of developing more effective partnerships between statutory service providers, voluntary agencies and informal carers (Holman, 1993). Research by the Children's Society, based upon its work in different child care projects and family centres also demonstrates that this approach can be preventive—preventing crisis through strengthening communities as well as cost effective in terms of reducing the number of official referrals and statutory intervention (cited in Holman, 1995).

Further research by the Department of Health (1995) suggested that families without adequate community support were being drawn into the child protection system (Gill, 1996). It is also known that economic and environmental deprivation act as 'powerful stress factors which…make it more difficult to be an effective parent' (Utting *et al.*, 1993 cited in Southwell, 1994). There is also evidence that families referred to family centres by social workers as a child protection strategy, have similar problems to other families from the same community and therefore should have access to the same facilities (Southwell, 1994). Moreover, there is evidence that variations in rates of child mistreatment are associated with the strength of social support networks and general poverty levels (Garbarino, cited in Jack, 1997).

Community social work in the 1990s

Despite evidence of effectiveness, by the early 1990s CSW staff began to experience the same forces of marginalisation and fragmentation as affected the communities in which they worked. According to Hadley these were a consequence of 'the conjunction of central government policies which combined to reduce local authority autonomy, cap spending, prescribe essential separate services for children and other users and introduce market mechanisms into social care' (Hadley and Leidy, 1996: p825).

Holman (1993) suggests three reasons for the apparent decline of CSW: first, the media focus on child abuse post Cleveland which persuaded social services departments to concentrate resources on statutory interventions; second, the belief that CSW undermined efforts to improve the status of the profession; third, the growth of managerialism which promoted a more centralised and marketised approach. It is significant to note that during the 1990s CSW was overtaken by two other developments: First, the movement for enhancing citizenship rights and promoting user empowerment. Second, the community care reforms and development of care management with the social worker being redesignated as a care manager.

Whilst in theory such developments are mutually reinforcing and consistent with producing a needs-led service, in practice they have been fraught with contradictions. This is principally because the system of care management developed by local authority social service departments in the UK contains an inbuilt tension between empowerment and cost containment (see Chapter Two). Consequently, it is important for social workers to find some creative ways of reconciling these tensions and introducing a more empowering dimension into their work. Utilising opportunities for networking provides one way of doing this although it is not without its difficulties and ethical dilemmas.

Networking

Coulshed and Orme suggest that any effective use of CSW skills requires an understanding of networks. Networks emerge when we 'stand in the client's shoes…seeing the various people with whom that person is in touch, focus on actual or potential links which exist or could be fostered, keep in mind the communities of interest which develop between people who share similar interests or (our addition) because they share similar problems' (Coulshed and Orme, 1998: p222). Smale argues that it is the quality of the relationship between people in the network that is important and the processes the worker engages in which determine the objectives of CSW (Smale *et al.*, 1988).

One type of networking which seems particularly applicable to a community social work approach is referred to as network construction. Here the social worker may help the service user to draw a network map (or ecomap combined with geneogram) with key people placed in suitable positions according to the nature of the relationship. The connections can be strong, weak or stressful. This may assist the user to reassess the quality of different relationships, and importantly, identify potential sources of help and support.

The social worker can help to organise a meeting of the network to discuss particular issues and then assist the group to draw up an appropriate action plan. Further support might be directed towards sustaining the network as well as undertaking agreed tasks in collaboration with group members. Support networks are often a crucial resource for maintaining independence, especially during periods of crisis, as the following case example illustrates.

Practice Focus Two

This case involves a vulnerable and disabled woman, Mabel Green, 80, and her daughter Rita, 55, who has a learning disability.

Following referral, a social worker called at the home but was turned away at the doorstep by Mabel Green who was quite hostile stating that they were managing and did not want any help.

Four weeks later a neighbour referred the case to the same office. They were apparently begging for money and being bullied by a son, Tom, who lived on the other side of town. The referral described Mabel as unkempt, smelling of urine, disabled, and likely to be very suspicious of any formal intervention, and Rita as someone who seemed frightened and unable to cope. Both were, in effect, housebound.

A social worker called to see them and was surprised to be made welcome in a very bare, dark and poorly maintained cottage. They began to tell their story. Two or three weeks earlier they had found Mabel's husband dead on the floor. After his death extensive debts came to light and they did not know what they were going to do. It seemed they were more angry, confused and frightened than grief-stricken.

In listening to the Greens' story and beginning to make an assessment of their needs it emerged that they had once been active in the community. Mabel and Rita, in fact, welcomed suggestions for breaking their isolation, so long as no one contacted Tom. Sue, the volunteer facilitator at the local Health Centre, joined the social worker for a second visit. Mabel said she would like to join a lunch club. This would enable Rita to pick up visiting an old friend of hers once a week. No sooner had Mabel attended the Lunch Club than Sue reported back to the social worker that many people were saying they knew Mabel and what a friendly, sociable person she had been.

It was time to bring the latent, sustaining resources of the community back into the lives of Mabel and Rita to restore them to living independently again. Apart from the formal interventions of a community nurse, and of an occupational therapist to provide aids for Mabel and adapt the environment of their cottage, the rest of what Mabel and Rita required arose out of a meeting of those in the local community who had rediscovered their knowledge of the Green family and also wanted to help them find their independence again.

With support from the local community Mabel and Rita lived independently and the case was on the point of closure. At this stage, however, Rita found the trust and confidence to disclose that in her teens on one occasion Tom had returned home on leave from National Service and, in the absence of their parents, sexually assaulted her.

The ability to mobilise appropriate community support is clearly critical in enabling Mabel and Rita to regain their independence. Another valuable aspect of CSW is that the quality of the relationship with the service user can create a climate where other problems may be revealed and tackled—in this case the current behaviour of Tom and the previous incident of sexual abuse against Rita.

Re-establishing community social work: some possibilities and dilemmas

Given the unrelenting pressure on public resources, in combination with 'best value' initiatives and modernising policies (often in the name of producing fair and responsible communities) as well as greater demands and obligations on the citizen, 'no rights without responsibilities', it is inevitable that social workers will also be subject to corresponding pressures to demonstrate evidence of effectiveness based upon 'what works'. However, rather than accept a narrow definition of social work, with its inevitable short-term orientation, we argue for a broader, more integrative CSW approach, one which combines individual care management tasks with a wider community development role. Such an approach is far more suited to conditions of uncertainty and fragmentation which are to be found in disadvantaged communities.

The following model is offered which draws on the work of Bryant and Holmes (1977), Vickery (1983), Smale (1988), Sawdon (1986), Mayo (1998). The main circle in diagram one shows the CSW process and some of the activities which might spring from it.

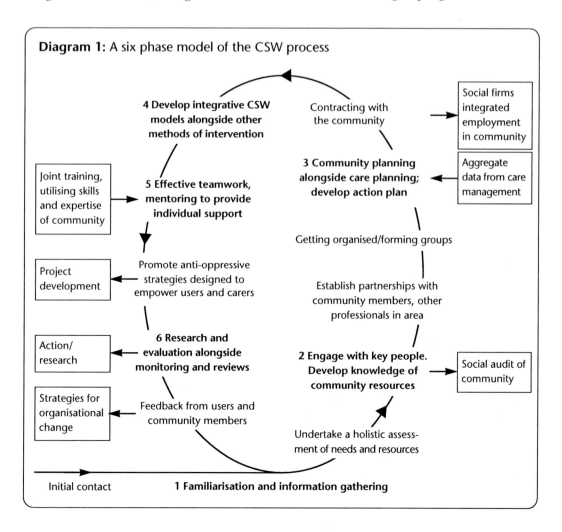

Diagram 1: A six phase model of the CSW process

4 Develop integrative CSW models alongside other methods of intervention

Contracting with the community

Social firms integrated employment in community

Joint training, utilising skills and expertise of community

5 Effective teamwork, mentoring to provide individual support

3 Community planning alongside care planning; develop action plan

Aggregate data from care management

Getting organised/forming groups

Project development

Promote anti-oppressive strategies designed to empower users and carers

Establish partnerships with community members, other professionals in area

Action/ research

6 Research and evaluation alongside monitoring and reviews

2 Engage with key people. Develop knowledge of community resources

Social audit of community

Strategies for organisational change

Feedback from users and community members

Undertake a holistic assessment of needs and resources

Initial contact

1 Familiarisation and information gathering

There are six phases to the model which to some extent overlap and may not follow in sequential order – for example, phase 6, the research to evaluate effectiveness would clearly need to be set up at the outset. The six phases are:

1. Familiarisation and information gathering.

2. Engagement and assessment.

3. Organisation, planning and partnerships.

4. Intervention in collaboration with community members.

5. Mobilising team resources for empowerment (users and staff).

6. Research and evaluation.

The individual practitioner will need to adapt the model to particular situations with vision and skill, noting that at each stage in the process there are additional opportunities or requirements depicted by the seven rectangles, which open up new possibilities for constructive action—for example, after phase 2, it may be useful to carry out a social audit of the wider community to map out the full range of needs and resources; after phase 3, opportunities for contracting could involve setting up social enterprises to provide employment for local people; during phase 5, training strategies might include planning joint sessions with user groups and other community members. In certain respects the CSW model can be seen to have similar features to the care management process. However, there are important differences, especially the introduction of additional elements designed to assist community development and promote a more integrative model of practice.

Conclusion

Encouragingly, the latter half of the 1990s has seen the re-emergence of CSW ideals both in Britain and the USA. This is in part a response to the limitations of market-led, centralised services but also to a general disenchantment with new managerial methods. CSW continues to develop, albeit in the shadow of the market economy, and Holman (1999) reports the continuing relevance of this approach in his work in Glasgow. Hadley *et al.*, refers to CSW experiments in Pennsylvania State, USA (Hadley and Leidy, 1996) while Banks and Wideman (1996) describe macro social work in Ontario, Canada.

In Europe community-based social work as part of efforts to regenerate local communities

remains popular and importantly supported by government through the EU social fund. With New Labour's commitment to social inclusion a well publicised policy at the heart of government thinking perhaps it is time for social workers to take up the challenge and rediscover their change agent role once again. CSW can promote the notion of a diverse and critical community, opening up possibilities for the inclusion of marginalised groups as part of a wider struggle against oppression and exclusion.

References

Abrams, P., Abrams, S., Humphrey, R., and Snaith R. (1989). *Neighbourhood Care and Social Policy*. HMSO: London.

Banks, C., and Wideman, G. (1996). The Company of Neighbours: Building Social Support Through the Use of Ethnography. *International Social Work*, Vol. 39: pp317–328.

Barclay Committee (1982). *Social Workers: Their Role and Tasks*. London: Bedford Square Press.

Batten, T.R. (1967). *The Non-directive Approach to Youth and Community Work*. Oxford: Oxford University Press.

Bayley, M. *et al.* (1987). *Practising Community Care*. University of Sheffield Unit for Social Services Research.

Bayley, M. (1982). Helping Care to Happen. In Walker, A. (Ed.). *Community Care: The Family, the State and Social Policy*. Oxford: Blackwell.

Bell, C., and Newby, H. (1971). *An Introduction to the Sociology of the Local Community*. London: Allen and Unwin.

Beresford, P., and Croft, S. (1986). *Whose Welfare? Private Care or Public Services*. Brighton Polytechnic, Lewis Cohen Centre for Urban Studies.

Beresford, P., and Croft, S. (1993). *Citizen Involvement: A Practical Guide for Change*. Basingstoke: Macmillan.

Bornat, J. *et al.* (1997). *Community Care—A Reader* (2nd edn.). Basingstoke: Macmillan.

Bryant, R., and Holmes, B. (1977). Fieldwork Teaching in Community Work. In Briscoe, C., and Thomas, D. (Eds.). *Community Work: Learning and Supervision*. National Institute Social Services Library, 32.

Cooper, M. (1983). Community Social Work. In Jordan, B., and Parton, N. (Eds.). *The Political Dimensions of Social Work*. Oxford: Blackwell.

Coulshed, V., and Orme, J. (1998). *Social Work Practice: An Introduction* (3rd edn.). Basingstoke: Macmillan.

Davies, B., and Challis, D. (1986). *Matching Resources to Needs in Community Care: An Evaluated Demonstration of a Long Term Care Model*. Aldershot: Gower.

Department of Environment. Transport and the Regions (1998). *Modernising Local Government Improving Local Services Through Best Value* (DETR). London: The Stationery Office.

Department of Health (1998a). *Modernising the Social Services*. London: The Stationery Office.

Department of Health (1998b). *Partnerships in Action.* London: The Stationery Office.

Dominelli, L., and Hoogvelt, A. (1996). Globalisation and the Technocratisation of Social Work. *Critical Social Policy*, 47(16): pp245–262.

DSS (Dept. of Social Security) (1998). *A New Contract for Welfare*, Cm. 3805. HMSO.

Etzioni, A. (1995). *The Spirit of Community*. London: Fontana.

Finch, J., and Groves (1980). Community Care and the Family: A Case for Equal Opportunities? *Journal of Social Policy*, 9(4): pp487–511.

Gill, O. (1996). Child protection and Neighbourhood Work: Dilemmas for Practice. *Practice*, 8(2): pp45–52.

Gilroy, P. (1987). *There Ain't No Black in the Union Jack.* Hutchinson.

Graham, H. (1997). Feminist Perspectives on Caring. In Bornat *et al. Community Care: A Reader*. Basingstoke: Macmillan.

Hadley, R., and Leidy, B. (1996). Community Social Work in a Market Environment: A British–American Exchange of Technologies and Experience. *British Journal of Social Work*, 26(6): pp823–842.

Hadley, R., and McGrath, M. (1984). *When Social Services are Local—The Normanton Experience*. London: Allen and Unwin.

Hadley, R., *et al.* (1987). *A Community Social Workers Handbook.* London: Tavistock.

Henderson, P., and Thomas, D. (1983). Out into the Community. *Community Care*, April.

Henderson, P., and Thomas, D. (1987). *Skills in Neighbourhood Work*. London: Allen and Unwin.

Henderson, P., and Armstrong, J. (1997). Community Development and Community Care: A Strategic Approach. In Bornat *et al. Community Care: A Reader*. Basingstoke: Macmillan.

Henwood, M. (1995). *Making a Difference? Implementation of the Community Care Reforms Two Years on.* Nuffield Institute.

Hillery, J. (1955). Definitions of Community. *Rural Sociology*, 20(1): pp111–123.

Holman, B. (1993). Pulling Together. *The Guardian*, January 20th, 1993

Holman, B. (1995). *Putting Families First*. Basingstoke: Macmillan.

Holman, B. (1999). *Kids at the Door Revisited.* Lyme Regis: Russell House Publishing.

Hughes, G., and Mooney, G. (1998). Community. In Hughes, G. (Ed.). *Imagining Welfare Futures.* London: Routledge.

Hughes, G. (Ed.) (1998). *Imagining Welfare Futures.* London: Routledge.

Itzhaky, H., and York, A. (1994). Different Types of Client Participation and the Effects on Community Social Work Intervention. *Journal of Social Services Research*, 19(1–2): pp85–98.

Jack, G. (1997). An Ecological Approach to Social Work. *Child and Family Social Work*, 2(2).

Jones, D., and Mayo, M. (1974). *Community Work One.* London: Routledge.

Jordan, B. (2000). *Tough Love: Implementing New Labour's Programme: Social Work and the Third Way.* London: Sage.

Jordan, B. (1998). *The New Politics of Welfare.* London: Sage.

Lee, D., and Newby, H. (1983). *The Problem of Sociology.* Unwin Hyman.

Mayo, M. (1998). Community work. In Adams, Dominelli, and Payne. *Social Work: Themes, Issues and Critical Debates.* Basingstoke: Macmillan.

Midgley, J. (1997). Social Work in International Context. In Reisch, M., and Gambrill, E. *Social Work in the 21st Century.* USA: Prine Forge Press.

Oakley, A., and Rajan, L. (1991). Social Class and Social Support: The Same or Different? *Sociology*, 25(1): pp31–59.

OPCS (Office of Population Sensus Surveys) (1992). *General Household Survey: Carers in 1990.* London: Government Statistical Service.

Payne, M. (1995). *Social Work and Community Care.* Basingstoke: Macmillan

Pearson, G. (1983). *Hooligan: A History of Respectable Fears.* Basingstoke: Macmillan.

Pereira, C., Peace, S., and Williams, F. (1998). Unpacking Community Care, *Workbook I*, Part I K259 course in Community Care. Buckingham: The Open University.

Popple, K. (1995). *Analysing Community Work: Its Theory and Practice.* Buckingham: OU Press.

Sawdon, D. (1986). *Making Connections in Practice Teaching.* London: Heinneman, NISW.

Smale, G., *et al.* (1988). *Community Social Work: A Paradigm for Change.* London: NISW.

Snaith, R. (Ed.) (1997). Neighbourhood Care and Social Policy. In Bornat *et al. Op. cit.*

Southwell, P. (1994). The Integrated Family Centre. *Practice*, 7(1): pp45–54.

SSI and NHS Executive (1995). *Community Care Monitoring Report.* London: DoH.

Stepney, P., Lynch, R., and Jordan, B. (1999). Poverty, Exclusion and New Labour. *Critical Social Policy*, 19(1): pp109–127.

Tönnies, F. (1957). *Community and Society.* Harper Torchbook.

Twelvetrees, A. (1991). *Community Work.* Basingstoke: Macmillan.

Vickery, A. (1983). *Organising a Patch System.* London: NISW.

Walker, A. (1997). Community Care Policy: From Consensus to Conflict. In Bornat *et al. Community Care: A Reader.* Basingstoke: Macmillan.

Weeks, J. (1996). The Idea of a Sexual Community. *Soundings*, Issue 2: pp71–84.

Williams, F. (1997). Women and Community. In Bornat *et al. Community Care—A Reader.* Basingstoke: Macmillan.

Williams, R. (1983). *Keywords.* Flamingo.

Willmott, P. (1984). *Community in Social Policy*, Discussion Paper No. 9. Policy Studies Institute.

York, A. (1984). Towards a Conceptual Model of Community Social Work. *British Journal of Social Work*, 14(1): pp241–255.

Young, M., and Willmott, P. (1957). *Family and Kinship in East London.* Harmondsworth: Penguin.

Chapter Twelve

Existentialist Practice

Neil Thompson

Introduction

Although existentialist philosophy has had a significant impact on both social thought in general and particular individual disciplines such as counselling (see, for example, May *et al.*, 1958), its influence in social work has never been of major proportions (Thompson, 1992a). Nonetheless, a case can clearly be made for its relevance and value as a body of knowledge and a theoretical framework which can cast light on many aspects of social work, particularly its dilemmas, insecurities and uncertainties. In particular, what existentialism can be seen to offer is a framework of understanding which chimes well with the social worker's experience of practice as complex and uncertain, with an absence of clear-cut or guaranteed solutions. This chapter, then, seeks to map out some of the key concepts and issues arising from an existentialist approach and to consider their implications for practice.

The first part of the chapter provides a brief overview of the main tenets of existentialism as a social philosophy by commenting on some of the key concepts and providing examples of their applicability to practice situations. The second part explores and summarises the implications of eight 'Principles for practice' first introduced in Thompson (1992a).

These are not presented as simple formulas or recipes to be followed uncritically. Rather, they are intended as an introduction to the complexities of existentialist thought as an underpinning foundation for practice. What is presented therefore needs to be seen in the context of reflective practice: a set of ideas to be drawn upon critically and reflectively as part of the continuing challenge of integrating theory and practice, as opposed to a set of ready-made technical solutions (Thompson, 2000). Indeed, it is a principle of existentialism that there can be no pre-defined answers—human existence is characterised as a continuous struggle to maintain a coherent thread of meaning in a confused and confusing stream of events and developments.

Social work operates at the intersection of the personal and the social, and where issues of loss, pain, distress, crisis, deprivation, discrimination and social inequality are to the fore. But much the same can also be said of existentialism:

- It addresses the meeting point between the individual (the subjective level) and his or her socio-political context (the objective level).

- Experiences of crisis, loss, pain and distress are recognised as major features of existential subjectivity (the individual).

- Similarly, deprivation, discrimination and social inequality feature strongly as important elements of the objective world (the socio-political context).

In similar fashion, Mahon (1997) describes existentialism as 'a kind of philosophy which is preoccupied with the most salient and poignant features of human existence, such as death, love, responsibility and despair' (p8).

Social work is a professional activity which seeks to respond to social problems through a personalised approach (Adams, 1996). As such, it wrestles with a wide range of complex and demanding issues, many of which are beyond resolution, and few of which fit neatly into formula solutions. Indeed, Schön's (1983) critique of 'technical rationality' is very relevant here, as it is clear that the type and range of problems encountered in social work do not lend themselves to relatively straightforward technical solutions. Rather, they tend to be, as Schon would put it, 'messy'—characterised by complexity, uncertainty, ambiguity, conflicting perspectives, and constantly subject to change. What is needed, then, is not a theoretical framework that seeks to provide a neat set of technical-type solutions, but rather one that helps to equip practitioners for the very messy reality of human existence which befalls them.

Existentialism does not offer direct solutions, but does provide a basis from which we can develop a critically reflective practice, in the full recognition that there are no easy answers (and just as importantly, that answers which appear easy are very likely dangerous over-simplifications). Existentialism recognises that, being unable to come up with neat, simple solutions is not a sign of weakness or failure on the worker's part, but rather an indication of the bewilderingly complex uncertainties of human existence in general and, in particular, the existential challenges that social work clients face.

There is therefore great potential for drawing on existentialist concepts and themes in seeking to guide and make sense of social work practice.

What is existentialism?

Existentialism is a complex philosophy with a long history (see Macquarrie, 1973). Consequently, it is a very difficult task to explain it briefly. What follows is therefore a very basic and limited account and should be used as a gateway to other literature on the subject, rather than regarded as a sufficient introduction in its own right.

Perhaps the most fundamental and far-reaching element of existentialism is its emphasis on human freedom and the 'fluid' nature of the self. Sartre's view was that we are 'what we make of what is made of us'. The 'what is made of us' part refers to the influence of the context in which we operate: social, political, economic, interpersonal and organisational factors that have a bearing on how we act and how we perceive ourselves. The 'what we make' part refers to our own role in responding to (and, in part, shaping) these wider factors.

Such a view of the self is:

1. *Dialectical*. It is based on a dynamic, interactive view of the self in which change and movement are basic characteristics.

2. *Non-essentialist*. It does not see individual personality as fixed or immutable (an 'essence'). Rather, it presents selfhood as a process in which we both influence and are influenced by the external circumstances in which we find ourselves.

The existentialist model of the self is therefore one based on the key concept of the dialectic of subjectivity and objectivity (Thompson, 1998a)—a theme to be developed below.

Another important concept is that of 'contingency', the idea that life is characterised by change, uncertainty and insecurity. Where we have a degree of stability and continuity, this can be attributed to the series of choices and actions that have contributed to establishing and maintaining such stability–continuity, where it exists, is the result of our actions, rather than simply a 'natural' state. Continuity is *constructed* in and by our actions, rather than a 'natural' state of affairs.

This relates closely to the concept of 'ontological security', the sense of 'rootedness' each of us seeks to maintain to hold together the various strands of our experience and retain a coherent identity in the face of contingency and change:

> *Ontological security refers to the individual's ability to maintain a coherent thread of meaning and a relatively stable sense of self over time and across a range of situations. It is a sense of being a person in one's own right and feeling comfortable with oneself and one's current circumstances. It is through ontological security that we maintain a sense of self or identity.*
>
> (Thompson, 1998b: pp169–170)

We seek to maintain a degree of ontological security by adjusting and responding to the changes in our lives that we constantly encounter.

A further important 'ingredient' of existentialism is that of phenomenology, a term which refers to the study of perception, and is therefore concerned with how we make sense of our experience, how we construct meaning:

> *Phenomenology is concerned with 'phenomena' which, taken literally, means 'appearances'. Phenomenologists stress the importance of perception and the relationship between appearance and reality. Frameworks of perception, how meaning arises, how time is construed, the role of ideology are all significant areas for phenomenological analysis.*
>
> (Thompson, 1992a: pp38–39)

Our subjective perceptions of the world play an important part in shaping our behaviour, attitudes and responses. Phenomenology is therefore a theoretical approach which has much to say about social reality. It is an approach which seeks to cast light on everyday experience by exploring and emphasising the significance of the subjective dimension of our lives—the role of interpretation and meaning construction.

However, this is not to say that phenomenology ignores the objective dimension of human experience, the external social world. Indeed, a central theme of existentialism is that of the dialectic of subjectivity and objectivity—the dynamic interplay of the subjective dimension (the individual's perceptions and the meanings attached to these) and the objective dimension (the wider social world, the context in which the individual exists). My actions (or 'agency') play a part (albeit a small part in the overall scheme of things) in shaping the wider social field (the objective dimension) and, in turn, the objective dimension plays a part in shaping my subjective experience by influencing and constraining my actions in various ways.

One important distinction to draw is that between choice and choices. Choice (that is, the ability/necessity to choose) is seen, in existentialist terms, as *absolute*, while the range of choices or options available at any give time is constrained and structured by wider social factors, such as class, race and gender - and is therefore *relative* (that is, relative to our position in the social structure and the differences in life-chances we will experience as a result of this). While the range of options available to a given individual will owe much to his or her social location, the necessity to choose will remain absolute, in the sense that we cannot choose not to choose (for example, avoiding making a decision is in itself a form of choice). As Billington (1990) puts it: 'Even leaving things in the 'pending' tray until it is too late for any meaningful decision to be made is a decision' (p102).

A central feature of existentialist philosophy is the concept of 'bad faith'. This refers to the tendency to deny human freedom, to think and act as if other factors were responsible for our actions (genetic, environmental or other forms of determinism), thus seeking to minimise the role of choice and decision making. Bad faith is therefore a form of self-disempowerment. Consequently, we can recognise that one of the implications of existentialist philosophy is the need to avoid and undermine bad faith—to promote *authenticity*. An authentic existence is

one in which choice, responsibility and freedom are taken seriously and efforts are made to follow through the implications of such freedom, rather than seek to deny, distort or minimise it. As we shall see below, the aim of existentialist social work can be defined as supporting clients in developing and sustaining authenticity—moving away from the self-defeating and limiting tendencies of bad faith.

Existentialism is a *dynamic* philosophy. That is, it is concerned with change and movement. This is exemplified in the use of what Sartre (1982) referred to as the 'progressive-regressive method' (see also Sartre, 1963). This refers to an understanding of human existence in which our present is influenced by both future plans/intentions/aspirations (progressive) and past learning and experience (regressive) and the interaction between the two. That is, my future plans will have been influenced by my past experiences, but I will also 'reconstruct' my past in line with my future expectations. This is not to say that I will distort my own biography to fit in with future plans, but rather that the significance we attach to past experiences will depend in part on our future intentions. For example, which aspects of my past life I draw upon in the present will depend largely on where I am hoping to go in the future, as in a job application where I would emphasise the aspects of my past which are relevant to and supportive of that application.

The progressive–regressive method is therefore an analytical tool for understanding the present circumstances by reference to the combined influences of the past and our proposed future:

> Human existence can be characterised as a process in which the present moment represents a focal point between the outcomes of past actions and the influence of future intentions. This 'progressive– regressive' conceptualisation can be used as an analytical framework to guide assessment and subsequent interventions.
>
> (Thompson, 1998a: p704)

It should be apparent from this brief overview that existentialism is a complex philosophy, but it is to be hoped that it is also apparent that it is an approach to understanding social reality that offers much by way of themes and concepts which can cast considerable light on the intricacies of practice, with all their subtleties, multiple layers and interconnections.

Principles for practice

Existentialism is not only a complex philosophy but also an evolving one. We should therefore be wary of coming up with simple and definitive prescriptions for practice. What follows, then, should be seen as guidelines to feed into an informed reflective practice rather than a set of 'rules' to be applied mechanistically and uncritically.

1. Freedom and responsibility are basic building blocks of human experience.

Our lives are characterised by the constant pressure to make decisions and to live by their consequences. The responsibility to choose is one that we face each day, to make choices within what Sartre (1958) calls the 'structured field of possibilities'. In this context, the broad role of the social worker can be seen to be twofold. First, there is a part to play in helping people recognise those areas of their lives in which they have a degree of control, especially where this capacity for choice and control may be masked by bad faith to the extent that the individual, family or group concerned may not even be aware that they have choice. Second, there is likely to be a role in seeking to influence the range of options available, for example through access to resources, advocacy or the use of influencing skills generally.

This principle requires practitioners to recognise that clients are not simply passive recipients of services, but active agents who play a central role in determining the course of their lives. The ability to make choices and the range of choices available are therefore key factors to take into consideration.

Consequently, assessment and subsequent interventions should take account of both the subjective and objective dimensions. In order to do justice to the complexity of human existence and the reality of clients' circumstances, it is necessary to look at: a) the *subjective* element—how the situation is experienced by those involved, the significance they attach to it; and b) the *objective* element— the range of broader factors that have a bearing on the current situation. This helps to avoid two pitfalls: the dangers of, on the one hand, addressing broader issues without taking account of the uniqueness of the situation for the individual concerned and, on the other, focusing exclusively on the personal elements without recognising the significant role of cultural and structural factors. Effective social work practice needs to address both dimensions.

2. Freedom is both liberation and heavy burden.

The necessity to choose gives us tremendous potential for changing aspects of our situation, for taking as much control of our circumstances as the objective constraints of the social world will permit—it is the basis of personal liberation and empowerment. However, this freedom is also a heavy burden to bear in the sense that it brings responsibility for our actions and their consequences. The social work task can therefore be seen to include efforts to convert negative aspects of the experience of freedom (anxiety, fear, insecurity and so on) into positive ones (confidence, self-esteem, self-control and so on). In some ways, this reflects traditional approaches to the psychology of human development which lay stress on the need to boost confidence and self-esteem. However, what we are proposing here goes beyond this, in so far as it recognises anxiety and related factors as basic elements of human existence, rather than as signs of individual weakness or inadequacy. They are *ontological* matters, rather than purely psychological.

Indeed, in terms of ontology, many of the problems social work clients encounter can be related to the existential challenges they face. As we move through life, we face a series of challenges, some of which act as turning points or 'crises' which can have a significant bearing on our subsequent attitudes and actions and the meanings we attach to the life events we encounter (Thompson, 1991). In order to respond appropriately to the situations which arise in practice, it is necessary to establish the existential basis by relating the circumstances to specific challenges and/or crisis points. For example, work with older people needs to take account of the particular challenges that arise in later life, such as retaining a sense of identity and self-esteem in an ageist society (Thompson, 1995).

3. Authenticity is the key to liberation while its opposite, bad faith, is the common (unsuccessful) strategy for coping with the burden.

While the tendency to deny human freedom (bad faith) is relatively common, an authentic existence—that is, one based on an acceptance and recognition of freedom and responsibility—is what is required to deal with the challenge of the responsibility our freedom brings. While attempts to boost confidence and self-esteem may well at times be invaluable in helping people cope with the burden of freedom, a wider commitment to promoting authenticity is called for. That is, what is needed is a form of empowerment based on seeking to replace bad faith with authenticity. This is not necessarily a straightforward or short-term task but social work can contribute positively to this process, rather than run the risk of reinforcing bad faith and its destructive effects in limiting opportunities for growth, development and active problem solving. This calls for more than encouraging or supportive words and actions—it requires a concerted effort to explore the presenting situation for opportunities to assist clients in gaining greater control over their lives and a sensitivity to those factors that stand in the way of authenticity.

Henry (1997) comments that: 'Kierkegaard's concept of dread concerns the anxiety that paralyses the human self as it senses its aloneness in the face of the cosmic dance of life' (p158). Part of the social work task, then, is to help tackle that sense of dread or anguish and thus support people in taking responsibility for making progress towards their goals.

In addition, of course, we need to recognise that we cannot promote authenticity in others unless we take seriously the challenge of our own authenticity. There is little point in seeking to support others in empowering themselves if practitioners disempower themselves through their own bad faith. Social work is a skilled activity that requires a degree of sensitivity and self-awareness. It is therefore important that we should not place barriers to our own development of skill, sensitivity and awareness

by denying our own freedom and responsibility. This is not to say that we should attempt to put our own house completely in order before we are able to try and support others. This would be unrealistic, as it has to be recognised that the development of authenticity is a long term project and not simply a one-off decision. The notion of 'continuous professional development' is an important one in terms of the development of knowledge, skills and values in general, but it can also be seen as significant in terms of continuing to learn about ourselves. Indeed, this is fully consistent with the existentialist view of the person as a process of growth and development, rather than a fixed entity or 'essence'.

4. Despite freedom, existence is characteristically experienced as powerlessness and helplessness.

The terms, 'freedom' and 'liberation' can be misleading, in so far as they mask the strong sense of powerlessness that is so often characteristic of human existence. However, as Payne (1997) comments:

> Clients struggle with immense problems. Workers must help them start to take responsibility in whatever limited areas are possible. As this is achieved, further progress in taking more collective responsibility (e.g. for solidarity in a family, or eventually for political action) can be achieved.
>
> (Payne, 1997: p196)

Feeling powerless and *being* powerless are, of course, not the same thing. The task, therefore, is to attempt to overcome feelings of powerlessness by supporting people in establishing control gradually and steadily as part of a process of empowerment. Bad faith, as a form of self-disempowerment and thus of feelings of powerlessness, must therefore be challenged. Although bad faith can clearly be seen as a barrier to progress, it is none the less evident in so many people's day-to-day lives. To leave bad faith unchallenged is therefore a serious mistake in so far as this is likely to undermine any attempts to implement a positive plan of intervention. This is not to say that the social worker can or should make major changes to clients' self-perception or expect radical transformations in how they conduct their lives. However, it nonetheless has to be recognised that to fail to address bad faith is to collude with it and therefore to reduce the chances of success as far as any programme of intervention is concerned. Skills in gently and constructively challenging bad faith and supporting people in the development of a more authentic approach to their lives should therefore be at a premium.

5. Existentialism proposes a shared subjective journey—a partnership in helping.

The important role of perception and meaning indicates the uniqueness of each individual, that each of us is ultimately alone in the world. It is therefore a fundamental principle of existentialism that we need to work together, to build alliances in tackling the range of existential challenges we face in our lives. This partnership approach operates at two separate but interrelated levels. First, it is important to work collaboratively with *clients*, to move away from a model in which it is assumed that the worker is the 'expert' who has the 'answers'. Involving clients directly in the social work process is a fundamental element of empowering forms of practice. Second, partnership needs to involve other *professionals*, to develop a shared perspective so that resources for change and development can be harnessed from a wide range of sources.

6. The dynamic tension between authority/control/statutory duties on the one hand and creative, non-directive work on the other is one to be recognised. It is a conflict that has to be managed in our everyday work rather than resolved once and for all.

Mahon (1997) makes the point that: 'the human world is a human construction which continually demands reconstruction, and in thus reconstructing the world I inescapably side with some human beings against others' (p7). That is to say, conflict is an inevitable feature of human experience. It would therefore be naive in the extreme to assume that issues of control will not arise. In order to protect some people it is necessary to control others (as in child protection, for example). As representatives of the state or other formal organisations, social workers are inevitably involved in the use of authority. However, this

is not an inevitable barrier to empowerment, provided that such power is not abused or misused. Indeed, the power of the worker can often be an important factor in creating situations in which empowerment becomes a possibility (see Thompson, 1998c). Power and control should be used appropriately and constructively, rather than naively wished away.

Existentialism recognises that power is an everpresent feature of human interaction, and would therefore take account of power imbalances and the potential for the deliberate abuse or unwitting misuse of such power. The task, then, is not for the social worker to use his or her power to coerce or cajole clients into following a particular course of action, but rather to use such power constructively in identifying and working towards agreed goals as part of a process of partnership. Where it is not possible to agree goals (as a result of a statutory duty being in conflict with a client's wishes, for example), the use of power should be clear and explicit so that there is no confusion or underhandedness, which in themselves could constitute a misuse of power. However, to ignore, deny or trivialise the power dimension of human interactions is to run the risk of dangerous practice, possibly doing more harm than good by failing to recognise the significance of power and control in a social work context.

7. Existence is movement. There is no 'natural' stability as our life-plans are constantly being reconstructed and so development, disintegration or stability are perpetual possibilities—contingency is everpresent.

While clients may at times be understandably resistant to change or defeatist about the possibility of positive change, the fact remains that existing stability in a given situation is reinforced by people's actions and attitudes and can therefore be undermined if that is what is required to make progress towards agreed goals. It is therefore important for social workers to be realistic about the possibilities for change, being neither unduly defeatist about the potential for change nor setting people up to fail by failing to take adequate account of the barriers to change. Assessing the potential for change therefore needs to take account of both the subjective dimension (the factors that are within the individual's control) and the objective dimension (the range of factors, some of which may facilitate change, while others may act as a barrier). An 'essentialist' view which regards people as being unable to change can be a significant obstacle to progress by ruling out important possibilities for moving forward (another example of bad faith).

An important implication of contingency as a basic feature of human existence is that meaning has to be recognised as a key issue in making sense of, and responding to, the uncertain 'shifting sands' of life in general and the situations encountered in practice in particular. In seeking to develop an adequate understanding of each practice situation, attention therefore needs to be given to the specific meanings attached to events or circumstances. For example, as Bevan (1998) comments in relation to social work in a palliative care context:

> A person who is dying may question the meaning and purpose of their own lives and those close to them. Their own personal systems of meaning may be questioned at this time. This may or may not involve formal or informal religious beliefs. It seems that what we are exploring here is the freedom for those who are dying to seek peace.
>
> (Bevan, 1998: p28)

This passage illustrates the importance of appreciating, and respecting, systems of meaning which will change and adapt to new situations, rather than simply seeking to impose our own interpretation of events.

8. Existential freedom—the process of self-creation—is a prerequisite to political liberty. To deny the former is to foreclose the latter and thus render an authentic social work impossible.

If we rely on deterministic notions which deny freedom and responsibility, we create artificial barriers to progress at a socio-political level. That is, if we regard individuals not as self-creating processes who exercise choice and agency, but rather as pawns pushed here and there by forces beyond their control, then we rule out the possibility of changing or influencing the broader circumstances which are often a significant source of pressure and difficulties (poverty, deprivation,

discrimination and so on). Recognising that we have a degree of control over our actions (and responsibility for their consequences) enables us to work towards a collective approach to social problems. The recognition of such freedom at a personal level is not a denial of the importance of wider cultural and structural factors, but rather an acknowledgement that the three levels (personal, cultural and structural) are intertwined and interdependent.

As Birt (1997) comments:

> There can be no liberation of consciousness separate from the total struggle for social liberation, just as there can be no social liberation without a liberating consciousness. There can be no radical transformation of identity without an entire struggle to radically transform the social order. And no radical transformation of the social structure is possible (nor would it have a purpose) without the transformation of identity—the self-creation of a new kind of human being. It is this self-creation and renewal that is the aim of all effort.
>
> (Birt, 1997: p211)

Social work, by helping clients realise their potential as free individuals thereby contributes to the broader emancipatory project of social transformation towards a greater degree of social justice.

Conclusion

An authentic social work practice cannot dodge the difficult issues of human existence and experience—crisis, loss, grief, pain, suffering, fear, frustration, uncertainty, alienation, deprivation, discrimination and oppression. What is needed, then, is a theoretical base which similarly does not shirk such difficult issues, and which, in fact, places such concerns at centre stage. Clearly, existentialist philosophy is one such theoretical framework. As the name implies, it begins with human existence. It takes the fact that we exist (ontology) as its basic starting point and then seeks to make sense of that existence, to see how meaning operates as a central feature (phenomenology). It then seeks to draw out the implications of all this for our day-to-day lives as we wrestle with the ambiguities, uncertainties, contradictions and paradoxes that confront us in the course of maintaining a coherent thread of meaning and rising to the existential challenges.

Social work is a complex and demanding endeavour. It is therefore understandable that some practitioners should seek simple, straightforward answers to complex problems. However, existentialism recognises the subtle intricacies of human existence in general and problem solving activities such as social work in particular and therefore alerts us to the dangers of over-simplification. Two such dangers are reductionism and essentialism. The former refers to the tendency to reduce a complex, multi-level phenomenon to a single level or explanation. For example, the view that 'all social workers are racist' fails to take account of the different levels of discrimination and oppression and thereby reduces a personal, cultural and structural issue to simply a personal one. The latter refers to the tendency to regard phenomena which are fluid and open to change as if they were fixed and immutable. For example, aspects of an individual's identity may be seen as beyond change, thus failing to recognise that identity is not a fixed entity and is influenced by a wide range of social and psychological processes— and is therefore partly within the control of the individual. Existentialism cannot be a simple philosophy offering simple solutions, because it seeks to make sense of the immensely complicated and intricate nature of human existence—it is therefore clearly antithetical to such dangerous processes as reductionism and essentialism which fail to appreciate the enormously complex nature of social reality.

However, although existentialism cannot offer simple answers, what it can offer us is a number of important themes and concepts which can be extremely useful in looking for ways forward in getting to grips with the challenges that face us in social work as we deal with not only the complexities of human experience in general, but also those particular situations which reflect the extremes of life, where pain, suffering, deprivation and oppression are to the fore. The demanding territory of social work practice is also very much the theoretical territory of existentialism, with its focus on those aspects of life which can challenge our ontological security. Such ontological security is necessary to nourish and sustain the sense of identity and rootedness which enables us to respond to the existential challenges that we all face at certain times in our lives, but which many people face far more frequently, and perhaps more intensely, as a result of their social location and the effects of discrimination and oppression in a society characterised by structural inequalities.

Existentialism is a practical philosophy. It seeks not only to understand the world but also to change it. It is this practical focus, together with its emphasis on the inherent suffering, unpredictability and risk of human existence, which makes it a useful basis for taking forward our thinking…Existentialism is a philosophy of *empowerment*. It recognises the fundamental freedom of human existence but also takes cognisance of the internal or subjective self-made barriers of bad faith and the external or objective constraints of social divisions and the attendant inequalities and oppressions of sexism, racism and so on. Existentialism offers a way forward in the perpetual struggle to maintain an authentic existence which avoids the indulgences and false salvation of bad faith, and which challenges and undermines the oppressions which seek to constrain or destroy our freedom (Thompson, 1992b: pp36–37).

Existentialist practice, then, is not a form of practice based on easy answers or stock responses, but rather an approach which recognises the complex demands of human existence and seeks to wrestle with them in an informed way—informed by our understanding of the nature of human reality as discussed, described and debated in the wealth of existentialist literature we have at our disposal.

References

Adams, R. (1996). *The Personal Social Services*. Harlow: Longman.

Bevan, D. (1998). Death, Dying and Inequality. *Care: The Journal of Practice and Development*, 7(1): pp27–38.

Billington, R. (1990). *East of Existentialism: The Tao of the West*. London: Unwin Hyman.

Gordon, L.R. (Ed.) (1997). *Existence in Black: An Anthology of Black Existential Philosophy*. London: Routledge.

Henry, P. (1997). Rastafarianism and the Reality of Dread. In Gordon (1997).

Lesnik, B. (Ed.) (1998). *Countering Discrimination in Social Work*. Aldershot: Arena.

Macquarrie, J. (1973). *Existentialism*. Harmondsworth: Penguin.

Mahon, J. (1997). *Existentialism, Feminism and Simone de Beauvoir*. London: Macmillan.

May, R., Angel, R., and Ellenberger, H.F. (1958). *Existence: A New Dimension in Psychiatry and Psychology*. New York: Touchstone.

Payne, M. (1998). *Modern Social Work Theory* (2nd edn.). London: Macmillan.

Sartre, J-P. (1958). *Being and Nothingness*. London: Methuen.

Sartre, J-P. (1963). *Search for a Method*. New York: Vintage.

Sartre, J-P. (1982). *Critique of Dialectical Reason*. London: Verso.

Schön, D. (1983). *The Reflective Practitioner: How Professionals Think in Action*. New York: Basic Books.

Thompson, N. (1991). *Crisis Intervention Revisited*. Birmingham: Pepar.

Thompson, N. (1992a). *Existentialism and Social Work*. Aldershot: Avebury.

Thompson, N. (1992b). *Child Abuse: The Existential Dimension*. Norwich: University of East Anglia Social Work Monographs.

Thompson, N. (1995). *Age and Dignity: Working with Older People*. Aldershot: Arena.

Thompson, N. (1998a). The Ontology of Ageing. *British Journal of Social Work*, 28(5): pp697–707.

Thompson, N. (1998b). *Promoting Equality: Challenging Discrimination and Oppression in the Human Services*. London: Macmillan.

Thompson, N. (2000). *Theory and Practice in Human Services* (2nd edn.). Buckingham: Open University Press.

Chapter Thirteen

Empowerment: Help or Hindrance in Professional Relationships

Lena Dominelli

Empowerment is a trendy catchword that has acquired resonance across the political spectrum, regardless of whether its adherents espouse traditional or progressive philosophies. Its potential to have meaning for all shades of political opinion makes it an intellectually messy concept that can frustrate attempts aimed at critically examining its usefulness in professional social work relationships. Nonetheless, in this chapter, I intend to consider empowerment in helping relations in terms of its capacity to describe the attempts of caring professionals to engage in power sharing activities with those whom they claim to serve—their 'clients' (1). I conclude that empowerment is necessary but contradictory and insufficient in bringing about the realisation of emancipatory social work.

The reason for embarking on this exercise is that I think that the power relations between professionals and their 'clients' are central to the kind of helping relationship that can be developed between them. Understanding these dynamics identifies the conditions under which 'clients' can engage in the process of asserting control over and being responsible for their own affairs. It is also a key ingredient in their ability to hold professionals accountable for their actions and demand services that are user-led. In the course of conducting this exploration, I also seek to explain why empowerment is acceptable to both rightwing politicians promoting discourses of choice and market solutions to the delivery of welfare services as well as to those supporting social justice for marginalised or socially excluded groups.

Empowerment: what is it?

Empowerment is a difficult term to define. It was popular in discourses around community action in the late 1960s and 1970s, but the New Right appropriated it for its own radical

agenda during the 1980s. The definitions of the former have conveyed ideas of a transfer of power across social categories; those of the latter, the assertion of control by individuals. Individualising definitions of empowerment have tended to focus on interpersonal relations, that is, what an individual can do when interacting with (an)other(s), whilst the former have concerned themselves with transformational changes at the structural or societal level. Those following either one of these two conceptions of empowerment have usually been at odds with the other, each criticising their opponents for their failure to take on board the dimension it has raised.

Stuart Rees (1991) has been a main advocate of the view that empowerment is about producing structural change. Individuals are empowered in the process of achieving that objective. Wallerstein and Bernstein (1994: p198) focus on the structural dimensions of the phenomenon by defining empowerment as a:

> ...social-action process that promotes participation of people, organisations and communities towards the goal of individual and community control, political efficacy, improved quality of community life and social justice.

However, structural approaches run the risk of excluding individual empowerment either at the personal level or as part of a collective process. If individual empowerment occurs, it is often as a by-product of the collective process rather than being one of its direct objectives.

Those particularly interested in an individual's psychological development have argued that empowerment is a process aimed at facilitating personal change by enabling individuals to take control of their activities (Riger, 1993). Individualising views of empowerment have also been fostered through managerialist pronouncements that have introduced complaints procedures and other bureaucratic forms of control over professional behaviour. Dominelli (1996; 1997) has critiqued managerialist approaches for ignoring process issues and focusing on bureaucratised forms of empowerment because these fail to address systemic inequalities and structural sources of individual disempowerment. Dominelli (1997) also argues that these lock individuals into tokenistic forms of empowerment because control over the creation and design of services rests with management.

This view does not endorse arguments legitimating professionals' capacity to act as autonomous beings who are unaccountable to 'clients' as Lloyd, 1998 claims. Rather, it suggests that professionals exercising critical judgement and discretion are more likely to allow for the possibility that people's needs can be met when their circumstances do not reflect normative behaviour because 'clients' have the opportunity to engage in a real dialogue with them and have their views heard. At the same time, professionals in these situations need to be aware that they can also exercise discretion in discriminatory ways and avoid doing so. It is important, therefore, to have empowerment operating at *both* personal and structural levels.

Concentrating on collective empowerment amongst 'black' people, Solomon (1976) argues eloquently that individuals must become involved in the empowerment of their communities, thus bridging the gap between the two polarised positions of either structural or personal change. To reach these objectives, Solomon suggests that community groups begin the process by redefining the issues to be addressed in terms of what they want to achieve. By acting along these lines and participating in collective action, people who have been marginalised individually and collectively are empowered because they begin to assert their own definitions of what is to be done, thereby challenging their being cast as pathological individuals and communities. Consequently, Solomon (1976) challenges commonly accepted definitions of socially excluded groups by constructing their 'difference' or deviation from the dominant norms as a source of strength and not the basis of their powerlessness. Empowerment in these types of situations becomes a matter of process and outcomes. Professionals may be involved in the organising process, but as facilitators of an agenda set by the community groups themselves.

Power relations and who has the power to define them in particular ways are crucial to issues of empowerment. But power itself is a disputed concept (Lukes, 1974; French, 1985; Clegg, 1989; Riger, 1993). Power has been conceptualised in three different ways as *power over*, *power to*, and *power of*. *Power over* involves relations of domination. Analysts like Talcott Parsons have presented *power over* as a 'zero-sum' entity, that is, a force that is imposed upon others or something that people *do to* other people (Parsons and Bale, 1955). It can be exercised in ways that impact on either individuals or groups. In many respects, this definition is the one that has gained commonsense currency. People assume that power is finite. It can only be taken away from those that have it through conflict of some kind. Although power involves action, *power over* is characterised by a certain fixedness which disables those at the receiving end of the ministration of more powerful other(s) and renders them passive against its onslaught. The application of *power over* others is usually experienced as disempowering by those at the bottom of a hierarchy of dominance.

Relations of domination that rely on the exercise of *power over* others are usually portrayed in dichotomous terms that sit in binary opposition to each other. One either has power or one does not. If one individual has *power over*, others can only take it away, that is, disempower him or her. Thus, people talk about taking control over one's life to counter this state of affairs. Those at the receiving end of such power relations are usually deemed passive victims who can do little about their situations. Passivity and the lack of vision depicting alternatives to their positions limit people's potential to see the possibilities for changing their environment. Discourses centring on *power over* others tend to focus on individual skills and cast those lacking power as inadequate or pathological. Moreover, through their interactions with more powerful others, individuals internalise dominant definitions of their positions and become less convinced of their capacity to resist the status quo arrangements or question the set of relations within which they are located.

Another set of theorists, particularly feminist ones, have questioned this 'zero-sum' view of power, postulating it as a complex force which emanates from many sources and which can be created and re-created through social interactions (French, 1985). Power which is considered multi-faceted involves people negotiating with each other so that power is created and recreated through the social relationships they form. Power can be both a positive and a negative source of energy and can be used creatively. Other people's powers can be diffused and their impact upon one's life limited. Thus, the issue is not simply a question of taking power away from someone else. Power can be shared and new forms of power can arise. People engage in power relations by exercising their agency either individually or collectively. In short, there is no passive victim of other people's actions, although their endeavours to assert their agency may or may not be successful. Moreover, there is nothing predetermined about the outcome of their negotiations with others (Dominelli and Gollins, 1997). Powerful people are not totally powerful and powerless people are not without power (Dominelli, 1986). Thus, neither the powerful nor the powerless are locked into positions from which they cannot move to advance or retreat. They can also stand still. Furthermore, their negotiations do not necessarily occur in a linear fashion. And, they take place in the routines of everyday life.

The structural positioning of individuals is also important in setting the scene for a negotiated encounter with others. This is particularly significant in the accessibility to and development of support networks. These networks can ease one's way in life, for they can assist in identifying the resources that are available, and enhance morale boosting efforts (Craig and Mayo, 1995).

In short, in a negotiation involving power dynamics, an outcome can go either way, depending on the situational circumstances and resources that the parties involved in the interaction bring with them. Since power in a negotiation can go either way, nothing is predetermined, although experience and statistics can demonstrate the probability that if an individual is poor and 'black', they will have less access to opportunities and resources than if they were 'white' (2). This reality will reduce 'black' people's capacity to effectively assert their power as individuals. But it is a dimension that can be challenged more effectively through collective action.

Personal relationships also matter in *power over* situations because they can be used to mitigate its potential to destroy those who have been subordinated. Creating these in adverse conditions can be crucial to an individual's chances of survival. For example, individuals abducted in hostage-taking incidents are more likely to be treated with less hostility or be released if they are successful in getting their captors to see them as persons with whom they can relate even when the immediate balance of power overwhelmingly favours the hostage-taker. In short, by engaging in a personal relationship, the *power over* relation can be diffused to some extent. These dynamics are an indication of how empowerment and disempowerment can feature simultaneously in any one given situation.

This rethinking of power relations has given rise to the idea that power involves doing something about one's situation and is reflected in the remaining two considerations of power. *Power to* entails resistance to subordination and oppression. It usually implies that individuals come together to collectively express their ability to take action in terms they set. This conceptualisation of power is a dynamic one which allows oppressed people to reject in myriad ways the position in which they find themselves and is thus deemed empowering. But the exercise of *power to* do something with others can easily shift into the dynamics of *power over* others.

Power of occurs as a result of individuals coming together as a united (not unified or homogeneous) category to form a collective organisation that is capable of challenging oppression, especially the imposition of *power over* them. Thus, Dominelli (1986) talks about the 'power of the powerless' in analysing a marginalised group of women's ability to organise themselves to challenge sexist social relations. Groups who create *power of* relationships for themselves experience their exercise of power as empowering because they are able to construct their own agenda for action.

Useful as these notions are in assisting in the task of understanding power, they are all problematic insofar as they fail to take on board the full complexities of power. These include the relevance of the three forms of power considered above and their interaction with each other in any specific incident. It is likely that a detailed analysis of any one situation will reveal that power as—*power over*, *power to* and *power of*, will be present simultaneously. Unpacking the concept is further complicated by the perception of power as an entity that operates within a dichotomous world. This is particularly pertinent in envisaging power relations as *power over*, the element that sits uneasily at the foreground of many people's understandings of power.

Consequently, in *power over* social relations, issues of oppression are considered in binary terms. A situation is described as either 'this' or 'that', in other words, as another instance of the 'us—them' mentality. According to this, with regards to power, people either have it or they don't. It is like having a good that can be traded or taken away. Therefore, an individual or group is either oppressed because they lack power or liberated because they have it. In these characterisations of the matter, liberation is simply a question of reversing the existing zero-sum configuration of social relations. Thus, in Marxist world-views, for example, the power of the bourgeoisie was to be challenged and replaced by the power of the proletariat.

In professional discourses, 'zero-sum' versions of power produce empowerment as a halfway house between being powerful and powerless. Yet, having control over one's affairs is not the same as feeling empowered within them. Indeed, in terms of professional bureaucratic responses, the empowerment objective can be thwarted by a concern with the mechanics of empowerment at the expense of process and outcome—the *how* and *who* of social relations. Thus, a disillusioned Oliver (1990) writes that the most that professionals can hope to achieve is to not disempower their 'clients'. Although couched in terms of *power over*, empowerment for Oliver (1990) is something that an individual can only do for him or herself within the context of collective action around their particular conditions.

Those committed to power sharing forms of empowering social interactions have sought to meet in this halfway house to ensure that the acquisition of skills, the allocation of roles or tasks and participation in decision making involve all members of a group (Belenky *et al.*, 1997). Through these, there is an attempt to validate experiential ways of knowing, not just

empirical evidence. There is often a reliance on mechanisms such as rotating formal positions to ensure that each person has a chance to learn different tasks and obtain the skills and knowledge that accompany these. Additionally, everyone is encouraged to participate in expressions of grief over their collective failures and joy over their group's successes. Empowerment in these conditions can impact on both personal and structural levels, as have, for example, feminists organising in political parties. Yet, even their successes in this arena have failed to transform social relations in an emancipatory way for women (see Dominelli and Jonsdottir, 1989).

A further obstacle in the unpacking of power dynamics relates to the organisation of social relations in ways that maintain a division between the public sphere and the private one. The setting of this boundary is especially significant in the exercise of *power over* others. For if public matters can be relegated to the private domain whether through discourses or other forms of action, issues of accountability lapse. Similarly, raising concerns usually located in the domestic sphere in the public arena, pushes issues of accountability and responsibility to the forefront of the public agenda. This was a tactic employed by feminists to raise public recognition of domestic violence and child sexual abuse within family settings at a time when denial about their existence was rampant (Rush, 1980; Kelly, 1988; Dominelli, 1989; Basu, 1995). In the process of meeting this objective, the women involved in such consciousness-raising activities began to feel confident in their abilities to set their own agendas and felt empowered as a result (Ruzek, 1986; Basu, 1995).

The issue of the public-private divide also becomes important in the creation of a welfare marketplace. For by defining care as a private responsibility, commercial providers are encouraged to develop facilities that seek to meet these needs. And, they can begin to charge for these in a way that assures the provider of a profit margin. Indeed, by transforming human interactions into commodity relations, social relationships become privatised, that is, become a matter between individuals who are then 'free' to negotiate a contract with each other. In this context, structural limitations, like the large numbers of people who are too poor to avail themselves of a 'free' choice do not even get into the picture, let alone penetrate the space to engage in the ongoing discourses in their own voices. In a globalised context, commodifying social relations tend to reproduce *power over* relations in which the managerial and corporatist voices dominate at the expense of both professionals and 'clients'.

Empowerment, defined as the ability to choose options within a range of available possibilities is therefore problematic for those seeking equality. For it assumes that the individuals can enter the commodity relationship on an equal basis, that is, they each have the same access to information and resources. Of course, this is far from the actual reality for a significant proportion of the majority of the world's population, as the latest United Nation's report on human social development indicates (UN, 1998). Thus, real choice, can only be exercised by the privileged few. But it is their capacity to conduct empowerment discourses in terms of presuming equality rather than demonstrating its presence in the commodity relation that makes the concept so attractive to right wing ideologues, policy makers and entrepreneurs.

The problems highlighted above raise queries about the conceptualisation of empowerment as a negotiating position that lies in the middle of a continuum with oppression at one end and liberation at the other. If its potential for action is derived from this location, then empowerment becomes a way of mediating power relations within tightly circumscribed constraints over which the individual as an individual can have only limited leverage. Such restraints in altering a situation relate to the individual's structural position rather than to his or her volition. This limitation in turn poses the question of the importance of collective endeavours in ensuring individual empowerment and success in a person's ability to exert control over his or her affairs. As part of the situational context, structural constraints also create major hurdles that have to be overcome by professionals who seek to work in empowering ways with their 'clients'.

This point emphasises another key difficulty in conceptualising power and empowerment as an individual or personal activity, that is, the decontextualisation of the person from his or her social context. Recognising the significance of situational contexts in an individual's capacity to assert control over their activities is often lacking in professional interventions (Thorpe, 1993). Social workers frequently act as if the context in which poor people or those suffering from structural inequalities exist is absent and treat them as if all individuals are the same when they are not. This is particularly evident when practitioners respond to people facing structural inequalities as if their life chances mirror those of the dominant group. This happens, for example, when they treat 'black' people as if they were 'white' (Dominelli, 1988; Ahmad, 1990), or women as if they were men (Hanmer and Statham, 1988; Dominelli and McLeod, 1989). Endorsed in the professional ideology of 'universalism', this stance ignores diversity and creates a totalising unity that negates the actual living conditions which individuals and groups experience. Ignoring the attendant conditions within which individuals are embedded results in a failure to acknowledge the boundaries within which the individual as an individual can take action to empower him or herself. A similar problem is endured by marginalised groups who also encounter these limitations in their capacities for resistance in their lived experience on a daily basis.

Additionally, a decontextualised view of power neglects to take account of the commodification of social relations which is occurring within the welfare market place at the same time. As a result of this, qualitative issues once deemed outside the commodity relation have been quantified and subjected to measurement, thereby enhancing bureaucratic forms of power which are usually controlled by agency managers and the professionals they employ. Bureaucracies are sites of entrenched forms of power which individuals have difficulty in challenging effectively when operating within the terms that those running them set. Furthermore, in the welfare market place, professionals in bureaucratic settings now interact with their 'clients' as individual consumers who are receiving a commodity for which they can expect to pay instead of a service delivered free of charge.

Engaging with 'clients' within commodity relationships requires different responses from professionals than those involved in forming professional relationships rooted in interpersonal relations. Whilst commodity relations can be empowering for individuals who have the capacity to exercise choice to avail themselves of services geared to their needs, the majority of 'clients' are not in a position to do so because their situational context is one of structural inequalities encompassed by the term poverty. Money determines the extent to which individuals can become purchasers in the service market place, despite their having being constructed as atomised consumers by the discourses of market place welfare entrepreneurs.

The commodity relation has also resulted in the de-professionalising of the profession by reducing complex professional tasks to their simplified constituent parts (Dominelli and Hoogvelt, 1997). This development has fed the proletarianisation of the once autonomous professionals who previously exercised a considerable degree of control over their own labour process. And, it has opened the door to the employment of less qualified individuals in caring situations demanding more professional expertise than ever because the 'clients' being referred to welfare agencies have increasingly complex needs (Teeple, 1995).

Many welfare state activities have now become subject to managerialist imperative and procedural forms of control (Culpitt, 1992; Teeple, 1995). These have made it difficult for those working within the welfare bureaucracies or seeking to access services, to challenge. Neither do they make it easy to hold professionals accountable for their interventions or failing to engage with 'clients' concerns. Thus, the Taylorisation of social work that has accompanied market relations in the welfare arena (Dominelli and Hoogvelt, 1997) has had devastating consequences for both professionals and 'clients'. For professionals, it has meant the loss of individual control over how they work. For 'clients', it has resulted in their having little real say over what is made available to them or who is entitled to access the facilities in question. However, 'clients' have made some gains from this process in that it has legitimated greater professional accountability, at least in principle. Nonetheless, the groups that have gained the most from this reorganisation of welfare relations are the politicians, corporate entrepreneurs and wealthy users. The politicians controlling the state apparatus have

gained for they have succeeded in shedding the state's responsibilities for ensuring the welfare of its citizens. Entrepreneurs are advantaged because a new source of getting rich opens up when they successfully land lucrative (mainly state) contracts, for these can yield substantial profits for the services they provide to targeted individuals, usually referred to as customers. Wealthy users gain because it has enlarged their choices quantitatively and qualitatively. And, they no longer have to receive services alongside their less affluent compatriots and experience the discomfort they associate with doing so. In short, the bureaucratisation of consumer power in the welfare sphere and managerialist control over professionals through performance-related pay, competence-based definitions of caring tasks and workplace-based training have meant a loss of control over the conditions in which both professionals and 'clients' conduct key areas of their lives (Dominelli, 1996).

To effectively challenge commodity relations in the welfare arena, change needs to occur at the individual or personal level and at the structural level. Thus, change has to take place in the 'client's' behaviour, the professional's repertoire of skills, the organisation of welfare services, and society's cultural and value systems so that the entire basis on which social relations are organised and conducted can be altered. Only then can the scene be set for empowerment, as liberation, to take place.

Accusations of reification, essentialism or reductionism in the debates over empowerment (see Lloyd, 1998) ignore the social construction of particular social categories at specific points in time by particular groups or individuals. It is not that these categories are totalising and immutable, for an examination of their composition reveals that they are simultaneously unifying and diverse. But they may be described as otherwise by those setting the terms within which discourses about them are conducted. Thus, they may be treated *as if* the category were homogeneous, thereby enabling *power over* relations to be reproduced. To create discourses that transcend such power relations, language has to go beyond simplifying symbols to describe complex realities. A symbol is both a signifier and representational of people's actions, behaviour, thought and meaning, each of which can only partially be conveyed through language. What lies 'hidden' behind these symbols is as important as the *partial* reality they convey, for this includes power relations which are also operative within a given interaction whether an individual is actively conscious of them or not.

For these reasons, empowerment theories should steer shy of theoretical frameworks which totalise social categories and despite evidence to the contrary, present them as if they were unitary. A useful framework would have to take on board the consideration that such categories are not simply a set of homogeneous groups. Within the unity of a category, diversity can be found. The existence of diversity within unity is a point that can be verified experientially and empirically. So, for example, referring to women as a group does not warrant the assumption that every woman in that category is the same. There are both similarities and differences that have to be acknowledged and taken on board. But it may be convenient for those doing the defining to treat women as a homogeneous group for particular purposes or because they have not thought out the implications of their categorisations. This occurred, for example, in the early days of the feminist movement when white middle-class American feminist writers treated women across the globe as if they occupied the same privileged position as they did (see Friedan, 1974). It was also evident when 'sisterhood' was declared 'universal' (Morgan, 1971) with little appreciation that the slogan denied the actual experiences of being a woman for the majority of women in the global context (Mohanty, 1995; Basu, 1995).

Honi Fern Haber (1994) utilises the concept of the 'individual in the community' to move away from a totalising universalism and related concepts linked to dichotomous thinking which privileges powerful people. Instead, she examines bonds of solidarity that recognise the uniquenesses symbolised by 'difference' as well as the unities within and amongst them. These can be developed to both empower and disempower individuals or groups. The main message that can be derived from her analysis is that any connection with others *must be created and not assumed.*

Thus, empowerment has to acknowledge the legitimacy of individual and group identity boundaries as well as valorise the strengths that are embodied within them at all levels. For professionals, this means desisting from thinking about 'difference' as a 'deficit' and pathology that must be eradicated (Dominelli, 1997, 1998). The acknowledgement of 'difference' places issues of identity at the forefront of the self-expression and the development of empowering power relations. The politics of identity can provide common objectives which will feed the webs of connection which can transcend 'difference' without obliterating it (Haraway, 1988). Unity of this kind differs from the assimilationist forms that were advocated by those running the nation state during its nation building ventures and those subsequently replicated through the welfare state (Lorenz, 1994). For these have denied 'difference' and based access to entitlements on exclusionary definitions of citizenship and reduced the rights of women and 'black' people to receive its benefits. Under assimilationist discourses of which totalising universalism was a part, 'difference' was suppressed, but it did not disappear.

Professionalism and empowerment

Are professionals promoting empowerment to be mistrusted as Oliver (1990) suggests or is it possible to transform professionalism so that power sharing with 'clients' becomes the norm as Dominelli and Jonsdottir (1989) imply? Clearly, as countless groups and the 'new' social movements have demonstrated, unlimited professional power, or the exercise of professional *power over* others is unacceptable to people demanding social justice. Social justice, according to Flax (1990), is a bridging concept which is rooted in the recognition of 'difference' and enables individuals to organise around identity issues experienced at both individual and collective levels. Empowerment which aims to realise social justice, therefore, has to address 'difference' in terms which will valorise its existence and value the strengths which arise from its recognition as a positive factor in people's lives. Professionals can contribute to this objective by appreciating and valuing 'difference' and relating to individuals in their social context.

Having this attitude will help practitioners utilise their experience in ways that contribute towards the well-being of their 'clients'. People want to work with experts who are accountable to them and can be held responsible for their behaviour (Oliver, 1990). In addition, as the feminist movements and disability movements have indicated, professionals should reconsider their definition of professionalism and turn it into one which is about placing expertise in the hands of the users. In other words, it is about professionals *servicing* the needs of their 'clients' rather than providing them with a service as a commodity. 'Clients' are quite capable of providing their own services—those that they design and run, once they have access to the necessary resources. A professional can become a resource like the other resources that 'clients' have at their disposal to achieve the purpose of enhancing their well-being.

This stance, however, can raise a number of awkward questions for practitioners. For example, are 'clients' always correct in identifying their own needs? Aside from queries aimed at determining who is the 'client', particularly in complex situations where there may be more than one 'client', should professionals simply go along with the needs identified by 'clients'? Whilst an affirmative reply may often be unproblematic, what happens if a social worker is working with a young male sex offender who identifies his need as having access to children against whom he commits sexual assaults? Or the man who believes he is 'right' to constantly beat his wife when he feels aggrieved? Both these behaviours would be deemed unacceptable to most professionals and their stance would be endorsed by their code of ethics. But in less clear-cut issues, for example, in a case of indirect discrimination occasioned by an employment policy requiring a qualification which is normally accessed primarily by 'white' men, the ensuing outcome of under-representation of both 'black' men and women is less likely to be noticed and condemned.

On the other hand, as countless inquiries into the abuse of children in residential care have demonstrated, 'clients' cannot assume that professionals will not abuse their *power over* them (see Haig-Brown, 1988; Kahan, 1989; Pringle, 1992). How can professionals demonstrate their trustworthiness to 'clients'? What kinds of relationships and controls are necessary to reduce their *power over* potential to

harm others? Obviously, compliance to a code of ethics, training and managerial controls can be used as measures to secure a professional's compliance with this objective. Empowering 'clients' to assert their voice and interests in their affairs is another powerful way of holding professionals accountable for their behaviour. But how 'client' control and empowerment can best be achieved remains highly controversial.

Another tricky issue for professionals to address is that of relativism, the idea that one position is as valid as another. Whilst laudable in ensuring that one world view does not dominate another, in professional encounters, relativism can lead to unhelpful uncertainty and indecision if applied indiscriminately to every situation—a condition which, I would argue, is more of a solipsism in which anything goes than it is relativism. In a post-modern world, ambiguity in practice is promoted as a positive skill (Parton, 1998). Ambiguity results from social workers acting as intermediaries between the state and civil society. However, ambiguity and uncertainty in daily discourses are usually taken to mean simultaneously holding more than one position. But operationalised in a practice context that disregards the situation that a 'client' is in, this can cause indecision that may be costly for vulnerable individuals. For example, how can a social worker imbued with a belief that 'truth' is relative deal with unacceptable behaviour amongst more powerful others whether this is men, sex offenders, or any other 'client' group abusing a less powerful one? On one level, social workers have always dealt with ambiguity and uncertainty as part of their daily routines. But at the end of the day, they have had to take action, to make decisions on which the livelihood and safety of others have depended.

This requires some appeal to universal principles such as the valuing of human life and others contained within a code of professional ethics and the United Nations Declaration of Human Rights. Whilst mistakes have sometimes been made, practitioners have tended to base their decisions on their assessment of an individual's situation not always taking account of their social context, but operating within a legal framework accompanied by a professional code of ethics and their own value system. Within this value system, valuing the lives of vulnerable people have been crucial elements that have transcended relativistic positioning. When the importance of going beyond a relativist position is not recognised and maintained for whatever reason, the lives of vulnerable individuals have been placed in jeopardy and social workers have been unable to adequately carry out their support and monitoring roles. At such points, social workers fail their 'clients'. This has happened to children on 'at risk' registers whose family members have gone on to murder them because social workers have failed to insist on their statutory obligations to investigate private relationships and thereby give priority to children's interests when these conflict with those of their carers. However, the difficulties in such cases are complex and social workers can become overwhelmed by their own needs for clarity over what they see as conflicting goals and a situational context which they experience as disempowering (see Blom-Cooper, 1986).

Social workers engage with both universal and relative values in the judgments they make as professionals. However, their actions must not occur within the assumption of the superiority of the worker's own views. That they do so is a failing which occurs far too often when they are working with diversity and 'difference' (see for example, Dominelli, 1988; Hanmer and Statham, 1988; Dominelli and McLeod, 1989; Ahmad, 1990). It also happens when they distance themselves from 'clients' because they label them as 'other', that is, those who are deemed pathological, inadequate and inferior. Instead, practitioners working within an empowerment framework need to engage with their 'clients' rather than distancing themselves by casting them as the 'other'. This means respecting the person, though not necessarily condoning their behaviour, confronting through dialogue unacceptable behaviour which attacks the dignity of vulnerable people; and following through with action aimed at ceasing their inappropriate behaviours.

A value system based on universal human rights can help them negotiate this task. Furthermore, empathy has to be achieved whilst holding ambiguity and then dealing with it by taking *specific action in a specific situation*. Empathy is a key dimension in the social work relationship (Egan, 1990).

However, empathy can only result if social workers can really get into another person's shoes whilst at the same time retaining their capacity for independent judgment in accordance with universalistic principles embedded in the realisation of human rights that acknowledge 'difference' within group and individual allegiances.

A universalism that addresses 'differences' and is rooted in universal human rights provides social workers with a concept that goes beyond the self and the sometimes sectarian politics associated with identity politics (3). However, this can only be relevant to their work as practitioners if they can recognise that universalism calls upon other values as prerequisites in the process of its realisation. These include solidarity, mutuality and interdependence. Each of these values is implicated in the creation of webs of support which enable empowerment to occur more readily under the control of those whom the professional seeks to serve. However, these values cannot be thought of in dichotomous terms that pit the interests of one part of the community against those of another. It is about recognising that there are a number of interdependent considerations that must be considered together as part of the whole picture.

So, for example, empowering a sex offender requires that his offending behaviour, that is, the sexual (and other forms of) abuse of others is terminated. But doing so also means taking on board the fact that the male sex offender is also a 'client' who needs a different set of support and resources than those required by the victim-survivors to enable him to stop abusing others. Thus, in terms of interdependence, the safety of the sexually abused child depends on the ensuring that the sex offender's need for rehabilitation through the learning of new, non-exploitative ways of relating to children and others less powerful than he is met as a matter of course. In short, the punishment given for committing crimes against a child becomes an opportunity for introducing behavioural change at the personal level rather than considering it solely a matter of incarceration as punishment for the offender and protection of the victim.

However, getting to this stage of redefining the problems to be addressed requires: personal change on the part of the offender;

structural change at the level of the institution so that this kind of response can become commonplace; and change at the cultural level so that sex offenders are considered people who also need help, even if it is offered by a different practitioner than the one who is working directly with the child and/or the non-abusing parent, usually the mother. Reciprocity occurs when the sex offender assumes responsibility for his behaviour and acknowledges its damaging impact on others; while society, via the professional acting on its behalf in working with him, facilitates his access to rehabilitative resources. Solidarity is expressed through a joint commitment to ensuring the safety and well-being of all.

Acting in accordance with the principles of universalism which acknowledge the specificity of context, can be risky and tricky. Even in the illustrations covered above, 'success' cannot be guaranteed. Consequently, to empower themselves in complex interventions, professionals have to come clean about their ambiguity and uncertainties. They do not always know the 'right' answer. They do not always live up to their own expectations when it comes to providing 'client'-centred services which respond to the unique needs of individuals. They do not always have the resources necessary to work with 'clients' in accordance with a mutually agreed plan of action.

The following case study in which all the characters have been given fictitious names, explores some of the ambiguities and uncertainties which complicate practice aiming to empower 'clients' so that it becomes contradictory and paradoxical (Lupton and Nixon, 1999), or even disempowering in a number of crucial respects:

Case study: the Goodson family

Clark Goodson was a 30-year-old white man living with his wife Selma, a 28-year-old white woman and their two children, Christine, aged three and Sally aged two. Clark was an unemployed miner who had been unable to get a job for over five years. Selma had become the family 'breadwinner' by working at four part-time jobs as a cleaner. As part of the working poor, their income was supplemented by Family Credit. However, it was difficult to

make ends meet. Selma often went without food although Clark was allowed the odd drink at the pub with his mates for old times' sake. Secretly, Selma was glad of this weekly ritual for it got Clark out of the house and gave her a few hours of peace with only the squabbling children to worry about. Selma was constantly tired and on edge. Her relationship with Clark was getting increasingly strained. She didn't feel he tried to find work hard enough. He complained bitterly that as a young man, he had been 'thrown on the scrapheap'.

The crunch came one evening when Selma's old banger which had been getting her to and from her various jobs broke down irreparably. Now carless, she didn't manage to get home until nearly midnight. Clark was furious when she returned. He had missed his pub night and the children had been impossible to get to bed. Indeed, they were still fussing about, though in their pyjamas. He started blaming Selma for all that had gone wrong with his evening. This proved too much for Selma and before long the worst row the two had ever had, erupted. It also got ugly. Clark started to hit Selma, punching her in the face and chest. The children who were witnesses to his violence started screaming. Christine ran to her mother just as Clark was punching her and one of his blows landed on Christine's skull. Christine fell over and bumped into a chair, hitting it with the side of her head, and slumped to the floor. Meanwhile, the neighbours who had heard all the screaming, shouting and other noises had called the police. Selma phoned for an ambulance. Both arrived at the same time.

Christine was rushed off to hospital where the examining doctor diagnosed several other signs of earlier bruising and violence—a fractured rib and arm that had healed. Eventually, Clark admitted that he had hit her several months earlier when Selma had been asked to work late on his pub night. Selma felt disgusted with him, mortified by his behaviour coming to light in these circumstances and guilty for having to go out to work instead of staying home to look after the children. And, she also felt angry that Clark had placed them in this position because he had been either unable or unwilling to land a job.

The family was referred to social services for an investigation as a case of non-accidental injury (NAI). The social worker who went to visit the family at home was a young newly-qualified childless 22-year-old 'black' woman of African descent called Angela. Though feeling sickened by letting his temper get the best of him and subjecting his family to what he thought would be a demeaning experience, Clark was in a belligerent mood. He kept telling himself he loved his family and he was not going to let any young 'whipper-snapper' tell him how to lead his life. 'NAI, indeed!' he expostulated. If they really wanted to help him, why couldn't someone just give him a job? He didn't need anything else. He'd had no problems when he was bringing home a good wage. Although the children had not been born at that point, he and Selma had had a great relationship and he was sure they would again if only he could bring in the money and hold his head high once more.

The social worker sensed Clark's hostility the moment he opened the door. She couldn't decide whether it was because he was anxious about what might happen; did not want a 'black' worker; lacked confidence in her ability to handle the situation adequately because she was relatively inexperienced; or had other reasons. However, she smiled at him and tried to put him at ease. Then she asked if she could go inside and meet the rest of the family. He reluctantly let her in. Selma's reaction to Angela was guarded. During the interview, she said very little. Clark took on the role of responding for them both.

Angela worked in as facilitative a manner as she could and tried to create the space that Selma and Clark needed to give their own views about what should be done to help them with their problems. However, she also made it clear to the two parents that her main concern was the welfare of the two children. She was looking for assurance that the children were not at 'risk' of further acts of violence being perpetrated against either of them.

However, the more she spoke to the couple, the more she realised that their problems were many and complex. She also realised that focusing simply on protecting the children from further harm was not going to work. The family was in need of a wider range of support services than she could offer within the remit of an NAI. Moreover, she didn't know how she could ensure that the children would be safe as long as the stresses and strains on the family continued as they were. Money was in short supply, but whilst Angela could make a one-off payment to safeguard the children's interests, she could not take on the commitment of supplementing Selma's meagre wages for an indefinite period. Moreover, Selma needed rest. Selma and Clark required marital counselling. And, Clark was in desperate need of a job.

Meeting most of these requirements was not the responsibility of the social services department. Yet, potential appeals to other agencies for additional resources were limited. Many charities were already overwhelmed by requests for assistance that they could not fulfil. Angela felt confounded by the situation that confronted her. Here she was intervening in the lives of people that she could scarcely help. She could place their children on the 'at risk' register or get them looked after by foster parents if she felt maintaining their safety warranted it, but she could offer little in the form of direct support to the family. At best, this could be attendance at a Family Centre a few days a week, a playgroup space and a volunteer to help out around the house. None of her options were ideal.

At the case conference subsequently held to discuss the family, Angela reported her findings and misgivings. Her colleagues shared her sense of frustration, but as the chair of the case conference said, they had to operate within the legal remit and resourcing that they had available. Thus, they concluded that the children would be placed on the 'at risk' register for a period so that the situation could be monitored. Meanwhile, the family would also be given the support services that Angela had identified. Although the outcome was as predicted, Angela's disappointment as she left the meeting was enormous. She dreaded having to tell Selma and Clark who chose not to attend the case conference, the result. She knew they would also feel disappointed, angry and perhaps betrayed. Betrayed by a system and people who had heard their calls for help but were unable to provide the support which would enable them to rise out of the low income trap into which they had fallen and restore Clark's sense of purpose and self-esteem.

Meanwhile, Selma had no alternative but to continue juggling the demands of home with those of work to try and salvage some shreds of dignity for herself and her family. She told Angela she felt betrayed by her intervention and that providing her with some relief in the care of the children was like putting a tiny plaster on a very large running sore.

In reflecting upon the Goodsons' predicament, we can see that Angela was able to respond in an empowering manner regarding the process of her intervention by listening to the couple's definition of the problems they faced and even agreeing with their assessment of their situation. But this was only possible at the interpersonal level. She had no impact on the structural inequalities that pervaded the Goodsons' lives. Although the Goodsons had been able to express their own views and exercise agency in their circumstances, the situational context was one that proved impervious to their wishes. Thus, processual empowerment can result in a disempowering outcome. The children's empowerment scarcely enters the scene, despite the focus of attention being upon their welfare. The adults are expected to cater to their needs by acting altruistically and in their best interests without necessarily involving them in any of the decision making processes. From the children's perspective, this can lead to patronising practice (Thorpe, 1993). In short, the empowerment of the Goodsons was only achieved to a limited extent.

Throughout this intervention, Angela felt disempowered as a professional by structural inequalities, personal prejudices and institutional failings. Yet, there were few opportunities for her to explore her ambiguities and uncertainties with others knowing that they would be addressed rather than simply being sympathetically received. Her own needs as a young, 'black' practitioner were poorly acknowledged and enacted upon. The empowerment of Angela as a professional was not even an issue to be considered.

The message of the failure of empowerment in professional helping relationships to liberate people from the daily grind of their life condition has been reinforced in this scenario. Although Angela felt she had tried to assist the Goodsons and done the best she could within the constraints evident in the situation, she also failed to respond to other important matters. Issues of identity figure prominently in the case scenario, particularly around class, gender, age and 'race', even though they are largely neglected. For example, the gendered roles within the family were critical to its

inability to meet the needs of its members. Clark's views on masculinity, Selma's on femininity were not enabling them to be responsive to their altered circumstances. Yet, if they had been helped to become more flexible in their gender expectations of each other with regards to valuing both men and women who undertake domestic work and sharing it more equitably between them, some of the stresses and strains of their daily lives would have been diminished. Clark might have even been enabled to adopt a new role that gave him status and promoted his well-being. However, their changing their lives in this respect would not have dealt with the fundamental problems of poverty, which also debilitated their development as a family whether as individuals within it or the unit itself. This case is a good illustration of the importance of change having to take place at the micro, meso and macro levels. Transforming the situational context that shapes the living conditions of the Goodson family is only possible when both personal and structural change can occur. Providing the 'clients' with a breathing space, as also affirmed by the opinion of the 'client', is *not* good enough.

Conclusions

Empowerment does not exist as a purely ideological phenomenon. It occupies contested terrain that is impacted upon by a variety of forces. These forces lead to its being realised as imperfect practice that can disempower as well as empower individuals and groups. The final outcome depends to a considerable extent on whether the practitioners and 'clients' who negotiate with privileged others during the course of their daily routines and interactions can get their agenda on the table as of equal concern to the proceedings. Moreover, any altruism that may have provided grounds for an optimistic interpretation of professional capacities and commitments to empowering those at the bottom of the social hierarchies carries little purchase in the market economy. As the Goodson case demonstrates, hard-nosed decisions are taken on the basis of the resourcing available to practitioners and not what people actually need or define as wanting.

Mark, a First Nations Mohawk in Canada questions the appropriateness of commodity relations in the caring relationship and issues a challenge to all professionals who believe in empowering 'clients' in the following terms:

> *The alcohol and drug abuse centres, everything that they do revolves around money. It don't revolve around compassion. They don't want to see alcohol and drug abuse end because the people that run those things are out of a job then. They're gettin' paid and that's wrong. I don't think there should be any payment have to be made for helpin' a brother or sister get away from alcohol or drugs. I think the payment is just seein' that they don't do it anymore. That's payment enough.*
>
> (Maracle, 1993: p184)

Mark has rejected paid professionalism as a phenomenon that commits a disservice to people. Although he is referring to a specific context of the oppression of aboriginal First Nations peoples in Canada, he is raising points that are of concern to all professionals. Who should provide welfare services that are non-exploitative and do not appropriate the energies of the 'clients' for their own ends? Should professionals assist in their creation? And if the answer is in the affirmative, how can they become involved in this task? Who will pay for the services that are needed? What will our responses to Mark's questions be? Is the problem having paid caring professionals or asking them to administer an unworkable system? Or both? For as Selma's predicament in the case study above makes clear, without transformative changes at both personal and structural levels, empowerment in the existing helping environment can be experienced as more hindrance than help.

Transformative social changes can also pick up on Mark's point about accessing services without having to pay for them at the point of need if universality of provision, rather than a user payment system, is enacted. Although it is unfashionable to propose such a solution in the current historical conjuncture, the solution of the market place is no solution for some people, the majority of whom are in poverty. Also, unless women are to be exploited indefinitely as unpaid care workers in the name of 'community support', a way has to be found for paying for the services that are created. It is irresponsible to argue that the state has no responsibility for picking up the tab. For in societies that have such gross inequalities of wealth as exist in the world today, the state has a major role to play in

ensuring that those who have considerable resources contribute to those that do not. Redistribution of this nature is a sign of the recognition of the interdependence of individuals, it is a symbol of solidarity with others and it involves reciprocity, for people who are empowered can contribute more fully to society and thereby increase the well-being of all those who live within it. The empowerment of the individual rests on the empowerment of and by the whole collective. It is time professionals put their efforts into the mutual empowerment of all.

Notes

1. I have placed client in quotes to indicate that it is a problematic concept.

2. I have placed quotes around the terms 'black' and 'white' to demonstrate that these categories are not unitary and homogeneous ones.

3. I am aware of the critique of universal human rights as a Western concept because it individualises rights. Whilst I accept that rights are both individual and collective, it can be helpful to focus on individual rights at times to assist oppressed collectivities in the defence of their rights. Women in industrialising countries have made use of individualised universal human rights to challenge collective collusion with the violation of their rights. For example, Bangladeshi women organised a Coalition Against Trafficking of Women of Bangladesh to halt the sale of women into forced prostitution (*Vancouver Sun*, 1999).

References

Ahmad, B. (1990). *Black Perspectives in Social Work*. Ventura Press.

Basu, A. (Ed.) (1995). *The Challenge of Local Feminisms: Women's Movements in Global Perspective*. Boulder: Westview Press.

Belenky, M.F., Clinchy, B.M., Goldberger, N.R., and Tambe, J.M. (1997). *Women's Ways of Knowing* (2nd edn.). New York: Basic Books.

Blom-Cooper, L. (1986). *A Child in Trust: The Report of the Panel of Enquiry into the Death of Jasmine Beckford*. London: London Borough of Brent.

Brecher, J., and Costello, T. (1994). *Global Village or Global Pillage: Economic Reconstruction from the Bottom Up*. Boston: South End Press.

Clegg, R.S. (1989). *Frameworks of Power*. London: Sage.

Craig, G., and Mayo, M. (Eds) (1995). *Community Empowerment: A Reader in Participation and Development*. London: Zed Press.

Culpitt, I. (1992). *Welfare and Citizenship: Beyond the Crisis of the Welfare State?* London: Sage.

Dominelli, L. (1986). Power and the Powerless:

Prostitution and the Enforcement of Submissive Femininity. *Sociological Review*, Spring: pp65–92.

Dominelli, L. (1988). *Anti-racist Social Work*. London: Macmillan.

Dominelli, L. (1989). Betrayal of Trust: A Feminist Analysis of Power Relationships in Incest Abuse. *British Journal of Social Work*, 19(4); Summer: pp291–307.

Dominelli, L. (1996). Deprofessionalising Social Work: Equal Opportunities, Competences and Postmodernism. *British Journal of Social Work*, 26(2): pp153–75.

Dominelli, L. (1997). *Sociology for Social Work*. London: Macmillan.

Dominelli, L. (1998). Anti-oppressive Practice in Context. In Adams, R., Dominelli, L., and Payne, M. (Eds.). *Social Work: Themes, Issues and Critical Debates*. London: Macmillan.

Dominelli, L., and Gollins, T. (1997). Men, Power and Caring Relationships. *Sociological Review*, 45(3); August: pp396–415.

Dominelli, L., and Hoogvelt, A. (1997). Globalization and the Technocratization of Social Work. In *Critical Social Policy*, 47(2); April: pp45–62.

Dominelli, L., and Jonsdottir, G. (1989). Feminist Political Organisation: Some Reflections on the Experiences of Kwenna Frambothid in Iceland. *Feminist Review*, 30; Autumn: pp36–60.

Dominelli, L., and McLeod, E. (1989). *Feminist Social Work*. London: Macmillan.

Egan, G. (1990). *The Skilled Helper* (4th edn.). Pacific Grove, CA: Brooks/Cole.

Flax, J. (1990). *Thinking Fragments: Psychoanalysis, Feminism and Postmodernism in the Contemporary West*. Berkeley: University of California Press.

French, M. (1985). *The Power of Women*. Harmondsworth: Penguin.

Friedan, B. (1974). *The Feminine Mystique*. New York: Dell.

Haber, H.F. (1994). *Beyond Postmodern Politics: Lyotard, Rorty and Foucault*. London: Routledge.

Haig-Brown, C. (1988). *Resistance and Renewal: Surviving the Indian Residential School*. Vancouver: Tillacum Library/Arsenal Pulp Press.

Hanmer, J., and Statham, D. (1988). *Women and Social Work: Woman-Centred Practice*. London: Macmillan.

Haraway, D. (1988). Situated Knowledges: The Science Question in Feminism and the Privilege of Partial Perspective. *Feminist Studies*, 14(3): pp575–99.

Humphries, B. (Ed.) (1996). *Critical Perspectives on Empowerment*. Birmingham: Venture Press.

Kahan, B (Ed.) (1989). *Child Care Research, Policy and Practice*. London: Hodder and Stoughton.

Kelly, L. (1988). *Surviving Sexual Violence*. Cambridge: Polity Press.

Lloyd, L. (1998). The Post and the Anti-analysing Change and Changing Analyses in Social Work. *British Journal of Social Work*, 28(5); October: pp709–27.

Lorenz, W. (1994). *Social Work in a Changing Europe*. London: Routledge.

Lukes, S. (1974). *Power: A Radical View*. London: Macmillan.

Lupton, C., and Nixon, P. (1999). *Empowering Practice?: A Critical Appraisal of the Family Group Conference Approach*. Bristol: Policy Press.

Maracle, B. (1993). *Crazywater: Native Voices on Addiction and Recovery*. Toronto: Penguin.

Mohanty, C.T. (1995). Under Western Eyes: Feminist Scholarship and Colonial Discourse. In Mohanty, C.T., Russo, A., and Torres, L. (Eds.). *Third World Women and the Politics of Feminism*. Bloomington: Indiana University Press.

Morgan, R. (1971). *Sisterhood is Powerful*. New York: Vintage Books.

Oliver, M. (1990). *The Politics of Disability*. London: Macmillan.

Parsons, T., and Bales, R.T. (1955). *Family, Socialization and Interaction Process*. New York: The Free Press.

Parton, N. (1998). Risk, Advanced Liberalism and Child Welfare: The Need to Rediscover Ambiguity and Uncertainty. *British Journal of Social Work*, 28(1); February: pp5–28.

Pringle, K. (1992). Child Sexual Abuse Perpetrated by Welfare Professionals and the Problem of Men. *Critical Social Policy*, 12(3): pp4–19.

Rees, S. (1991). *Achieving Power: Policy and Practice in Social Welfare*. London: Allen and Unwin.

Riger, S. (1993). What's Wrong with Empowerment? *American Journal of Psychology*, 21(3): pp279–92.

Rush, F. (1980). *The Best Kept Secret: The Sexual Abuse of Children*. New York: McGraw-Hill.

Ruzek, S.B. (1986). Feminist Visions of Health: An International Perspective. In Mitchell, J., and Oakley, A. (Eds.). *What is Feminism?* Oxford: Basil Blackwell.

Solomon, B. (1976). *Black Empowerment: Social Work in Oppressed Communities*. New York: Columbia University Press.

Teeple, G. (1995). *Globalization and the Decline of Social Reform*. Toronto: Garamond Press.

Thorpe, R. (1993). Empowerment Groupwork with Parents of Children in Care. In Mason, J. (Ed.). *Child Welfare Policy: Critical Australian Perspectives*. Sydney: Hale and Ironmonger.

United Nations (UN) (1998). *The 1998 Report on Human Social Development*. New York: United Nations.

Vancouver Sun (1999). Women Target Sexual Trafficking. *Vancouver Sun*, January 26th: A7.

Wallerstein, N., and Bernstein, E. (1994). Introduction to Community Empowerment, Participatory Education and Health. *Health Education Quarterly*, 21(2): pp141–9.

Chapter Fourteen

Conclusion: Tough Love: Social Work Practice in UK Society

Bill Jordan

The idea of social work as a profession in crisis has been a commonplace one, even a cliché, in the past two decades. Yet Brewer and Lait's (1980) question *Can Social Work Survive?* has never been more pressing than it is at the start of this century. In this chapter I shall analyse the fragmentation of the notion of practice, and its effects on the identity of the profession. I shall argue that there are opportunities as well as threats in the present context for practice, but that, as with all processes of change, something has to be sacrificed in order to gain new benefits.

At the core of the dilemma facing practitioners and the profession is a new moral climate and political culture in UK society. Seen from the top, from their perspective of the political elite and then special advisers, it is the Third Way (Blair, 1998; Giddens, 1998), with its *New Contract for Welfare* (DSS, 1998) and its agenda for *Modernising Social Services* (DoH, 1998). It involves changing from generalised, mediocre public services for passive recipients to high-quality, tailor-made provision that demands more (in terms of independence and achievement) from those who get it. More generally, it involves the notion of a 'responsible community' in which all must contribute. From the perspective of public sector professionals this often involves a hectoring, harassing and hindering regulation of their work, that calls them to account from day-to-day for the effectiveness of their practice. And from the standpoint of marginal and deprived communities, and the groups and associations that try to raise their morale and quality of life, it often sounds like the distant drone of a vicar's sermon, heard by a bunch of beggars huddled in the church porch.

However, what the change does also signal is a recognition that, in every transaction between a practitioner and a service user, important moral and social issues are at stake. There are no such things as neutral or routine encounters between agencies (public, commercial or voluntary) and citizens; every contact involves a significant transaction, conveying value and meaning, an exchange that has an ethical content, and a qualitative element. However mechanistically and obsessively the new standards and targets are applied, the idea behind them is that such exchanges should mobilise, energise, activate and empower service users, and contribute to cultural processes of inclusion, responsibility, regeneration and community-building. Practice should be stimulating and challenging, exciting and provoking, never dull and dispiriting.

As every practitioner is acutely aware, there is a yawning gap between these aspirations and the everyday realities of work in any front-line agency. But an equally wide chasm is now opening between the exhortations of government ministers and the lived experiences of citizens in many parts of UK society; as Tony Blair's speech to the Women's Institute conference painfully illustrated. This chapter will analyse the connections between the loss of credibility experienced by the government and the dissonance experienced by practitioners on the front line.

What seems to me to link these diverse phenomena is the requirement to provide the tangible, accessible sense of belonging, mattering and being valued that makes a more demanding, stringent and bracing culture of social citizenship justifiable. This applies as much to practitioners as to service users; if they feel shamed and scorned, they will not rise to the challenges of quality standards and effectiveness targets, any more than service users will feel motivated, activated or included. In order to change, people need to be secure that their efforts will be appreciated, and their vulnerabilities respected: that they will be cherished and supported as well as chided for backsliding. If stern remonstrations were the key to all personal development and cultural change, it would never have been necessary to invent social workers (or indeed families, associations or communities).

Elsewhere, I have tried to capture the New Labour government's aspirations and dilemmas on these issues in the slogan 'tough love' (Jordan, B., with Jordon, C., 2000). Its 1997 election campaign tried to tell UK citizens a new story about themselves and their society, that allowed them to make sense of their frustrations under the previous regime, and to turn their resentments into positive action. Specifically, it told taxpayers that their contributions would be well spent, because beneficiaries and service users would be given better incentives and opportunities to work and be independent, and made to take these opportunities. This should enable a style of practice that encourages responsibility and participation, because it promotes co-operation and trust, instead of the competition, insecurity and fear of an excessively individualistic environment (where there was 'no such thing as society'). The question is how the government conveys both elements in the equation, in the right balance. Practitioners are familiar with the issue of balancing support with challenge, care with control. New Labour, in turn, has to discover how to combine toughness with love, in a culture which bestows the secure sense of equal membership and recognition but evokes a vigorous contributory and participatory response.

There is therefore a strong parallelism between the political and the practice level, and, as I hope to show, an interdependence between them. After a long honeymoon, the Blair government has run into all sorts of problems, not least over the plausibility of its original model for national renewal through responsible community (Jordan, 1998). Practice must seek its resolutions of similar difficulties.

The identity of social work

For UK social workers, a point has been reached where the factors that gave their profession a strong identity and unified voice are now its weaknesses. Under New Labour, its close association with the public sector in general, and the local authorities in particular, make it part of the problem to be addressed, rather than part of the solution sought. This means that social work's potential salvation lies in giving up at least part of that identity, and embracing a new one, that will at first seem more vague and amorphous.

The post war history of UK social work's role in the welfare state made it unusual among European national patterns. In most of the latter, under the Christian Democratic tradition and the subsidiarity principle, social work services were provided by voluntary organisations (often with a religious basis), but under increasingly close state regulation (Badelt, 1994; Jordan, 1997). Organisationally, such services were scattered among a number of policy fields; such state social work services as existed were also attached to various public agencies (health facilities, criminal justice systems and social assistance programmes). Hence there was little correspondence between a professional and an organisational identity; the former had to override the fragmented nature of the latter. Furthermore, there was no unified professional training; public sector workers tended to be trained in technical high schools or polytechnics, while a proportion of voluntary sector professionals took university courses, which were far more academic. In addition to this, the existence of a separate profession and theoretical tradition (social pedagogy) within social work meant that the professional had an almost federal structure (Lorenz, 1994).

In the UK and the Scandinavian countries, local authority and other public sector agencies contributed the largest and strongest part of the profession, and served to identify it as part of the social state. But the apparently similar paths pursued up to the 1970s (when UK local authority services were consolidated following the Seebohm Report) diverged in the following decade. Margaret Thatcher's policies for embracing global market forces and dissolving many of the collective protections of the post war era meant that the public sector was essentially responding to social polarisation, exclusion, poverty, and disadvantage, rather than being part of a strategy for preventing them, as in Scandinavia. In the latter countries, the expansion of well-paid, secure, trade unionised and professionalised public sector employment, especially in social care, was an integral part of their regimes for combating the corrosive effects of globalisation (Esping-Andersen, 1990; 1996). In the UK, the same services, in particular local authority social services departments, were used to deal with the consequences of greater inequality, division and conflict: the so-called 'underclass' phenomenon (Jordan, 1987; 1990; 1996; 1998). In other words, in creating a social and economic ghetto of poverty and its attendant behavioural problems, the governments of the 1980s and 1990s in the UK residualised public-sector social work, recreating many of the issues of the era of the Poor Law, rather than (as in Sweden) using it to develop the scope of the welfare state. This was especially obvious in the field of child care and child protection (Parton, 1985; 1991; Parton, Thorpe and Wattam, 1997).

Two consequences have flowed from these developments. First, public sector practice has come under the increasingly prescriptive regulation of central government, as the cost effectiveness of the public services has become the focus of first Conservative and then New Labour governments. Both the stigma of being increasingly involved in attempts to contain the corrosive effects of poverty and marginalisation and control the most damaging manifestations of cultural disintegration, and the demands of being required to account for themselves in terms of quantifiable outputs, have transformed practitioners into managers of scarce resources and assessors of serious risks. Second, significant aspects of the former field of social work practice have quietly migrated out of statutory authorities, towards counselling, the voluntary and commercial sectors or private practice. Meanwhile, new agencies and community groups have arisen around new initiatives and issues, often not identified with professional social work, but using many of its principles and methods.

In other words, practice has itself become far more diverse, and is located in a much more diverse set of organisations. Above all, there has been a proliferation of new projects, outreach, drop-in and street-level teams and centres, support units and survivor organisations, all giving very direct and accessible assistance, and filling the vacuum left by public sector social work's retreat into office bound, arm's length, formal methods. Yet the identity of social work is still strongly linked to the public sector, and to local authorities in particular; their issues and requirements still dominate training and research agendas, and popular perceptions of the profession. This has become part of the

defence mechanism of an occupation under pressure, but it no longer reflects the realities of practice or the needs of service users. Indeed, it makes social work vulnerable in ways that will become more pressing as the Third Way reforms of New Labour themselves come under criticism and attack, and government ministers look round for scapegoats.

In the following section, I shall analyse how the possible elements in more viable and promising identity have become fragmented in New Labour's agenda for reform, and argue that it is not too late for social work practice to reclaim them.

Social inclusion in practice

On the face of it, there should be an easy fit and good compatibility between the values underpinning New Labour's programme and those that drive social work practice. Tony Blair's own account of the Third Way (1998) and his political speeches (1996, 1999) emphasise equal value, autonomy, responsibility and community; his government aims to shift the culture of our society towards enabling individuals to contribute more and to give higher priority to the needs of others. The strong promotion of social inclusion as a policy goal seems to offer a particular opportunity for social work, since its low status under the previous regime was so closely connected with the exclusion of its clientele. Yet the government's reforming and modernising agenda makes no mention of social work, except as a target for improving standards and new systems of quality control. Why is the profession not recognised as a suitable means of implementing New Labour's programme, and why are practitioners not seen at least as important allies in the culture shifts the government aims to accomplish?

The first reason is connected with the very partial analysis of social exclusion that lies behind the government's strategy. In this, the main factor in marginalisation is the phenomenon of 'workless households' (DSS, 1998), and hence the central thrust of policy for inclusion is increased employment through the New Deals. The problem of economic exclusion is understood in terms of weak incentives to take the low paid service work that has grown since the 1980s, along with the increased temptations of cash-in-hand undeclared earnings and other shadowy or criminal activities, lumped together as 'fraud'. Hence the goals of 'making work pay' (through tax credits and the national minimum wage) and cracking down on the informal economy, in the name of improved opportunities and better targeting of taxpayers' money to those in 'genuine need'.

It is easy to see why public sector social work has little to offer in this part of the programme, which emphasises formal employment as the main component of inclusion. Since the post war welfare state was founded, personal social services were directed mainly at those outside the formal economy, retired, disabled, sick, or caring for children at home, and not at issues of work. This was because the logic of the Keynes-Beveridge era was based on a 'full-employment' strategy of expanding industrial work for men, expected to earn a 'family wage'. But now that this sector is declining, women's employment and service jobs are growing, and the boundaries between work and family life are more problematic, this logic no longer so clearly applies. There is a task concerned with *negotiating* transitions between work and family (the New Deal for Lone Parents) and between the informal and the formal economy (the New Deals for Young People and the Unemployed, and the Employment Zones). It is here that New Labour has chosen to reject social work as the instrument of its flagship programme. Instead, it has decided to create a new specialised occupation, New Deal advisers, who will combine aspects of social work practice, such as 'individual tailor-made packages of help' (DSS, 1998: p24), with others of vigilant enforcement (withholding benefits from those who do not co-operate). This new species of practice, 'enforcement counselling' (Jordan, B., and Jordon, C., 2000), can be seen as the government's response to the hidden challenge of social inclusion: that the improved incentives of the Working Families Tax Credits and minimum wage, and the opportunities of new employment in part-time, low paid service work, will not on their own constitute sufficient inducement, or offer prospects for future advancement, enough to draw people out of marginality and poverty. But in this crucial part of its programme, the toughness that is required is not entrusted to social work, a profession seen as not suited to such hard-edged economic roles.

The second reason is closely linked with the first. Only formal, paid employment is to count as a valid contribution, delivering the claimant's part of the 'New Contract on Welfare', and demonstrating the responsibilities that are now conditions for receiving social rights. But this means that all the other kinds of work that go on in communities, the activism, support systems, voluntary efforts and group endeavours, do not count. In relegating the growing volume of such units and projects, both indigenous to local neighbourhoods and branches of broader organisations, to the role of fostering cohesion and reducing costly social problems, the government is devaluing the expanding and effective part of practice, and social work's most valuable contribution to social inclusion. It is also giving the lie to its own claims to promote empowerment, participation and the enhancement of the capacities of people living in deprived communities.

This is a blind spot of New Labour thinking, and it is one that spurns a great deal of what practitioners have to offer to its project for cultural change. The fact is that community, one of its key concepts, is potentially far more than a backward-looking bastion against lawlessness, disorder, violent conflict and isolated despair. It is a way of getting things done, a working alternative to both labour markets and public services as a means of providing a better quality of life, more satisfying and fulfilling work roles and a more effective pooling of resources in such neighbourhoods (Holman, 1981; 1988; 1998; Leonard, 1994; 1999). The government sees community as the expression of social discipline and the restraint of anarchic individualism (Driver and Martell, 1997). It conceives most of what happens in the way of community activity as a low cost solution to the problems of disorder, homelessness, truancy, delinquency, and child protection, rather than as a crucial form of social inclusion and empowerment. Many of its initiatives, such as the Employment Zones, cut across the work done by local practitioners, by insisting on maximising formal employment, even when this is at the expense of community engagement. It also sees regeneration primarily in terms of the market, rather than social interaction and active participation in local affairs (Ginsburg, 1998). It is very questionable whether in the long run the aim of converting informal activities into formal employment is either sustainable or desirable, and whether the poorest citizens benefit from such a strategy. In Third World countries the trend is in the opposite direction, with efforts to stimulate communities to provide environmental services (sewers, water supplies, conservation) for themselves, and it is proving successful, from a strictly economic standpoint. The same may apply even more strongly to social services.

The third reason is that New Labour's reform programme makes a sharp distinction between what is required of those capable of work, and those in 'genuine need': hence the slogan 'work for those who can, security for those who cannot' (DSS, 1998). Yet in practice the decision on who is and who is not capable of doing any kind of work (the All Work Test) has proved contentious, and it means that those who qualify for various kinds of disability benefits are excluded from access to the tax-based welfare system. Social work is identified with provision for those outside the workforce; yet what is surely needed is bridges between the two, especially through forms of activation and involvement which include people with disabilities and illnesses. Here again, the rigidity of the government's strategy limits the potential contribution of practice, as well as that of disabled citizens.

Tough love in practice

What I am arguing is that both the New Labour government and social work as a profession are struggling with the same set of issues: how to forge a convincing combination of valuing and cherishing members (citizens or service users) simply for who they are, and challenging them to give of their best, and pull together in the name of a common purpose. The way that the government's programme deals with social work, as a public sector activity that has been inefficiently performed and requires tighter regulation, quality standards and performance indicators, and the way it fails to recognise and regard all the various activities and contributions made by practitioners, are both indicators of this central problem. Conversely, social work's fragmentation into the managerism and

formality of the public sector and the diverse projects and units of voluntary and community sectors reflects the implementation dilemmas of the government's social policy programme.

The paradox for both is that the changes in individual behaviour and the culture shifts that they seek are extensive and far-reaching; yet they can only be accomplished by personal, face to face methods. Unlike the old welfare state, which was effective mainly as a way of restraining costly class and industrial conflicts and achieving mass solidarity through uniformity and averages, the Third Way tries to reach right down to the level of the individual, the family and the neighbourhood. The old welfare state could work through bureaucratic rules and systems; the new deals in personal development, change, and achievement. The old exercised blanket controls; the new requires conversion, transformation and motivation. But the government cannot trust the professionals in its services, teachers and doctors as well as social workers, to do this work on its behalf, because it sees them as still too compromised with old systems and methods, and as having too big a stake in the old order. In trying to prescribe and direct every aspect of their performance, it largely annuls any chance of developing the commitment, charisma and flair that might be able to deliver its objectives.

For social work practice there is the added twist that New Labour has adopted much of its rhetoric and values, empowerment, inclusion, participation, autonomy, as the basis for its new vision of society; yet it cannot recognise the contradictions between these principles and many of its regulatory methods. Above all, in the concept of community, the government claims to have discovered a foundation for a new ethic of belonging, trust and co-operation, based on reciprocity (something for something) and mutual concern. This sounds like the ideal ethical basis for a style of practice that most practitioners would in principle choose: one of negotiated give-and-take, shared power and partnership (Jordan, 1990). But the reality of the new regime consists in detailed rules and accountability, a medium of top-down control that contradicts the message of its morality.

In practice, as every head of a residential unit, day centre, or community support group is aware, the best combination is a set of fairly simple and self-explanatory rules, combined with a pervasive culture of challenging honesty that is always underpinned by empathy and support. The more widely and deeply this culture is shared by staff and service users, the less it is necessary to rely on formal sanctions and controls, and the more it is possible to deal with even the most serious issues through the informal, personal methods that sustain the everyday order of the regime. Far from trying to prescribe for each situation, the rules require interpretation and negotiation to fit the circumstances of the individual, and the contingencies of personalities, interactions and circumstances. So, for instance, in a family centre with such a culture, it is feasible to sustain more risky and tenuous relationships between parents and young children by informal approaches than would be possible through the arm's length monitoring and surveillance that has become characteristic of much child protection field work (Jordan, 1997).

Of course, such a culture is always answerable to the more general rules of government procedures and guidance, and ultimately to the law, but its binding force and uplifting influence on service users is experienced through the personalities of the staff, and the tangible qualities they offer in day-to-day transactions. Good practice provides an invisible link between the formal order of the public authority and the informal order that sustains everyday life; it does so in such a way that the requirements of law and policy are not felt as some imposed, alien restrictions, but part of the way that service users make sense of their own worlds, and deal fairly and decently with each other, in reliable and rewarding ways.

At the general election of 1997, the government's transformative message seemed persuasive; it appeared to give UK society a story about itself that could mobilise energies that were blocked by frustration, and connect up forces that were pulling in opposite directions. But the mainstream voters who constituted New Labour's crucial new support were promised that social inclusion and responsible community could be achieved without any significant sacrifice of their advantages and comforts. As the reform programme has not yielded immediate recognisable improvements in the quality of social life or the performance of public

services, the government has been driven into more and more pompous postures of toughness and intolerance. And as the next election approaches, its message about community and inclusion has sounded increasingly jaded and unconvincing (the Prime Minister's speech to the WI), or serious analysis has been replaced by headline-grabbing gimmicks (telling an audience of German theologians about spot fines for drunken louts).

If community and inclusion mean anything, they refer to exactly the experiences of belonging and mattering that can only be conveyed through personal warmth and support, communicated by trusted fellow-members of a culture in which recognition of identity and value are exchanged in direct, face to face ways (Goffman, 1972). In so far as the government tries to achieve inclusion by compulsory employment schemes and the threat of tough sanctions against disorder and deviance, or public sector social work is driven into methods of checklisted rationing and risk management, both are doomed to ineffectiveness. But practice that takes place in isolated projects and units, in desolate and deprived neighbourhoods, cannot on its own offset the disadvantages and exclusions that its members suffer. The loving side of social work, its capacity for getting alongside those in trouble and distress, and achieving the street credibility that formal methods lack, can never deliver its full potential if it is treated as marginal to the mainstream of policy and service delivery. Somehow the government must find new ways to re-value difference, diversity, plurality and the potential of its marginal individuals and communities, and social work must reconnect its elements into a coherent force for change.

Conclusions

Social work practice has a double agenda: to serve the policy purposes of government, and to be a credible and relevant factor in the lives of people who use its services. As tough love requires practitioners to be more demanding of service users (asking them to contribute more and behave better) they must also become more meaningfully involved in their lives. It is not enough for practice to be more efficient and effective by government standards; it must also ring true in terms of the ways in which service users make sense of their worlds.

A large part of the White Paper *Modernising Social Services* (DoH, 1998) is concerned with raising standards of practice. A whole chapter is given over to reviewing the registration, qualification and training of practitioners in the field of social care, and how standards can be sustained and enforced. But this conceals a set of assumptions about what practice is, which are very restrictive and stifling. Indeed, practice cannot break out of its present patchy performance (much criticised by the government) if it accepts the government's limited vision of its nature and purposes.

The model of local authority practice that informs the government's ideas on training and supervision is concerned with policing the community to forestall breakdowns in its informal caring functions, and step into the breach to provide care of various kinds where such breakdowns occur, or protection is needed. For all the rhetoric about 'promoting independence', this boils down to various financial payments, material services and moral exhortations, mainly aimed at encouraging employment or family integrity. What is missing is a vision of a quality of life, a richness of conviviality, or a culture of civility, which can be improved through imaginative and creative methods of partnership and service. More than this, the nature of practice itself remains shadowy, portrayed either as risk monitoring or decisive protection, but never as sensitive, aware, flexible negotiation about everyday crises in ordinary lives.

This view of practice as a formal means of policy implementation helps explain the range of projects, units and homes that is rapidly emerging, between this managed world of contracts between public, voluntary and commercial organisations, and the problems that confront citizens in their neighbourhoods. These provide a link between those two worlds, supplying what is lacking in formal provision, and giving some street credibility to the policies and goals they represent. With the procedures and structures of public services dominated by ideas about assessing, commissioning and management, they get alongside service users, and operate in a fluid and provisional way, helping them cope with insecurity, change and the demands of new government programmes.

However, many of these practitioners, project workers, support workers, drop-in and outreach workers, are not employed as social workers, and do not think of themselves as social workers; many are highly educated and motivated, but have no intention of taking a social work training. There is, in fact, no recognised training for their practice, and no unifying rationale within which they can share and reflect their experiences as professionals. This is partly because they do, in a sense, represent a new kind of practice, perhaps even a new profession, of street-level worker, or social mediator.

Simultaneously, the government's broader programme is creating another large cohort of practitioners in the public sector: New Deal counsellors, Single Gateway advisers, Asylum Support workers, and so on. Much of their practice is concerned with social inclusion through participation in employment, education or training, or the enforcement of conditions around benefits and services. Here again, there is no unified or coherent supervision, training a professional development of these practitioners.

This is not to argue that either of these two groups should be trained on social work courses like the existing ones. But it does call for a recognition of the common ground between all these practitioners, and the development of coherent new ideas about how the various elements in their work can be co-ordinated, so that they reflect a consistent set of values and goals. Above all, it indicates the need for a more imaginative and flexible approach to issues of social exclusion and cultures of resistance among people at the margins of society. New Labour's rigid perceptions of these issues, and mechanistic methods of re-integrating and activating citizens, shows a lack of understanding of their needs for identities, supports and activities that they can generate for themselves, together, and in negotiation with the public authorities.

Tony Blair's government has had some humiliating experiences, stemming from its self-imposed mission to appease the irritable sensibilities of mainstream citizens on unemployment, lone parenthood, asylum and public order, and to demonstrate the effectiveness of its reforms of welfare services. Its pigeon-holing of public sector social work, and fragmentation of the other elements in practice, reveal the fault lines in its own programme for social inclusion. A broader version of social work practice could rediscover its own integrity, while making a valuable contribution to the loftier aspirations of that programme.

References

Badelt, C. (1990). Institutional Choice and the Non-profit Sector. In Anheier, H., and Seibel, W. (Eds.). *The Non-profit Sector: Comparative Studies in Non-profit Organisations*. Berlin: de Gruyter.

Blair, T. (1996). Speech to Labour Party Conference.

Blair, T. (1998). *The Third Way: New Politics for the New Century*, Fabian Pamphlet 588. London: The Fabian Society.

Blair, T. (1999). Speech on moral standards. *The Guardian*, September 6th.

Brewer, C., and Lait, J. (1980). *Can Social Work Survive?* London: Temple Smith.

Department of Health (1998). *Modernising Social Services: Promoting Independence, Improving Protection, Raising Standards*, Cm. 4169. London: Stationery Office.

Department of Social Security (1998). *A New Contract for Welfare*, Cm. 3805. London: Stationery Office.

Driver, S., and Martell, L. (1997). New Labour's Communitarianisms. *Critical Social Policy*, 17(52): pp27–46.

Esping-Andersen, G. (1990). *The Three Worlds of Welfare Capitalism*. Cambridge: Polity Press.

Esping-Andersen, G. (Ed.) (1996). *Welfare States in Transition: National Adaptations in Global Economies*. London: Sage.

Giddens, A. (1998). *The Third Way: The Renewal of Social Democracy*. Cambridge: Polity.

Ginsburg, N. (1998). Putting the Social into Urban Regeneration Policy. *Local Economy*, May: pp17–28.

Goffman, E. (1972). *Interaction Ritual: Essays on Face-to-face Behaviour*. London: Penguin.

Holman, B. (1981). *Kids at the Door: A Preventive Project in a Council Estate*. Oxford: Blackwell.

Holman, B. (1988). *Putting Families First: Prevention and Child Care*. Basingstoke: Macmillan.

Holman, B. (1998). *Faith in the Poor*. Oxford: Lion Books.

Jordan, B. (1987). *Rethinking Welfare*. Oxford: Blackwell.

Jordan, B. (1990). *Social Work in an Unjust Society*. Hemel Hempstead: Harvester Wheatsheaf.

Jordan, B. (1997). Partnership with Service Users in Child Protection and Family Support. In Parton, N. (Ed.). *Child Protection and Family Support*. London: Routledge.

Jordan, B. (1998). *The New Politics of Welfare: Social Justice in a Global Context*. London: Sage.

Jordan, B., with Jordan, C. (2000). *Social Work and the Third Way: Tough Love as Social Policy*. London: Sage.

Leonard, M. (1994). *Informal Economic Activity in Belfast*. Aldershot: Avebury.

Leonard, M. (1999). Informal Economic Activity: Strategies of Households and Communities, paper given at the 4th ESA Conference, Will Europe Work?, Amsterdam, August 18th–21st.

Lorenz, W. (1994). *Social Work in a Changing Europe*. London: Routledge and Kegan Paul.

Parton, N. (1985). *The Politics of Child Abuse*. London: Macmillan.

Parton, N. (1991). *Governing the Family: Child Care, Child Protection and the State*. London: Macmillan.

Parton, N., Thorpe, D., and Wattam, C. (1997). *Child Protection, Risk and the Moral Order*. London: Macmillan.

Index